# Greek Romance Influence in Shakespeare and Sidney

Jesse G. Hanna

ABSTRACT

This study argues that the Greek romances of late antiquity were an important source in the works of William Shakespeare and Sir Philip Sidney. I specifically address how the chaste marriage plot of Greek romance reflected the social and religious ethics of the Jacobean and Elizabethan era. The renewed interest in Hellenistic romance coincided with an emerging Protestant sexual ethic of mutual love in marriage and wedded chastity. The genre of Greek romance also imparted the theme of erotic suffering. This theme manifests itself in the ideal romance plot pattern of love-leading-to-marriage. The young hero and heroine triumph over adversity in their quest to remain faithful to the principle of true love. I discuss Sidney's use of the Greek romance model in the *New Arcadia*, particularly his interest in the model of erotic suffering as a paradigm of female virtue. Sidney explicitly invokes a Heliodorian model of ideal love. I also discuss Shakespeare's use of the Greek romance paradigm of sexual love in his romance plays, *Pericles*, *Cymbeline*, and *The Winter's Tale*. In these late plays, Shakespeare draws on source material that is rooted in the Greek romance tradition of ideal marriage and erotic suffering. The heroes in Shakespearean romance often find psychological or spiritual redemption in affliction. The heroine in Shakespearean romance is often made to suffer for love on account of patriarchal abuse. It is the heroine's virtuous fortitude in adversity that gives the play its regenerative closure.

INDEX WORDS:     Sir Philip Sidney, William Shakespeare, Greek romance, erotic
                 suffering, adventure novel, Heliodorus, Longus, Achilles Tatius,
                 *New Arcadia*, *Pericles*, *Cymbeline*, *The Winter's Tale*, Robert
                 Greene, Laurence Twine, Gower, George Wilkins, Boccaccio.

# TABLE OF CONTENTS

Page

CHAPTER

CHAPTER 1

Introduction: Tales of Erotic Suffering

Not only was the influence of romance deep; it was wide and intricate too,
for romance literature was a diverse and complex stream of verse and
prose, the product of five changing centuries and of half a dozen European
countries of varying culture and civilisation. (E. C. Pettet, *Shakespeare
and the Romance Tradition*)

E. C. Pettet's account of romance literature in Elizabethan England points to the
difficulty of isolating any one romance tradition in the early modern period. Despite the
confluence of influence, the many rivulets that make up the stream, Pettet narrows the
scope of interest down to four categories: medieval chivalric, Italian epic, Petrarchan
poetry, and Continental novels and novella. Although the subgroups of romance are
distinct in their own right, they can all be categorized under the over-arching umbrella of
sexual love: As Pettet succinctly states, "Above all else romance literature was a
literature of love and love-making."[1] The Renaissance found the literature of sexual love
in different modes of romance writing. In particular, a vital reserve of stock material and
romantic focus came from a specific genre of romance, the Greek prose romances of the
Roman Imperial period. While Pettet does not include the Greek genre as a subgroup of
romance, these ancient stories of erotic suffering lie at the heart of Sidney's *New Arcadia*
and Shakespearean romance. More than any other Elizabethan or Jacobean writers, these
authors engaged vigorously with the Greek romance paradigm.

Why did Renaissance writers such as Sidney and Shakespeare look specifically to the Greek romance model of sexual love? The romances of the Hellenistic era brought to the early-Christian world a heterosexual paradigm of amatory relations. According to Michel Foucault, this paradigm shift created "a new erotics": unlike the old ideal, one that glorified love between men and boys, the new ideal extolled erotic passion between a man and woman.[2] This "new erotics" carried with it an ethic of chastity. The passion between the young romance hero and heroine is fulfilled in matrimony, and this marital joining is based on the necessary factor of parental consent. The Greek romances are often referred to as "ideal" by modern critics because the protagonists usually uphold the virtues of fidelity and chastity.[3] As such, these stories of mutual love enjoyed a resurgence of popularity in the Renaissance when humanist scholars began to translate the Greek texts into Latin and the vernacular. In the Elizabethan and Jacobean period, the newly-translated stories provided an ideal model of erotic desire: there is a hero and heroine who meet and fall in love; they suffer ordeals of separation and loyalty; through their trials, the lovers remain true and are finally brought together often in celebration or in marriage.

One of the divergent forms that Greek romance took in the Middle Ages was the genre of hagiography, or saints' lives.[4] These popular stories often describe the various forms of torture and torment that medieval martyrs endured for religious faith: their allegiance to the suffering body of Christ. The hagiographical narratives usually depict men and women who view suffering as a condition of devotion to religious piety. As Judith Perkins states, "to be a Christian *was* to suffer."[5] Like the Greek romance heroine, the virgin martyr is subjected to near rapes, but is always able to defend her chastity and defy enemies. For instance, the story of Paul and Thecla recalls the Greek romance pattern of separation, adventure, and reunion. The legend tells of Thecla's dedication to Paul's preaching, her separation from him, attempted assaults on her virginity, and physical punishment for her fidelity to Christ. We see that the chaste heroine of Hellenistic romance evolves into the menaced virgin of the saints' lives, an aesthetic vision of Christian piety and humility.[6] While there are similarities between the ancient romance genre and the literature of hagiography, the differences between these genres are significant. Lovers in Greek romance suffer adversity in order to remain faithful to an erotic attachment, and their hardships are rewarded in the fulfillment of wedded love. The medieval martyr, especially the menaced virgin, finds reward in a symbolic and spiritual marriage to Christ.

Another popular form of romance that influenced Elizabethan and Jacobean writers was, of course, medieval chivalric romance. This genre of romance drew heavily from the courtly love (*fine amors*) tradition as famously set down in Andreas Capellanus's *De Arte Honeste Amandi* (13th century). For Capellanus, the experience of romantic love followed a codified set of rules. Love had the potential to be an ennobling experience, for it encouraged the (male) lover to perform deeds of knightly virtue. According to John Stevens, the aesthetic of courtly love followed a basic pattern: "a young man falls hopelessly in love with a beautiful young woman and for her sake is willing to undergo the most excruciating misery, to pay the last farthing of the costs that she exacts of expects in discipline and 'derrying do.'"[7] This romantic tradition understood relations between a man and woman in terms of power: the hero performs perilous deeds in order to please a woman, a person who may or may not return the knight-lover's affection. Moreover, the experience of romantic love in the medieval romance was often unequal or illicit. As C. S. Lewis argues, love in romance of the Middle Ages expressed itself largely through adultery.[8] Unlike the symmetrical attraction that occurs between the hero and heroine of Greek romance, the lovers in medieval romance are represented as asymmetrical—whether on account of an adulterous liaison or unrequited love.

This dissertation argues that there are two fundamental reasons why Sidney and Shakespeare turned to Greek romance as a paradigm of sexual love. First, the Greek romance plot of love-leading-to-marriage coincided with an emerging Protestant sexual ethic of marriage and wedded chastity. Second, the plot formula of erotic suffering produced a new model of heroism. Unlike the chivalric display of male valor, one in which the hero proves his prowess in martial exploits,[9] the Greek romance model of heroism requires that both the male and female prevail equally in trials of fidelity and chastity. For Sidney, this example of virtuous suffering is primarily a prototype for female heroism. It is critically evident that Shakespeare looks back to Sidney's Elizabethan prose romance in his romance plays. As Geoffrey Bullough states, "[Shakespeare] enjoyed prose works of Greene and Lodge, and especially Sidney's *Arcadia*."[10] Shakespeare, however, brings new material to the Greek romance model by complicating the pattern of male and female romantic passion: while suffering is a feminine trait for the hero, the heroine gains strength from her pain and adversity: Shakespeare modifies the paradigm of the suffering male into a metamorphosed hero who experiences spiritual penitence.

# I

Before turning to an analysis of Greek romance in Sidney and Shakespeare, I would like to show how an early Elizabethan romance play, *Common Conditions* (1576), can be used as a template for looking at the rise of the love-leading-to-marriage plot and the development of the suffering heroine. In this anonymous play, named after the Vice character, the central storyline retains all of the essential ingredients of the Greek romance love plot: love-at-first-sight; separation of the lovers; trials of fidelity and chastity; reunion (this play has a particularly unusual ending that will be discussed further on). Overlaid upon the play's romance plot structure are the familiar early Elizabethan dramatic conventions and character. Instead of prose, we have heptameter couplets; instead of Fortune, the Vice character, Common Conditions, manipulates the action; instead of priests and priestess, there are knights and ladies; instead of slaves or lewd servants, low comic characters make merry. Notwithstanding its native English flavor, the play recalls in its broadest sense the Greek romance story of Theagenes and Chariclea. It describes the true love of Clarisia (a name in tonal quality reminiscent of Chariclea) and Lamphedon, a pair of lovers who prove their constancy and fidelity to each other in the face of adventure and adversity.

In *Common Conditions*, the lovers' expression of love at first sight illustrates the reciprocal nature of the hero and heroine's passion. It also prepares the audience for the lovers' mutual fidelity by showing the sudden, explosive strength of their shared sentiment. In the hero's soliloquy, Lamphedon describes his awakening to true love by emphasizing the ocular and its role in the creation of desire. He states: "a lady faire whome I espied this day, / As I in forest hunting was persuing of the pray. / Whose bewty hath bewitched me, even mawger Dians chaste / To yeeld and be a courtier now unto dame Venus grace" (ll. 516-20).[11] The invocation of the Actaeon-Diana myth hints at the potential threat for men of female sexuality, but Lamphedon dispels any notion of danger or of possessing a base desire of the heroine: "And this the first time is (Alas) of her I had a sight, / Whose cumly lokes & bewty brave hath wrought to me this spight / Ha lady brave, would gods through knewest the love I beare to thee" (ll. 532-34.). Immediately following the hero's confession of amour, Clarisia mirrors Lamphedon by reiterating an identical sentiment. Comparing the intensity of the passion to the "hauke whose rowling eyes are firs on Partredge fast," she declares, alone: "so I through sight of valiant knight within this forest here, / Have first my eye, untill I die, uppon Lamphedon deere. / Ha valiant knight, whose comly corps hath won my hart for ever, / Whose sight hath prest my tender brest, that I shal fayl thee never" (ll. 624-29). The couple's instant declaration of love presages their physical compatibility and unity. The verbal mirroring and repetition in which Clarisia and Lamphedon engage will also point to the betrothed's capacity for mutuality in love, their shared commitment to the precepts of loyalty and sexual constancy.

The hero and heroine's reciprocal love culminates in a perfectly orchestrated exchange of marital vows. When Lamphedon and Clarisia chance upon one another in the next scene, the two secretly declare their steadfast and eternal devotion:

> Lamphedon doth professe he will to thee be faithfull knight,
>
> Not once for to forsake thy love, for wronge ne yet for right.
>
> And therefore Lady yeelde to mee like promise here agayne,
>
> To rest to me as I to thee, a lover true certayne.  (ll. 650-53)

Clarisia matches this oath with the same reverence:

> Clarisia doth protest, as she is Lady true,
>
> To rest they love while life indure hap so what shall ensue
>
> And therefore my sweet lovying knight, have no mistrust in mee,
>
> For I do whole betake my selfe unto the use of thee.  (ll. 664-665)

Like Heliodorus's Chariclea, Clarisia makes sure that her pledge of marriage includes wedded chastity. She says, "So that thou wil performe the bondes of wedlocke in this case, / I am content that none but thou my corps shall sure embrace" (ll. 664-665). Lamphedon assents: "And therefore Lady, here is my hande, eke faith and trouth I give, / To rest and by thy loving knight, whilst I have day to live" (ll. 670-71). The rhetorically-balanced dialogue conveys to the audience the deeply mutual nature of the couple's love. There is thus an interesting movement toward a state that is paradoxically narcissistic--as each sees in the other a vision of perfection--and mutual, as the lovers engage with each in a symmetrical exchange of married love, loyalty, and constancy.

The symmetry of the hero and heroine eventually symbolizes their suitability for marriage; as it will turn out, Lamphedon and Clarisia share similar social and economic backgrounds, but in the play there is the suggestion that Lamphedon's parents oppose the marriage on account of Clarisia's inferiority in rank. After their clandestine marriage, the separation of the hero and heroine is caused by the Vice's successful manipulation of the hero's mother, who is all too easily convinced of Clarisia's supposed immodesty: "[T]he Duchess is fallen out with Clarisia long of mee," says Common Conditions, having told the Duchess's waiting maids that people believe Clarisia "excels the Duchess grace" (ll. 897-99). The play's clandestine marriage takes on wider significance within the context of sixteenth- and seventeenth-century controversies on marriage. Whereas early Christian canon upheld the legality of the secret marriage, one based on the free and mutual consent of a man and woman without witnesses, the religious reformists, notably Calvin and Luther, renounced this doctrine in favor of public marriage.[12] Luther contended that legal marriage entailed the presence of witnesses, including the parental consent of both partners. He proposed that a marriage performed without parental authorization and blessing should not be legally enforceable.

Miles Coverdale's Tudor translation of Heinrich Bullinger's *The christen state of Matrymonye* (1541), provides a detailed justification for the necessity of parental consent in marriage: "To a ryght mariage," he states, "must children also have the consent of theyr parents."[13] The author questions the papacy for its unsound logic, and he wonders what "papistical bokes & lerned men dyd meane whan they taught, that consent only of both the parties, doth fasten the matter & coupleth them together in marriage." The problem is that if a young couple contracts a foolish or nonadvantageous marriage, they remain legally bound together: "The consent of the parentes also say they is good wythall, but yf they two have consented & one hath take the other, the knot cannot be unknite, nether maye [the] parents separate them free a sunder" (sig. B3v). He continues to expound on the problem of young people's lack of discretion in marriage: "For in as much as the children are not yet come to perfyct discretion, they can not contract mariage which requireth understanding, yea they can nether counsell nor helpe them selves. So that in this behalfe the consent of they parents is not only necessary but also good and profitable for them" (sig. B3v). He concludes by urging mutual respect between children and parents in marriage: "the children must have respecte to their parentes and not wilfully despie them or cast them of: so shulde not the parentes without any pite compell their children to mariage afore their tyme nether wickedly neglect them, or leave them unprovided for in due season" (sig. B8).

In Thomas Paynell's English translation of Lodovicus Vives's *The office and duetie of an husband* (1554), Vives goes even further in his condemnation of the clandestine marriage: "secrete contractes of matrimony made betwene those that be young, are seldom fortunate & luckey, and feawe to be unlucky that are made, and established by their friendes and parents."[14] Therefore, he admonishes a future husband to leave "the care of this election to his parents, [the] which have better judgement & are more free from the agitations and motions of al affections, they are."[15] The Council of Trent (1563) adopted some of this new thinking on marriage reform. It abjured the validity of the clandestine marriage by repudiating the practice that made the private exchange of vows legally binding; it thus made marriage lawful by requiring the presence of witnesses, not necessarily parents, but at least a clergyman.[16] In *Common Conditions*, the Duchess's disapproval of the heroine might be warranted, given that Clarisia, fatherless, brings to the marriage no apparent dowery, position, or title, although the heroine claims the King of Thrace as her uncle (l. 920).

In keeping with the Greek romance tradition, the separation of Lamphedon and Clarisia after their secret marriage works to strengthen the couple's bond, even though their trials take on different forms. Like Clarisia, Lamphedon experiences ordeals that test his loyalty. But where the heroine suffers a direct threat to her body, thwarting assaults upon her virginity, Lamphedon does not. He attempts to keep his allegiance to Clarisia by ending his life. Believing that his beloved is drowned at sea, the hero finds solace in death: "Sith that her joy was joy to thee, let her death be thins also, / And with this goring blade of thine devide this hart from wo" (ll. 1124-5). As the heroine tenaciously keeps her pledge of fidelity and chastity, the hero tenaciously keeps his oath of everlasting love, even if it means his own demise (a plot feature found in romantic tragedies such as *Romeo and Juliet*). Although Clarisia's father attempts to poison the hero later in the play, the comedic nature of the story disallows a tragic ending. When Lamphedon is informed that Clarisia is alive, his contemplation of suicide turns into a determination to save his beloved from bodily harm (sailors have misinformed him that Clarisia has been imprisoned on the isle of Marofus in Cardolus's dark tower). In the context of the Greek romance genre, the tower acts as a symbolic threat to the heroine's inviolate chastity, even though Lamphedon does not find Clarisia in the tower. Although Lamphedon liberates the other captured women there, the fact that his beloved is not among the victims of Cardolus's cruelty does not avoid us from seeing Lamphedon as heroic. Yet it does make Clarisia's adventure and ordeal all the more heroic: she is not saved by the story's hero, but is rather the author of her own salvation (even though the Vice aids her when he wants to).[17]

Despite the sense of the lovers' reciprocity, the heroine's trials begin to gain greater centrality in the play, and these trials measure the heroine's ability to uphold her vow of loyalty and chastity. Here again, the heroine is neither acted upon nor merely saved by fortune, but is actively protecting herself from harm. For example, after escaping the threat of imprisonment in Cardolus's tower, Clarisia must repulse the romantic advances of an unlooked-for admirer. Posing as Metrea, the heroine unknowingly attracts the attention of her brother Sedmon, who is masquerading as the knight Nomides. Sedmon unwittingly falls in love with Metrea, Clarisia in disguise. Of course, Metrea shuns the flirtation and wooing of Nomides (whom she, of course, doesn't recognize as her brother). Lovesick, he begs Metrea to harken to his plea:

> Accept, my sute, O pereles dame, denay not my good will,
>
> But yeeld to me my wished pray which I desired still.
>
> And let me not for your sweet sake, O Lady, dye for love.
>
> (ll. 1478-80)

Metrea curtly dismisses his request: "I am al redy linkt in love with one who faithfull is. / For whose sweet sake Ile never love if of his love I mis" (ll. 1482-83). In addition, Leostines, Metrea's master, is really her own father; he possesses an overly zealous interest in the heroine, though he does not realize that he and she are related. Thus disguised as the servant Metrea, Clarisia now finds that she must defend her vows of chastity from the intentions of her new master. This paternal threat is at once more sublimated and more menacing. Because Leostines takes pity on Metrea and sees that "virginitie in [her] does still appeare" (ll. 1591), he plans to marry her to a knight of noble stock. To avert this threat to her plighted troth, Clarisia prevaricates in a state of desperation: "Lo here, deare lorde, do graunt to her in virgins state to rest, / For why I think and deme in minde that for my state is best. / And not for that I think my wit should pas your noble skill, / But from infancy till now have I request it still" (ll. 1636-39). Clarisia soon soliloquizes the real reason for her refusal to wed: "No, no Lamphedon, for thy sweet sake Ile ever faithfull rest" (1. 1652). Unsure whether or not Lamphedon is alive, Clarisia chooses a life of chastity rather than break her oath of constancy to the hero.

However extraordinary the hero's and heroine's vows of marital chastity seem, the uniqueness of their faith only intensifies when contrasted with another pair of lovers in the play. The play's subordinate plot, which follows the unrequited love of Sabia for Nomides, provides a counterplot to the perfectly balanced affection between Clarisia and Lamphedon. As counterplot, it brings forth a set of values that are antithetical to the valorization of fidelity and chastity by the hero and heroine. The subplot runs as follows: Sabia, a Phrygian maiden, has fallen helplessly in love with Nomides. Unfortunately for Sabia, not only does Nomides disdain love, but he abuses the name of woman by denigrating the female sex. According to Nomides, "Helena," "Cressida," "Phedria," "Media," as representatives of their gender, were all deceitful (ll. 800-05). He therefore adduces that "Men still are just though women must their plighted vows neclect [*sic*] (1. 807). After the audience has just witnessed the sincerity of Clarisia's and Lamphedon's "plighted vows," Nomides'' logic presents itself as circumstantial and faulty. Sabia tells him as much. Recalling the unfaithful men of myth and legend--"Eneas," "Jason," "Theseus," and "Deomedes"--she berates Nomides for his one-sided ignorance:

> Tush tush you see to trust to men whose fickle brains are so,
>
> That at the first sight of every wight their plighted vowes for go
>
> And therefore you must wey in minde, though wemen sometime misse
>
> Men wil do so though to their wo it doth ensew I wisse.  (ll. 824-27)

Sabia treats the theme of constancy without equivocation: men and women are not equally faithful, but can be equally unfaithful. At this point, Nomides admits defeat, but along with his capitulation comes rebuke. While men win honor in battle, women, according to Nomides, use sophistry, "suttle slights," to gain victory over men (l. 833).

Drawing on the rhetoric of early modern controversies about women, as well as the Petrarchan tradition, the interaction between Sabia and Nomides clearly does not adhere to the Greek adventure romance paradigm; in fact, their debate, coupled with Nomides' disparagement of love, calls into question the very possibility of equity in love.

Unfortunately, the text of *Common Conditions* remains unfinished. Because the play cuts off abruptly, we can only surmise the way in which the subplots are resolved. The hero has just been "poisoned" by the possessive Leostines, who has flown into a jealous rage upon seeing Lamphedon and Clarisia together. The play concludes in such disarray that it hardly bears out the intent of its title as "An excellent and pleasant Comedie." Even the epilogue states apologetically that "Time is pictured foorth to vew all bare and bauld behind, / With sickel in his hand to cut when it doth please his mind. / With that his sickell all are cut, and all thing brought to end. / As wee are now by Time cut of from farther time to spende" (ll. 1889-92). Given the conventions of the genre, we can speculate on an orthodox ending: Lamphedon revived; the lovers happily reunited; Nomides unveiled as Sedmon; Sedmon's union with Sabia, Leostines discovered as Clarisia's father; Leostines' aristocratic standing restored; Clarisia reconciled with the Duchess; the parental consent of the match; and the celebration of the lovers' nuptials. As far as the play goes, the hero and heroine successfully keep their marital vows of fidelity and chastity. Insofar as the lovers share an equal burden in the suffering, Clarisia defends her chastity twice. The hero does not. The heroine blocks the threat of a brother and father, and this comic blocking represents the heroine's fortitude in her constancy to the hero.

**II**

The play *Common Conditions* exemplifies the prevalence and popularity of the Greek romance plot in the Elizabethan era. Dramatists freely visited the traditional love and adventure plot line. The maiden heroine who suffers for love had a particularly widespread appeal in a society burgeoning with Protestant morality and the ideal of chaste love. In Chapter 2, "Love, Chastity, and Woman's Erotic Power: Greek Romance in Elizabethan and Jacobean Context," I examine the three surviving Greek romances that were translated into English in the Elizabethan period: Heliodorus's *Aethiopica, or Theagenes and Chariclea*; Achilles Tatius's *Leucippe and Clitophon;* and Longus's *Daphnis and Chloe*. I analyze the dominant characteristics of the genre as represented by these texts: a love-leading-to-marriage plot, the motif of symmetrical attraction, and trials of chastity. I look at the way in which the Greek romance paradigm of love and marriage, as expressed in these stories, reflected the new religious thinking on matrimony and sexuality: because virginity, or abstinence, was no longer the ideal expression of virtue, reformists viewed lawful marriage as an ideal state. These stories can be seen as a metaphor of the theoretical idea of mutuality in love and wedded chastity. Heliodorus's *Aethiopica* was the most popular of the Greek romances in the early modern period precisely because the author strongly emphasized the sexual purity of the noble hero and heroine. In this chapter, we also see how the theme of erotic suffering develops from this plot paradigm, and is connected with the construction of female heroism.

Chapter 3, "Sir Philip Sidney and Female Heroism: Erotic Suffering in the *New Arcadia*," argues that Sidney uses the Greek romance paradigm, specifically that of Heliodorus, as a model of female heroism. Ultimately, Sidney does not find in the Greek romance paradigm a suitable model of male conduct; he prefers to cast his male protagonists in the chivalric mode of virtue-in-arms. Sidney, however, discovers in Greek romance an appropriate expression for the heroic female. On the one hand, this heroine is disobedient because she violates her parents' wishes (often her father's) in order to wed the worthy hero. On the other hand, she is obedient to the moral code of chastity, conforming to a strict ethic of sexual abstinence before marriage. In order to remain constant to her standard of morality, she is made to suffer for her ideal belief in mutual love and sexual fidelity.

Shakespeare complicates Sidney's use of the Greek romance paradigm. While Sidney tends to separate the different models of male and female heroism, one based on chivalric romance, the other on Greek romance, Shakespeare uses the Greek romance pattern of erotic suffering as a criterion for male and female heroism. This gesture represents Shakespeare's response to and his revision of Sidney's understanding of Greek romance. In his romance plays, *Pericles, Cymbeline, and The Winter's Tale,* Shakespeare blurs gender lines by feminizing the young hero as he, like the heroine, suffers adversity in the name of love. The main stress is still given to the suffering of the heroine, but Shakespeare often eroticizes the male hero. In Chapter 4, "Romantic Symmetry in Shakespeare's *Pericles*," I look at how Shakespeare uses source stories rooted in Greek romance, specifically the *Apollonius of Tyre* tale, to create a hero who conforms to the Greek romance paradigm: throughout his many ordeals, Pericles adheres to the principles of faithfulness and wedded chastity. His heroism stems from his heroic, if not feminine, endurance in suffering.

In Chapter 5, "'The casting forth to crows thy baby daughter': Female Suffering and Child Abandonment in Shakespeare's *The Winter's Tale*," I show that Shakespeare drew from Greek pastoral romance, using Robert Greene's *Pandosto* as the primary source. In this play, greater emphasis is given to the suffering of mother and child, Hermione and Perdita, as they undergo affliction instigated by the jealous tyranny of Leontes. The redemption in the play derives, though, from the erotic suffering of the young generation, as they offer a new vision of amatory relations based on mutual love and shared affliction. Chapter 6, "The Comedy of Romantic Suffering: Imogen in Shakespeare's *Cymbeline*" argues that Shakespeare integrates into his plot line two models of romantic suffering. I contend that he bases his dramatic text on an early Elizabethan play, *The Rare Triumphes of Love and Fortune*. This play is, like *Common Conditions*, based on a Greek romance model, and Shakespeare overlays this story with the medieval wager story; the combination creates a hero who must suffer not only external obstacles but the threat of romantic disintegration from within. Imogen manifests manly valor, while Posthumus must suffer the wrongs that he has committed against his wife.

Pettet's statement concerning the diversity and ubiquity of romance in Renaissance England suggests the difficulty of discerning particular traits in the wide body of literary traditions. While Sidney and Shakespeare incorporate a variety of influences in their works, this study focuses on one crucial genre of romance. It is from this Greek romance genre that we find the marriage plot and the theme of erotic suffering that will be discussed in these chapters.

---

[1] E. C. Pettet, *Shakespeare and the Romance Tradition*, (Brooklyn, NY.: Haskell House Publishers, 1976), 12-13. In *Shakespearen Romance*, Howard Felperin finds that there are

three romance traditions that can be traced in Shakespeare: Greek romance, medieval chivalric romance, and the miracle play (based on classical romance). Felperin posits, however, that the miracle play, with roots in Greek romance, exerted the greatest influence on Shakespeare: "The miracle play actually derives on one side from Greek romance, since the stories of the trials and tribulations of the Christian martyrs and saints that it dramatizes were assimilated very early in the Middle Ages to the plot structure and Mediterranean setting of Greek romance, the accidents of fortune yielding to the providence of God" (Princeton: Princeton University Press, 1972), 13.

[2]Michel Foucault, *The Care of the Self*, trans. Robert Hurley, vol. 3. (London: Penguin Books, 1984), 228.

[3]Simone Swain, ed., *Oxford Readings in The Greek Novel* (Oxford: Oxford University Press, 1999), 5.

[4]See Tomas Hägg, "The New Heroes: Apostles, Martyrs and Saints," in *The Novel in Antiquity* (Berkeley and Los Angeles: University of California Press, 1983), 154-65.

[5]Judith Perkins, "Representations in Greek Saints' Lives, in *Greek Fiction: The Greek Novel in Context*, eds. J. R. Morgan and Richard Stoneman (London and New York: Routledge, 1994), 255-71.

[6] For a full account of the menaced virgin of the saints' legends, see Kathleen Coyne Kelly, *Performing Virginity and Testing Chastity in the Middle Ages* (London and New York: Routledge, 2000), esp. 40-62. Fo accounts of the lives of some well-known female saints, see Karen A. Winstead, ed., *Chaste Passions: Medieval English Virgin Martyr Legends* (Ithaca and London: Cornell Unviersity Press), 2000.

---

[7] John Stevens, *Medieval Romance: Themes and Approaches* (London: Hutchinson University Library, 1973), 33.

[8] C. S. Lewis, *The Allegory of Love* (Oxford: Oxford University Press, 1936), 13.

[9] See Erich Auerbach, "The Knight Sets Forth," in *Mimesis* (1953; Princeton University Press: Princeton and Oxford, 2003), 123-42.

[10] Geoffrey Bullough, *Narrative and Dramatic Sources of Shakespeare*, vol. 8 (London: Routledge & Kegan Paul, 1975), 347. For the influence of Sidney on Shakespeare, see also John F. Danby, *Elizabethan and Jacobean Poets* (London: Faber and Faber, 1964), 74-107. See also Pettet, *Shakespeare and the Romance Tradition*, 1-35. Sidney's *Arcadia* would have been well known to Elizabethan readers as *The Countess of Pembroke's Arcadia* (1593). This is a hybrid text put together by Sidney's sister, the Countess of Pembroke, after her brother's death. It consists of the first three books of the *New Arcadia* with the ending of the *Old Arcadia*, plus the Countess of Pembroke's emendations. In my discussion, I cite from the *New Arcadia* (1590) in order to acknowledge how Sidney reworks his romance material into a model based on ideal love and female heroism. For a discussion of the publication history of *Arcadia*, as well as Sidney's revisions, see Maurice Evans, ed., *The Countess of Pembroke's Arcadia* (Harmondsworth: Penguin, 1977), 9-50.

[11] *Common Conditions*, ed. Tucker Brooke, Elizabethan Club Reprints (New Haven: Yale University Press; London: Humphrey Milford; Oxford: Oxford University Press, 1915). Citations of the play by line number will be indicated parenthetically within the text. I follow the editor's numbering in these citations.

---

[12]James A. Brundage, *Law, Sex, and Christian Society in Medieval Europe* (Chicago and London: University of Chicago Press, 1987), 562-63.

[13]Miles Coverdale, trans., *The christen state of Matrimony, wherin housbandes & wyfes maye learne to kepe house together wyth Love* (London, 1541), sig. B3. Further citations will be indicated parenthetically within the text.

[14]Lodovicus Vives, *The office and duetie of an husband, made by the excellent philosopher Lodovicus Vives, and translated into Englyshe by Thomas Paynell* (London, 1554), sig. D5.

[15]Ibid., sig. D4v.

[16]Brundage, *Law, Sex, and Christian Society*, 564.

[17]As David Konstan argues in *Sexual Symmetry*, the inability of the hero to save the heroine from danger constitutes an important aspect of the Greek adventure romance convention: "A valiant defense of rescue of the beloved would have run counter to the spirit of the genre." Konstan goes on to explain that "The novel avoids any sign of differentiation between the roles of hero and heroine when their bond to one another is challenged." That is, the lovers must exhibit equal courage and bravery during their trial (Princeton: Princeton University Press, 1994), 24, 26.

CHAPTER 2

Love, Chastity and Woman's Erotic Power:

Greek Romance in Elizabethan and Jacobean Context


That the Greek romance exerted a strong influence on Elizabethan and Jacobean

prose fiction and drama, including Shakespeare, has been well documented.[1]

Notwithstanding individual variations, the Hellenistic authors who were most influential

in the Renaissance--Heliodorus, Longus, and Achilles Tatius--use plots that share an

underlying structural pattern: a pair of youthful lovers meet, fall in love, separate, suffer

trial and tribulation, and eventually reunite in lawful marriage. According to the classicist

John J. Winkler, the Greek romances of North Africa and Asia Minor introduced "a quite

specialized form of erotic story: these are love-leading-to-marriage stories, in which the

necessary goal of passion itself is lawful matrimony."[2] The erotic stories that constitute

the ancient prose romance genre include Heliodorus of Emesa's *Aethiopica* or *Theagenes

and Chariclea* (4th century AD); Longus's *Lesbiaca* or *Daphnis and Chloe* (3rd century

AD); Achilles Tatius of Alexandria's *Leucippe and Clitophon* (2nd century AD). Two

additional romances with less direct bearing on early modern drama and fiction are

Xenophon of Ephesus's *Ephesiaca* or *Habrocomes and Anthia* (2nd century AD) and

Chariton of Aphrodisia's *Chaereas and Callirhoe* (2nd century AD).[3] Typically, the hero

and heroine of Greek romance persevere through a series of conventional ordeals (storms,

shipwrecks, pirates, bandits). The protagonists' victory over their ill-fated mishaps ensure that their sexual attraction, which strikes instantly and with reciprocal force, is formidable enough to endure into the bond of matrimony. As David Konstan explains, "the reciprocal love between the primary couple is constituted in the Greek novels as the basis for an enduring relationship of marriage."[4] The formulaic motif of equal love in marriage guarantees the lovers' success in adversity and the story's triumphant ending.

The longstanding appeal of Hellenistic romance stretched well into Renaissance England. In *Shakespeare and the Greek Romance*, Carol Gesner has proposed an archetypal interpretation of the genre's popular storyline. Gesner draws on Northrop Frye's notion of the heroic romance quest by applying the tripartite pattern of the adventure "quest" to Greek romance: the "perilous journey," "crucial struggle," and "final discovery and recognition."[5] This mythic interpretation of the plot pattern runs counter to what Bruce R. Smith sees as the specific cultural significance in Renaissance England of "romances like *Clitophon and Leucippe*." Such Greek romances are sites of carnival "sexual license" where misrule and lawlessness reign within the constraints of the Elizabethan "power structure": because these romance narratives represent a temporary release from societal mores, they are, in Smith's words, "not real life," "a place apart," and "time out."[6] Although Greek romance may have functioned as a "place apart," or even a wish-fulfillment "quest," there are aspects of its love-in-marriage story that engaged directly in the moral codes of the period. More specifically, the generic plot scheme reflected a critical commonplace in sixteenth- and seventeenth-century Protestant sexual ethics: the valorization of legal matrimony and wedded chastity over celibacy and single life. The ancient romance plot--as it arises in the *Aethiopica, Leucippe and Clitophon, and Daphnis and Chloe*--presented a version of erotic love that conformed to the new ideas of married chastity and the sanctity of holy matrimony. It also promoted

fidelity as a dominant characteristic in the cultivation of romantic and married love; in

addition, Greek romance endorsed the state of virginity as a prerequisite for honorable

female (as well as male in Heliodorus) conduct in courtship.

Mikhail Bakhtin's discussion of Greek romance provides a theoretical lens

through which to analyze the ancient genre in relation to Protestant views on romantic

love. According to Bakhtin, Greek romance falls under the rubric of the "adventure novel

of ordeal" since its literary *chronotope* or "time space" corresponds to the pattern of

novelistic "adventure-time."[7] Bakhtin locates the nature of adventure-time within the plot

framework: "The first meeting of hero and heroine and the sudden flareup of their

passion for each other is the starting point for plot movement; the end point of plot

movement is their successful union in marriage"(89). In essence, all the action of the

novel transpires between these two poles, meeting and matrimony. For Bakhtin, the

concept of adventure-time entails that the hero and heroine undergo a series of ordeals

that test virtuous behavior. Between the two poles of plot movement, the awakening of

passion and its fulfillment in lawful matrimony, the young lovers experience a variety of

situations and adventures. The hero and heroine meet not only with perils throughout the

course of the story but also with a variety of temptations and enticements; as such, they

often find themselves in compromising situations and yet somehow manage to keep their

integrity. While the young lovers exemplify a variety of physical virtues--fortitude,

strength, and boldness--the moral qualities most often tested are fidelity and chastity. The

loyalty and constancy of the hero and heroine contribute to a principal characteristic of

Greek romance and demonstrate the lovers' mutual rectitude and probity. Thus, the symmetrical love of the hero and heroine remains unaltered throughout the novel, so that "[t]heir chastity is also preserved, and their marriage at the end of the novel is *directly conjoined* with their love--that same love that had been ignited at their first meeting at the outset of the novel"(89).

The narrative scheme of love-in-marriage would have found favor with a Renaissance Reformation audience who theoretically regarded matrimony as a state equal to (if not surpassing) celibacy, and considered mutuality in love as an integral condition within the bonds of marriage itself.[8] For religious reformers such as Luther and Calvin, the state of marriage was not conceived as a remedy for the ills of copulation, according to the standard interpretation of Gratian's *Decretum* (c. 1140), but rather a beneficial condition and blessing in itself.[9] No longer a sacrament, matrimony became the natural endpoint of erotic impulses. Thus, sixteenth- and seventeenth-century religious reformers embraced a more optimistic view of sex and marriage than was conventional in medieval canonical thought, although they realized that sexual passion had the power to vex human relationships, generate brutal behavior, and divert attention away from spiritual concerns.[10] As such, reformed theologians asserted the necessity of piety and reverence in sexual conduct; yet, they also considered sex in marriage a positive aspect of nuptial relations, so that lawful sexual union between a man and woman was not a defect in human nature caused by original sin, but a gift in its own right.[11]

The reformists' idea of chaste marriage, a doctrine that "claimed for marriage the spiritual prestige which had previously been reserved for celibacy,"[12] is consistent with the two most important elements of the Greek romance plot: the moment of love (or love-at-first-sight) and the moment of mutual union in marriage. The ancient romance plot, as it progressed from erotic passion to solemnized marriage, subscribed to the idea of

conjugal love and chaste marital relations as crucial factors in matrimony. Likewise, the

Protestant view of marriage as a validation of sexual relations between husband and wife

not only championed the notion of romantic love as a positive force in marriage, but it

also laid open to criticism the belief that sexual desire is *ipso facto* a destructive power in

human relationships, reducing lovers to irrational or lustful conduct. Sex, a natural and

powerful drive, gains legitimacy within the institution of holy matrimony.[13] The concept

of married love occupied a fundamental position in courtship and marriage in the Tudor

and Stuart period. In view of the elevated status of love in marriage, early modern

historian David Cressy contends that love, in the sixteenth and seventeenth centuries,

appears to have been "a common and expected ingredient in the majority of matches."[14]

I

The newly translated Greek romances enjoyed a tremendous readership in early

modern England and in Continental Europe. English translations of Greek romance first

appeared in Elizabeth I's reign. Angell Daye's edition of Longus's romance *Daphnis and

Chloe* was issued in 1587; this translation was based largely upon Jacques Amyot's 1559

popular and influential French rendering, *Les Amours pastourales de Daphnis et Chloé*.

William Burton's *The most delectable and pleasant Historye of Clitiphon and Leucippe*

appeared a decade later and was followed by Anthony Hodges's English version of

Achilles Tatius's romance in 1638. Prior to Burton's translation of *Leucippe and

Clitophon*, the romance had been widely available: it had been translated into Latin in

1554, Italian in 1546, and French in 1568. By far the most popular and esteemed of the

Greek romances in the early modern period was Heliodorus's *Aethiopica*. The first translator of the complete *Aethiopica* into English, Thomas Underdowne, closely followed the 1552 Latin translation of the romance undertaken by the Polish knight Stanislaus Warschewiczki.[15] Underdowne's 1569 version, *An Aethiopian historie*, was reprinted numerous times: in 1577, 1587, 1605, 1622, and 1627.[16] The decision to translate Heliodorus in the vernacular was, in all likelihood, inspired by such successful translations as Jacques Amyot's *L'Historie Aethiopique de Heliodorus, contenant dix livres, traitant des loyales et pudiques amours de Théagènes Thessalien, et Chariclea Aethiopiene*, a version that saw print no fewer than twenty-five times between 1547 and 1626, or Leon Ghini's popular Italian rendering, *Historia di Heliodoro delle cose Ethiopiche*.[17]

The *Aethiopica* was an exemplary piece of romantic fiction in the Elizabethan period, largely due to the sexual purity of its hero and heroine. What is particularly noteworthy about Underdowne's English translation is that it helped fashion the moral tenor of the *Aethiopica* by defending its amatory content. As the full title of Amyot's *L'Historie Aethiopique* indicates, Underdowne was not the first early modern translator to interpret the story of Theagenes and Chariclea as a commentary on loyal and modest love ("loyales et pudiques amours"). Nonetheless, in the 1577 and later reprints of *An Aethiopian historie*, he praises the book anew for its chaste love story, while noting its secular subject matter:

> I am not ignorant that the stationers shops are to full fraughted with books
>
> of smal price, wither you consider the quantitie or contents of them, and
>
> that the loosenesse of these dayes rather requireth grave exhortations to
>
> vertue, then wanton allurements to leudness, that it were meeter to publish

notable examples of godly christian life, then the most honest (as I take this to be) historie of love.[18]

Unlike other books that encourage "wanton allurements to leudness," the *Aethiopica* chronicles, as Underdowne has it, the most honest history of love. According to the *OED*, the word "honest" in the sixteenth century included the meaning of "chaste" and "virtuous," especially in reference to a woman's sexual conduct. Since the *Aethiopica*, however, is a story about the reciprocal love of Theagenes and Chariclea, "honest" presumably refers to the virtue and chastity of both the hero and heroine. The idea of mutual chastity reinforces Underdowne's moralistic proclivity, and he goes on to contrast the teaching of the *Aethiopica* with other stories of "smal price": "If I shall compare it with other of like argumente, I thinke none commeth neere it. *Morte Darthure*, *Arthur* of little *Britaine*, yea, and *Amadis* of *Gaule*, [etc.] accompt violent murder, or murder for no cause, manhoode: and fornication and all unlawfull luste, friendly love" (sig. iii). These chivalric romances fail to provide sound ethical instruction to the reader since they equate violence with manhood and unlawful passion with love. "These bokes," writes Lodovicus Vives about such fiction, "do hurt both man & woman, for they make them wylye & craftye, they kyndle and styr up covetousnes, inflame angre, & all beastly and filthy desyre."[19] The chivalric tradition, in general, tended to privilege the escapades of a knight in love with a lady already married over the story of chaste lovers, shared adventures, and their union in lawful matrimony.[20] Accordingly, their gratuitous violence and illicit sex differentiate them from Heliodorus, whose "booke punisheth the faultes of evill doers, and rewardeth the well livers" (sig. iii).

As Underdowne's appraisal of the *Aethiopica* indicates, early modern readers of Heliodorus frequently interpreted the story's theme of honest love as a paradigm of romantic relations. This interpretation, one repeatedly applied to Heliodorus, extended well into the seventeenth century. For example, in his 1638 verse translation, *The famous historie of Heliodorus* (originally titled *The Faire Ethiopian* in the edition of 1631), William Lisle appends the document "Testimonies of Learned men concerning Heliodorus." These testimonies substantiate the value of the *Aethiopica* by enumerating its wide range of virtues, including, of course, its chaste love story. A testimonial from the scholar Thomas Dempster states cogently: "Heliodorus the Phoenix of Phoenicia: an Elegant writer of chast Love, and in the contexture of this History, a most elaborate Author."[21] Later in the century, Nahum Tate and a "Person of Quality" affix similar testimonials to their 1686 translation of the romance, *The Aethiopian History of Heliodorus*. This title undergoes a transformation in the 1687 second edition to read in full: "The Triumphs / Of Love / And / Constancy: / A / Romance. / Containing the Heroick Amours of Theagenes & Chariclea / In Ten Books." Along with the "Heroick Amours" of the hero and heroine, the title proclaims love and constancy as its main premise, and the testimonials of "Eminent Persons, Ancient and Modern" corroborate this claim. One such person, "Vicentius Obsopoeus," the first editor of the *Aethiopica* in print (1534), is quoted as saying:

> I Recommend The Aethiopian History of Heliodorus, as the most absolute
> Image of all humane Affections; a perfect Example of Conjugal Love,
> Truth and Constancy being Wonderfully drawn in the Characters of
> Theagenes and Chariclea.[22]

This Protestant critic defines the story as an ideal model of romantic love: the devotion of the hero and heroine is "the most absolute" of human affections and a "perfect Example" of marital love, truth, and constancy.[23] Concomitantly, another testimonial from a Dr. Peter Heylin indicates that the lovers' "honest and chaste affection" is suitable for even the "chastest Ear":

> A piece indeed of rare contexture and neat contrivance, without any touch of loose or lascivious Language, honest and chast affection being the subject of it, not such as Old or Modern Poets show us in the Comedies or other Poems: for here we have no Incestious mixtures of Fathers and Daughters: no Pandorism of Old Nurses: no unseemly action specified, where heat of Blood and opportunity do meet: nor indeed any one passage unworthy of the chastest Ear. (sig. a5)

Although there is no direct reference to a specific comedy or poem in this comparison, it appears that Heliodorus's romance would afford the stage worthy material, for the story supersedes less virtuous tales of passion, including presumably those of New Comedy in which the subject of love is often sexualized and usually illicit.

Other English translations of Greek romance share a similar emphasis on the merit of honest love. In Daye's *Daphnis and Chloe* the title page emphasizes the virtue of honorable courtship, among other themes: "Daphnis and Chloe / Excellently / describing the weight / of affection, the simplicities of love, the purport / of honest meaning, the resolution of men, and disposition of Fate."[24] Likewise, the title page of Hodges's seventeenth-century translation of Achilles Tatius's *Leucippe and Clitophon* accentuates the romantic love between the hero and heroine: "The Loves / of Clitophon / And

Leucippe. / A most elegant History, written in / Greeke by Achilles Tatius."[25] In the same translation, a sonnet accompanies an illustration on the frontispiece. It depicts the hero and heroine in the throes of a storm at sea: "See for the sceane a troubled Sea, whereon / Float faire Lecuippe and her Clitophon." Clutching one another, the lovers receive little succor from the element: "But churlish Neptune (who for Venus sake / Me thinkes on Lovers should some pitie take) / Quels not the raging Ocean, while each wave / Presents the ship, and passengers, a grave." The sonnet concludes with Venus's dispatch of Cupid to the lovers' rescue: " . . . Loves Queene . . . Sets Cupid at the sterne; who well may free / These paire of Turtles from the tyranny / Of angry Neptune . . . " (sig A1v). The shipwreck off the coast of Alexandria refers to Leucippe and Clitophon's first adventure and separation, and it initiates the series of trials that lead up the couple's marriage. The powerful drive of erotic love--which in the Petrarchan or Ovidian tradition is often associated with the frenzy, sickness, and derangement induced by Cupid's arrow--is now depicted as a benevolent and benign force that saves lovers from the threat of destructive elements. As the placement of the sonnet and illustration indicates, these Renaissance printers and translators of Greek romance stressed the amorous virtues represented in these stories, including the triumph of mutual love tested by adversity.

Even though Achilles Tatius, Longus, and especially Heliodorus received praise for the didactic nature of their stories, such writers also incurred the condemnation of early modern critics. An infamous critique can be found in Stephen Gosson's *Playes Confuted in Five Actions* (c. 1582). Gosson singles out the "*Aethiopian historie*" as one in a group of indecent, low-brow stories and dramatic works that had been "throughly ransackt" to supply material for the London playhouses:

> The *Palace of pleasure*, the *Golden Asse*, the *Aethiopian historie*, *Amadis of Fraunce*, the *Rounde table*, baudie Comedies in Latine, French, Italian and Spanish, have been throughly ransackt, to furnish the Playe houses in London. How is it possible that our Playemakers headdes, running through Genus and Species & every difference of lyes, cosenages, baudries, whooredomes, should present us with any schoolemistres of life, looking glasse of manners, or Image of trueth?[26]

In part, Gosson's complaint is that such common fiction not only contains vile subject matter, "lyes, cosenages, baudries, whooredomes," but presents an illusory and thus false image of reality because it distorts the "looking glasse of manners, or Image of trueth." About this much-quoted passage, Hallett Smith states that "[t]he Greek romances would have been scorned by the enemies of the stage, like Gosson," who regarded them as extravagant and foolish.[27] Although Gosson denounces the *Aethiopica*, his criticism suggests that at least one Greek romance provided playwrights with a repertoire of incidents and characterizations. Indeed, in *The Lost Plays and Masques, 1500-1642*, Gertrude Marian Sibley lists a play called *Theagines and Cariclea*, performed at court in 1572 for the Christmas festivities, and also one titled *The Queen of Ethiopia* (identified with *Theagines and Cariclea*), acted by Lord Howard's men for the mayor of Bristol in 1578.[28] It was theoretically conceivable that Gosson's "Playemakers" were reading and scripting Underdowne's English translation of Heliodorus, which would have been available to them in 1569 and again in 1577. Underdowne's 1577 epistle to the reader in support of the *Aethiopica* also appears in approximately the same period that Gosson launches his attack on playwrights. Whether or not Underdowne was ambivalent about the transference of his work to the stage, or whether his translation did in fact encourage dramatic adaptations of the prose romance, he upholds the *Aethiopica* as a celebrated testimony to "honest love."

Heliodorus's *Aethiopica* seemed to set the standard for the Greek romance genre. Apparently, Heliodorus created its paragon, "the most honest . . . historie of love" (Underdowne, sig. iii), as well as "a perfect Example of Conjugal Love" (Tate, sig. A5v). Indeed, one compliment paid to Hodges on his translation of Achilles Tatius was the author's comparison to Heliodorus: "Friend, I thy boke compare with swilk of yore, / With mighty deeds of worthy Heliodore" (sig. A6v). Moreover, in Burton's 1597 translation of *Leucippe and Clitophon*, the translator compares the merit of Achilles Tatius's work to Heliodorus's: "(as Crucius saith uppon Heliodorus) there is none who is learned, and desirous of good instructions, which once having begun to read him, can lay him aside, untill he have perused him over."[29] This reverence for Heliodorus canonizes the *Aethiopica*, even though chronologically it was written after both the works of Achilles Tatius and Longus.[30]

Given similarities in plot and theme, why did Heliodorus's *Aethiopica* stand apart from its romance counterparts in the early modern period? An explanation of the *Aethiopica*'s singularity may lie in the story's emphasis on the virginal purity of both the hero and heroine. At this point, a further distinction needs to be made within the genre of Greek romance. In his study of the Greek novel, David Konstan argues that the primary virtue of the Hellenistic romance hero and heroine resides in the preservation of their mutual fidelity, not necessarily in the strict enforcement of their physical chastity. He states:

In the Greek novels, the body is not the primary site on which the problem of love and fidelity is transacted. In the absence of a strong opposition between love and lust, where sex is constructed as the specific object of lust and is resisted in the name of true love, the Greek novel does not focus on sex per se as the hallmark of virtue. In certain situations, the protagonist, male or female, accepts a sexual association with another partner, but this is not registered in the text as a failure of fidelity.[31]

In support of this observation, one could cite Clitophon's seduction by an Ephesian wife or Daphnis's copulation with a married woman. Rather than an absolute adherence to chastity, the integrity of the Greek romance hero and heroine consists in maintaining a commitment to their pledge of fidelity. In essence, a sexual peccadillo, usually committed in extremity, does not damage the lovers' unshakable resolution to remain together. Konstan, however, perceives that in Heliodorus a different type of relationship between the hero and heroine develops, one in which virginal purity begins to take the place of mere fidelity as the story's principal virtue. What makes this shift in emphasis especially significant in Heliodorus is that the ideal of pre-marital virginity applies equally to the male as well as to the female protagonist. As will be shown, the importance given to both female and male chastity in the *Aethiopica* distinguishes the story from its Greek romance counterparts in *Leucippe and Clitophon* and *Daphnis and Chloe*.

In the *Aethiopica*, the love-leading-to-marriage plot fosters the motif of reciprocal chastity, and the emphasis on the virginal purity of the hero and heroine occurs almost as soon as the protagonists meet. Theagenes, a Thessalian and descendant of Achilles, has come to Athens to perform ceremonial rites in honor of his ancestors. Chariclea, an

Athenian priestess of Diana, oversees the ritual. In actuality, the heroine is an Ethiopian princess born with white skin because her mother, Persina, gazes on a picture of Andromeda during her daughter's conception. Chariclea's light skin color forces Persina, who fears accusations of adultery, to convey her daughter secretly from their native land, an action that places Chariclea under the guardianship of an Athenian, Charicles. During the festivities of the Pythian Games, Theagenes and Chariclea fall in love at first sight (Book Three). The narrator describes Cupid as the "moderatour" and "Arbiter" of the festivities in order to show that the couple's romantic and eventual sexual union is ultimately controlled by a higher, goodly power. By having a judicious Cupid oversee the love match, Heliodorus sets the scene for the couple's chaste and discreet pairing: "The nexte daie Apolloes games did ende, but youthfull disportes begane, Cupide (in mine opinion) moderatour, and Arbiter thereof, beeing in full determination, to declare his force, in most ample wise, by these two champions, which he had sette together" (F8v). Consequently, in Book Four the modest Chariclea resists her ardent passion for Theagenes, fearing that her love sickness will denigrate her virginal state. She says to the Egyptian sage Calasiris: "Although mine increasing disease doth muche greeve me, yet that greeveth mee more, that at the firste I overcame it not, but am yeelded unto love, which by hearing onely doth defile the honorable name of virginitie" (sig. G6v). Calasiris convinces Chariclea of the naturalness of her desire and that her strong affection for Theagenes can only find legitimization in holy matrimony. Therefore, he pacifies the heroine:

> But now we consider howe presently you may best order your businesse,
> in as much as at the firste, not to be in love, is a kind of happinesse, but

when you are taken, to use it moderately, it is a point of excellente

wisedome, which thing you may well doo, if you will beleeve mee, by

putting away the filthy name of luste, and imbracing the lawfull bande of

wedding, and turning your disease into matrimony.  (sig. G6v-G7)

Calasiris does not prize virginity over wifehood, but he does indicate that sexual desire

should be properly channeled via the rite of marital union.

In a larger context, Calasiris's differentiation between virginal and wedded

chastity would have been acknowledged by Elizabethan and Jacobean readers as a

legitimate distinction, especially, though not exclusively, for women. In Marie

Loughlin's definition, virginal chastity in the early modern period involved "sexual

abstinence usually undertaken by religious women and men," while wedded chastity

referred to "virginity aimed . . . at the dissolution of its integrity in the lawful sexual

initiation of marriage."[82] The logical conclusion is that wedded chastity was, writes

Loughlin, "a state that Protestants valued more highly than the older ideal of lifelong

abstinence."[83] We find, for example, a pertinent explanation of the place of chastity in

wedlock in a sixteenth-century treatise on marriage. In *Gods Arithmeticke* (1597), Francis

Meres explains that the Devil and his workers (the Catholic Church) "bannished out of

the bondes of Christianitie, that most famous and glorious Empresse Ladie Matrimonie

and exalted in her Throne fained Dame Chastitie, which beeing pure is not to be preferred

before holy Wedlocke."[84] According to Meres, because God ordained Adam and Eve to

increase and multiply, the Catholic dogma that elevates virginity over sexual relations in

marriage contradicts the Creator's commandment. Hence, "Virginitie is the daughter of

Marriage, and through marriage is made a Cittizen and In-dweller of Paradice."[85]

Interestingly, an Elizabethan translation of Heliodorus emphasizes the very idea of wedded chastity. In *The Amorous and Tragicall Tales of Plutarch* (1567), James Sanford appends Book Four of the *Aethiopica* to a series of Plutarch's tales. Significantly, Sanford's rendering of Heliodorus's romance places greater weight on the sanctity of wedded chastity than does Underdowne's translation, which follows Warschewiczki's Latin version more closely. Unlike Plutarch's more sordid tales of lust and murderous passion, the section of the *Aethiopica* that Sanford chooses to translate describes the spotless inception of Theagenes' and Chariclea's symmetrical love, their pledge of fidelity, and wedded chastity.

The scene in question occurs just before the lovers' elopement. When Chariclea's father arranges for her to marry his nephew, Theagenes and Chariclea decide to elope in order to remain together. Sanford's Chariclea insists that Theagenes not violate her until their nuptials have concluded: she demands that "Theagenes establishe with an othe [her] securitie and suretie, that he shall not bed with [her], untill the espousalls bee ended." Disappointed that Chariclea should suspect him so weak as to need an oath of chastity, Theagenes did "sware, that he had injurie shewed him, saying":

> That faith might be broken by preventing the oath, and onely to be performed willingly with promise of mind, neither that hee could commende that minde, which for feare of one more stronger seemeth to be compelled.

The narrator continues:

> yet he sware by Apollo of Delphos, and by Diana, & Venus hir selfe, that
>
> he would doe all things as Chariclea desired. And he and she calling the
>
> Gods to witnesse, made the agreement betwene themselves.[36]

In Heliodorus's story, Theagenes and Chariclea have not been publicly married during

the course of their adventures, though at this point in the narrative they exchange private

vows of fidelity and sexual continence. It is possible that an early modern reader of this

passage might interpret this literary presentation of the couple's private oath as a

clandestine marriage, one based on the late medieval and Renaissance theological precept

of *verba de presenti* (present consent) and *verba de futuro* (future consent): a theory of

legal marriage based on the sole mutual consent of a couple.[37] The historian David Cressy

writes that a lawful and binding marriage contract in the medieval and early modern

period "could be expressed in *verba de presenti*, making an immediate and indissoluble

commitment expressed by the words 'I do'; [or] *verba de futuro*, a promise of future

action expressed by the words 'I will.'"[38] Diana O'Hara states further that "Words of

future consent (*verba de futuro*) and conditional contracts did not instantly create valid

unions, but became absolute once sexual intercourse occurred and any specified

conditions were fulfilled."[39] She adds: "Local customs such as the use of gifts and rings,

and other formalities which involved familial agreement and betrothal before witnesses,

were called for but were not in fact essential for legal validity."[40] Alone, Sanford's

Theagenes and Chariclea exchange vows that countenance mutual sexual abstinence until

"the espousalls bee ended," so that the clandestine ceremonial pact between the lovers (in

the language of *verba de futuro*) reinforces the principle of mutual chastity before lawful marriage. The same passage, however, in Underdowne's *An Aethiopian historie* gives a notably different reading. Here, Chariclea has Theagenes swear to his chastity in these terms: "that he shall not fleashly have to doo with me, untill I have recovered my countrie, and parentes, or if the Godds be not content herewith, at least untill I by mine owne free will be content he shal marrie me. Other wise never" (sig. H3). Not only does Chariclea wish to choose the time of her marriage, but she concedes, it seems, to the possibility of sex before the event of a solemnized marital union, one formally witnessed by her parents. In Underdowne, Chariclea possesses more sovereignty than in Sanford's characterization of her. Although *Amorous and Tragicall Tales* was published two years before the first printing of Underdowne's *An Aethiopian historie*, the variations in the two passages reveal Sanford's concern with fashioning a more orthodox picture of the hero and heroine's equal commitment to marriage and sexual temperance.

In another Elizabethan translation of Heliodorus, the subject of wedded chastity arises once again as a significant theme. Abraham Fraunce in *The Countesse of Pembroke's Yuychurch* (1591) appends a small excerpt from Book One of the *Aethiopica* to his *Amyntas Pastorall*, a dramatic poem based on Torquato Tasso's *Aminta*. While this small excerpt from the love story of Theagenes and Chariclea may have been merely a literary exercise in Greek translation, its inclusion in Fraunce's publication is more than fortuitous. Similar to the love-leading-to-marriage pattern in Heliodorus's romance, what is exalted in *Amyntas Pastorall* is not virginal chastity, but virginity that culminates in holy wedlock. This theme is not totally incongruent with the Catholic ideal of chaste conduct before and during matrimony, an ideal that one might find in a writer such as Tasso. About this issue, Ruth Kelso argues that "chastity, synonymous with virginity in the maid, was obviously not conceived by Catholics as ending with virginity on marriage, but . . . was counted the greatest virtue of the wife in her fidelity to her husband."[41] Initially, the virginal Phillis cruelly rejects the affection of Amyntas; yet, when she discovers that Amyntas's supposed death is brought on by her own proud disdain, Phyllis repents her scorn: "my scornefull pryde, that I then my Chastyty called, / And it Chastyty was, but Chastyty noe-pyty-taking, / Now I repent it alas, but now too late I repent yt."[42] After Phyllis realizes her folly, her lack of compassion in love, she gives herself to the revived Amyntas in marriage. Phyllis's self-realization corresponds to Chariclea's maturation from a reclusive virgin to a chaste bride. Before Chariclea falls in love with Theagenes in the *Aethiopica*, her father laments that "Shee hath bidden mariage farewell, and determineth to live a maiden stil, and so becomming Dianas servant, for the most parte, applieth her selfe to hunting, and doth practice shooting." He goes on to describe the heroine's resolve to remain celibate: Chariclea "commending virginitie with immortall praise, and placing it in Heaven by the Gods, calleth it immaculate, unspotted, and uncorrupted: as for love, Venus disporte, and every Ceremonie, that apperteineth to marriage, shee utterly dispraiseth" (sig. E4v-E5). As does Chariclea, Phyllis eventually abrogates the state of maidenhood for the sanctioned contract of marriage.

In "The second part of the Countesse of Pembrokes Yuychurch," based on a translation from Thomas Watson, the poem describes Amyntas's inconsolable grief over the death of Phyllis on their wedding day. This poem, when read together with Fraunce's translation of Heliodorus's Book One, has further thematic links with the notion of wedded chastity. Unwilling to live without his beloved, Amyntas mortally wounds himself, and, as a tribute to his undying faith, the gods transform the dying Amyntas into the Amaranthus flower; not remarkably, Cupid appropriates the flower. Even though this love story does not conform strictly to the Greek romance ending of happy-ever-after, it appears that Fraunce draws from the story of Theagenes and Chariclea to suggest the idea of mutual chastity even in death; for, the Heliodorian lovers uphold their pledge of fidelity to such a degree that they would rather choose death than lose their virginity to any other person. For example, in Fraunce's "The Beginning of Heliodorus his Aethiopical History," the reader meets Chariclea and Theagenes, learns of their devotion, and views their courage in the face of shipwreck and Egyptian thieves. One of the high points of this section occurs when Chariclea, threatening suicide, staves off capture by a large group of bandits, whose leader is Thyamis. Defending the wounded Theagenes and guarding her own person, the heroine, in Fraunce's words,

> cleaved fast to the yongman,
>
> And held yongman fast, and every way shee declared;
>
> Unles yongman went, she never meant to be going,
>
> Unles yongman went, herself shee meant to be murdring,
>
> And with a knife in her hand to her hart shee begins to be poynting.
>
> (sig. M3)

Similar to Amyntas, who stabs himself in the breast, Chariclea chooses death over the possibility of life without her betrothed, though she is saved here from actual suicide. Chariclea's defense of Theagenes also implies a defense of her own virginity. Surrounded by a group of bandits who profess utter astonishment over Chariclea's rare beauty, the heroine perhaps senses a palpable threat to her person and chastity. A little later, when Thyamis captures the hero and heroine, Chariclea declares her determination to remain true to Theagenes or else die: "but rather then any man should filthely know me, which Theagenes never did, truely with haulter I woulde ende my life, reserving my selfe pure and chaste (as hitherto I have done) even unto deathe, and thereby gaine a beautifull Epitath for my singular virginitie" (Underdowne, sig. A5). Importantly, Theagenes had been injured in an earlier skirmish when he was attempting to protect the heroine's maidenhead. At that earlier point, he and Chariclea took up arms "Syth force and violence were offered unto [her] person" (Fraunce, sig. M2v).[43] Theagenes' and Chariclea's single-minded tenacity to consummate their passion in marriage remains a thematic feature of the first book.

If readers were to continue where Fraunce's translation leaves off, they might observe that the preservation of the hero's and heroine's virginity often depends upon the lovers' ability to pass as brother and sister. The use of this plot device indicates the physical and psychological mirroring of the primary couple: beautiful, chaste, and valiant, Theagenes and Chariclea resemble each other to such a degree that they often succeed at simulating a brother-and-sister relationship. Although romantic love happens as the product of spontaneous attraction in Greek romance, it occurs within the confines of a predetermined social and economic boundary: not only do the hero and heroine physically resemble each other, but they belong to the same social and economic class.[44] For example, in the *Aethiopica* the couple Theagenes and Chariclea both claim noble ancestry; the hero is a direct descendant of Achilles, and the heroine learns that she is the daughter of an Ethiopian king and queen. In Longus's pastoral *Daphnis and Chloe*, the hero and heroine, as shepherds, both discover at the story's conclusion that each possesses an affluent father in Mytilene. In Achilles Tatius's *Leucippe and Clitophon*, the lovers are even half cousins. To further this sense of homogeneity, the romance hero and heroine often mirror each other by being the most attractive, pure, or virtuous of their sex. In the narrative context of Greek romance, the hero and heroine freely choose love; however, the objective of this love, lawful marriage, takes place within the bounds of the couple's established social order.

The lovers' similitude in the *Aethiopica* allows the hero and heroine to put on the guise of brother and sister in order to ward off potential threats to their chastity. Both Theagenes and Chariclea use this tactic. For example, when the robber Thyamis (who is really a high priest of Memphis) desires Chariclea as his lawful wife, the heroine invents a story that keeps Theagenes from harm and her virginity intact. About her "brother" Theagenes, she says to Thyamis: "When we came to the age of fourtene yeeres, by the lawe (whiche calleth such to the office of priesthood) I was made priest, to Diana, and this my brother of Apollo" (sig. B6). When Chariclea deceptively requests that Thyamis allow her to surrender her priesthood at an appropriate shrine of Apollo before she marries him, Chariclea gains valuable time to forestall a marriage with Thyamis, while simultaneously quelling Thyamis's jealousy of Theagenes. But Theagenes does not understand this dissimulation. Bewildered by Chariclea's apparent plan to wed another, Theagenes accuses the heroine of forsaking her pledge to him. Chariclea counters this accusation by restating her immutable loyalty to Theagenes. She states:

> In one thing onely I knowe, I have not ruled my selfe, that is, in the love
>
> that I have borne to you, from the beginninge, but notwithstanding it is
>
> both lawfull, and honeste: for I not like your lover, but at the first
>
> concluding marriage with you, have committed my selfe to you, and have

lived chastely without copulation hitherto, not without refusing you

oftentimes, profering me such things, and have waited for occasion to be

married, if any where it might lawfully be done, whiche thing, at the first,

was decreed betweene us, and above all things, by othe established. (sig.

B7v)

Implicitly, Chariclea reminds Theagenes that her scheme--to wed Thyamis--is merely a

ploy to keep her troth plight. Just as Chariclea safeguards her virginity by blocking an

unwanted suitor (and evidently also refusing Theagenes), Theagenes also blocks the

sexual advances of the character Arsace, sister to the king of Memphis. Theagenes

subdues the envy of Arsace by feigning that Chariclea is his sibling.

Books Seven and Eight of the *Aethiopica* focus largely on the preservation of

Theagenes' virginity and his sexual commitment to the heroine. When the hero and

Chariclea arrive in Memphis, the seductress Arsace becomes "inflamed when shee had

seene Theagenes excellent beautie, which farre passed all that ever shee had seene

before" (sig. M5v). Secretly plotting to entrap Theagenes, Arsace invites the couple to

stay with her after their guardian Calasiris dies. As Theagenes considers "howe wantonly

with steady eyes, continually shee beheld him, so that her becks declared scante a chaste

minde" (sig. M8), he apprehends Arsace's capacity for lust and her jealousy of Chariclea.

Prompted by the heroine, Theagenes tells Arsace's bawd that they "be brother and sister"

(sig. M8v). The bawd "was very gladde to heare the names of brother and sister, thinking

then surely that Cariclia should be no impediment to Arsaces disports" (sig. M8v). When

by necessity Theagenes reveals to Arsace that Chariclea is really his plighted wife, the

hero suffers torture but does not succumb to Arsace's repeated attempts upon his virginity: "by reason of his chastity," Theagenes delights in his torture: "he now had occasion to declare what good will he bare to Cariclia" (sig. O6-O6v). This physical trial only serves to strengthen Theagenes' dedication to Chariclea and reinforces his pledge of chastity: "he tooke a lofty stomach to him, and rejoyced, and gloried in that fortune" (sig. O6-O6v). In order to draw attention to the reciprocal nature of the couple's commitment, Heliodorus has Chariclea incarcerated with the hero on a trumped up charge of murder. Fettered togther, the couple interprets their perseverance in adversity as a testament to a shared allegiance to constancy and virginal integrity:

> But they compted this a comfort, and to be pained alike they thoughte it a vauntage, and if either had lesse torments then the other, eche supposed hym selfe vanquished, and as it were more faint, and weake in love. For nowe was it lawfull for them to be together, and encourage eche other to take in goodly wise what fortune so ever came, and refuse no perill which shoulde insue of their unfained chastitie, and stedfaste faith.  (sig. P2)

The passage underlines the common trials of the hero and heroine. Each experiences pain and hardship on account of the other, and each wishes the other to suffer less. The lovers' anguish only fortifies their impervious bond, their "unfained chastitie" and "stedfaste faith."

The final test of the couple's chastity takes place in the last book. This episode supports the ethic of male and female celibacy before marriage. In a series of events too complicated to summarize here, Theagenes and Chariclea arrive as prisoners in the heroine's native Ethiopia. Once again, they act as brother and sister. Chariclea's father, Hydaspes, has just won victory over the Persians and intends to sacrifice both a male and a female virgin to his country's gods. Unaware that Chariclea is his own daughter and Theagenes his future son-in-law, Hydaspes hopes to offer the heroine to the Moon, the hero to the Sun. But before Hydaspes initiates the sacrifices, he tests the pair for their sexual purity: "the lawe willeth that shee be as well cleane also, that is offered to the Moone, as he that is sacrificed to the Sunne" (sig. R7v). To test their innocence, the hero and heroine must walk through fire because "it would burne every unchast person" (sig. R7v). Not surprisingly, the couple proves chaste. What amazes the spectators, though, is not the virginity of the heroine, but the hero's maidenhood: "After Theagenes also put his foote to the fire, and was founde a maide, there was great wondering, both for that he being so tall and beautifull, as also because he was young and lusty, and had never to do with any woman" (sig. R8). The logic is that the young, attractive hero should have by now submitted to his carnal passions. The public trial of virginity not only affirms the spotless attachment of the hero and heroine, but it also paves the way for their lawful wedding at the story's conclusion.

The concepts found in Bakhtin's treatment of Greek romance seem to relate particularly to Heliodorus's story of reciprocal love and sexual continence; in his words, the main protagonists "are placed in the most ticklish situations, but they always emerge with their honor intact" (106). Yet this model does not wholly correspond to the presentation of love and chastity in the storylines of Longus and Achilles Tatius. This is not to say that the concept of mutual sexual temperance does not figure largely into the design of their narratives. It does. In these romances, however, the hero's desire for sexual intimacy with the heroine or his physical indiscretion with another woman, which usually occurs at a moment of crisis in the course of his ordeals, is excused or tolerated as a common aberration in male conduct.

In *Leucippe and Clitophon*, the lovers learn to cultivate the virtue of chastity during the course of their adventures. If Theagenes and Chariclea possess an innate understanding of the necessity of wedded chastity, Achilles Tatius's plot teaches the primary couple to abstain from sexual relations before marriage. In Book One, Clitophon falls head-over-heels in love with Leucippe during their first encounter, and he is coached into seducing her by his sexually-sophisticated cousin, Kleinias. In his attempt to bed the heroine, Clitophon convinces Leucippe that, if the couple exchange private vows of love, they can licitly consummate their passion. No longer satisfied with mere kissing, he urges her to "do the rest which lovers most of all desire: therfore first let us contract our selves togither, for if we will sacrifice to Venus, we shall not find any god more favourable unto us then this" (sig. F1). The hero mitigates Leucippe's anxiety about premarital sex by assuring her of the legality of their secretly plighted troth. Soon after Leucippe agrees, their attempt at lovemaking is stymied by Leucippe's mother, Panthia. Due to the circumspection of Panthia and because Clitophon's father wants him to marry his half-sister, the pair decide to elope. It is during the first separation of the lovers that a new alliance is forged between the couple, one based on the prospect of wedded chastity or mutual sexual abstinence before lawful matrimony. Unlike Theagenes' and Chariclea's vow of chastity before their elopement, the hero and heroine in Achilles Tatius's novel come to their agreement on abstinence only after their elopement and only after the onset of their initial trials, which include a shipwreck, capture by Egyptian outlaws, and the heroine's faked immolation. When the pair eventually reunite after their first set of adventures, Leucippe forestalls Clitophon's request for sex, his "frutes of Venus" (sig. K1v), by relating to him the contents of a dream. In this dream, the goddess of chastity, Diana, reveals herself as Leucippe's guardian: "in my dreame Diana seemed to appeare unto me, saying; doo not weepe, for thou shalt not die, I my selfe will helpe thee, keepe thou as yet thy virginitie, until I shall otherwise appoint thee, for thou shalt marry none but Clitiphon" (sig. K1v). Although privately betrothed to the hero, Leucippe at once resolves to remain a virgin until lawful matrimony. Coincidentally, Clitophon has had a similar dream. He recounts that, while standing in a temple of Venus, a woman appears before him, saying that "as yet it was not lawfull for me to enter into the temple; but if that I would stay a little space, it should come to pass, that the doores would open of theyr owne accord, and also that I should be created a Priest unto the goddesse" (sig. K2). The apparition in the dream forewarns Clitophon of the illegality of intercourse before marriage. On account of Leucippe's vision of Diana and Clitophon's dream in the temple of Venus, the hero now determines to exercise sexual temperance with the heroine: "neyther did I strive to offer her [Leucippe] violence any more" (sig. K2). Leucippe retains her virginity throughout her ordeals, but not without much suffering and tribulation.

As we begin to see, the heroine's ability to defend her virginity is a key ingredient of this love-in-marriage plot. The trials over which Leucippe prevails largely measure the heroine's ability to defend her virginity; for, after the revelation of the dreams, a series of assaults is made upon the heroine's maidenhead. At this crucial point in the narrative, the issue of wedded chastity gives way to the problem of the preservation of the heroine's virginity from outside forces. Leucippe manages to protect her virginity from malefactors through a sequence of bizarre and chance events. Just before her arrival in Ephesus, an Egyptian general, Charmides, who has just saved Clitophon from a band of marauders, seeks the heroine for his own pleasure, but before he is able to violate her, Leucippe must overcome yet another attempt upon her maidenhead. This time, an Egyptian soldier falls in love with Leucippe; in order to seduce her, he concocts an "amorous Potion" (sig. L3). Unfortunately, the heroine receives too much of the love tonic and consequently is afflicted with madness. From this event, a third assay on Leucippe's virginity comes to pass when an Egyptian doctor treats the heroine's disease only because he, as well, has fallen in love with her: "[he] gave her the medicine hoping to have occasion therby to come into acquaintance with her, and that he might preserve her for himself" (sig. M2). Since the Egyptian doctor understands that Leucippe's virtue remains unassailable, he devises a scheme to kidnap her by transporting the heroine onboard a ship. Prior to her attempted ravishment, a group of pirates on the sailing vessel intervene (as can now be expected) and sell her to a steward in Ephesus.

The most powerful defense of Leucippe's virginity unfolds during her stay in Ephesus. Once she reaches Ephesus, the city whose patron goddess is, of course, Diana, a slight change takes place. The heroine can no longer rely merely on chance to save her. Now she must actively begin to oppose assaults upon her virginity. Leucippe is enslaved at a great house of Ephesus because she refuses to submit to its steward's "filthie desire" (sig. N3v). The steward, Sosthenes, purchased the heroine from the band of pirates for two thousand gold pieces. Not only has Sosthenes developed a licentious appetite for Leucippe, but the master of the same estate, Thersandros, has as well. Lovesick and fearing that Leucippe is truly married to Clitophon, Thersandros is consumed with such lustful desire that he forces himself on the heroine. To repulse the concupiscence of Thersandros, the heroine uses a progression of stratagems. She first reminds him of the profanity of his desires: "But heare you sir, doo you reverence Diana heere; and go about to ravish a virgin in a virgins Cittie?" (sig. Q4v). Leucippe furthers his sense of guilt by comparing her stalwart virtue with his brute savagery: "this is the most famous commendation and to be preferred before all, that Leucippe keepe her maydenhead against the force of Thersander, more savadge then all the pyrates" (sig. Q4v). Finally, the heroine brandishes her most important weapon against her despoilers, her volition and personal liberty: "I am both naked, alone, and a woman: and have no defence, except my liberty, which can neither be whipped with rods, nor cut with iron, nor burnt with fire: that will I never leese, and if you cast me into the middle of the flame: there will not bee force inough therein to take it from me" (sig. Q4v). Leucippe's obstinacy and declaration of liberty deter Thersandros from further physical assault, even though he later tries to abduct the heroine while attempting to have Clitophon executed for murder.

In the *Aethiopica*, both Theagenes and Chariclea successfully guard their virginity from various assailants. In Achilles Tatius's adventure romance, however, the hero struggles to remain chaste to his betrothed, but his dedication to chastity does not equally match the heroine's physical constancy when it is put to the test. When Clitophon wrongly believes that pirates have decapitated Leucippe, he mourns her death (and attempts suicide), yet he is ultimately persuaded into another marriage with a wealthy and beautiful woman who also believes her spouse has died: she is Melite, wife of Thersandros. Melite has fallen desperately in love with Clitophon. Although Clitophon successfully keeps her at bay for awhile, he ultimately falls prey to Melite's desire to wed and to his own youthful impulses. Clitophon's only stipulation to this new marriage concerns the solemnization of his marriage vow: "I sware when I lost Leucippe, that heere never any shoulde have my Virginitie" (sig. N1v).[45] In other words, Clitophon will not consummate the union with Melite in the same country where Leucippe has supposedly died. Despite his dedication to Leucippe's memory and loyalty to her love, Clitophon not only agrees to marry Melite in the temple of Isis, but it appears that he pledges to her his complete affection:

> I also tooke my oath that I loved her as sincerely as ever I did Leucippe before: shee likewise did sweare that I should bee her husband, and shee would make me Lorde of all her substance: all which was confirmed there betweene us, but the nuptials should not bee solemnized before wee came to Ephesus, and that there as I had sworne before, Melite should succeede in Leucippes place. (sig. N2)

Clitophon's marital oath resembles a contract made *verba de futuro* with the stipulation that the marriage would not be solemnized until consummation in Ephesus. While Burton's translation above emphasizes Clitophon's change of heart,[46] the hero does stay true to his temporary pledge of chastity--not to have sex with Melite in the same place where Leucippe has died. Just after his arrival in Ephesus, the city where Clitophon is to consummate his union with Melite, the hero discovers, to his chagrin, that Leucippe is actually alive. To express his utmost devotion and fidelity to Leucippe and to indicate that his "marriage" to Melite is not lawful since it was not consummated, Clitophon explains away his apparent betrayal of the heroine. In a letter to Leucippe, the hero writes that he has refrained from sexual intercourse with his new bride: "you shal find that my virginitie (if there be any virginitie of men) hath followed your example" (sig. O1v). At this moment, Clitophon's statement is true. He has not engaged in a sexual liaison with Melite. Despite Clitophon's physical continence up until this point (and as if to foreshadow the lacuna of "any virginitie of men"), the hero eventually capitulates to Melite's demand for sex. He rationalizes coitus with Melite by pointing out that he and Melite are no longer contractually bound together since Leucippe is still alive. Therefore, copulation with Melite would not indicate a legally binding act of marriage.

The disparity between the hero and heroine at this juncture intensifies when Leucippe is made to take a public virginity test at the story's conclusion. The hero is not. The heroine triumphs in her test of chastity when music issues forth from a cave of Diana, a sign that evidences a woman's bodily pureness. By contrast, Clitophon is never compelled to perform a chastity test, nor does he fail to omit his copulation with Melite when he recounts his adventures to a group of banquet guests, which include Leucippe's newly-arrived father, Sostratos. Clitophon says falsely: "I doo keepe my virginitie (if men have any as yet untouched, as Leucippe doth hers) since that I hadde learned long before to consecrate it to the honour of Diana" (sig. T1v). With so much emphasis given to the preservation of the heroine's virginity, it is paramount that the heroine stay virginal until a marriage has been conducted with at least one parental witnesses. As Clitophon says to Sostratos, ironically or not: "wee would not celebrate our marriages our father being away, hee is now heere present" (sig. T1v). The lovers return to celebrate their nuptials first in the hero's homeland of Tyre.

In *Daphnis and Chloe,* a similar preoccupation with the issue of the heroine's virginity emerges. Unlike the main protagonists' experience of love-at-first-sight in the plots of Heliodorus and Achilles Tatius, the love of the hero and heroine in Longus's

story develops more slowly, although there is a precise moment in the narrative when

each is suddenly and irrevocably taken by the beauty of the other (specifically during

Daphnis's bath at the shrine of the Nymphs and the prize of Chloe's kiss during the

beauty contest between the hero and Dorcon in the first book).[47] When Daphnis and

Chloe communicate to each other their shared love, they also exchange vows of mutual

commitment: "they iointly agreed to give eche to other an interchangeable oth" (sig.

M4v). But because Daphnis has sworn his faith by the "wanton" and "verie subtil and

amorous" god Pan, Chloe has Daphnis undertake a separate oath of constancy, so that he

"swore unto Chloe the othe and assurance she required" (sig. N1).

The conventions of the Greek romance genre require that the hero and heroine

withstand trials of their love, and the love trials in this pastoral romance are less

spectacular than the ones in the *Aethiopica* or *Leucippe and Clitophon*;[48] even so, Chloe's

relatively minor adventures leave her a virgin at the story's end, while Daphnis's ordeals

do not. Chloe's tribulations include the cowherd Dorcon's bungled attempt to violate her,

capture by warring Methymneans, and abduction by the cowherd Lampis. In these

instances, fate miraculously intervenes to deliver the heroine from harm. On the hero's

part, Daphnis survives injury from the Methymnean band of youths and even repulses the

wooing of Gnatho, his brother's male servant.[49] Aside from these obstacles, Daphnis

yields to the erotic longings of his married neighbor Lycaenion (she is appropriately

named the "she-wolf"), who seduces the hero into intercourse. In his 1587 version of the

romance, Daye omits this vital seduction scene from his version only to replace it with

"The Shepheards Holidaie," a group of songs and eclogues in praise of Elizabeth I.

One of the effects of this scene's exclusion from the Elizabethan edition concerns the forfeiture of viewing the hero's sexual initiation. If we look to a modern translation of the scene, it reads: "Daphnis did not resist [Lycaenion] but was delighted. Being a rustic, a goatherd, in love and young, he threw himself at the feet of Lycaenion and begged her to teach him, as soon as possible, the skill that would make him able to do what he wanted to Chloe."[50] The loss of the hero's virginity, like Clitophon's sexual involvement with Melite, is in some sense construed as the result of a young man's natural ardor; perhaps more important, it indicates a necessary and formidable step in Daphnis's sexual development, even a kind of sacrifice for his future wife. Although the adulterous act is omitted from its Elizabethan version, there is no apparent stigma in the Greek romance against a young man who is initiated into the art of lovemaking. Despite his lessons in love, Daphnis refrains from intercourse with Chloe due to Lycaenion's warning of Chloe's hymenal bleeding: "Chloe would easily have become a woman if the thought of blood had not disturbed Daphnis" (327). It appears that providence conspires to keep the pair of young lovers chaste until wedlock. As a result, Chloe's worth as a young woman, like Leucippe's, is based on the preservation of her maidenhood until the rites of lawful matrimony have been performed. The following episode concurs with this assumption. When Daphnis's father, Dionysophanes, considers Chloe's worthiness as his son's future bride, he asks a crucial question--if she be a virgin: "Daphnis swore that nothing more had taken place between them than kissing and vows; so Dionysophanes was pleased" (345). It seems reasonable to conclude that the heroine's virginity, not necessarily the hero's, makes possible the legitimate and hallowed marital union that constitutes a fundamental aspect of the Greek romance plot in Longus and Achilles Tatius.

Over and beyond the charm of its chaste love plot and its emphasis on the mutual affection of the hero and heroine, the Greek adventure romance engaged its audience with a patriarchal view of women and marriage that would not have been totally foreign to English readers in the sixteenth and seventeenth centuries. According to Brigitte Egger, the Greek romance of Hellenism generated a complex attitude toward marriage that blended together the patriarchal laws of classical Greece with the more liberal marital laws of Hellenism. In classical Greek or Attic law, the legal contract of marriage regarded the woman solely as an object of barter: it was a transaction between her legal guardian (most often her father) and the groom: "The dowry was entirely at her husband's disposal as long as the marriage lasted, and afterward had to be returned to her male relatives. She certainly had no right of choice; her consent either to marriage or to divorce was unnecessary."[51] The transition, however, from classicism to Hellenism brought about significant changes for women and marriage. Along with increased control over the dowry and the ability to own property, Greco-Egyptian women now participated in the marriage negotiations; the matrimonial contract became a consensual agreement between the male and female rather than an economic arrangement between the heads of families. A further indication of woman's new legal status was, in Egger's words, the idea of "the *autoekdosis* ("self-handing-out"): their capacity to give themselves in marriage, with a family member as a witness, but by their own authority."[52] We have seen earlier that Heliodorus's Chariclea invokes the premise of *autoekdosis* in her dealings with Theagenes when she declares her choice of a partner and the time and place of marriage (she states: "[Theagenes] shall not fleashly have to doo with me, untill I have recovered my countrie, and parentes, or if the Gods be not content herewith, at least untill I by mine owne free will be content he shal marrie me" [Underdowne, sig. H3]). In spite of the significant allowances authors of Greek romance made to accommodate an audience that enjoyed the entitlements of the new marital laws, the writers did not completely integrate the recent thinking on marriage into the construct of their fictional worlds. Egger finds that the stories often place restrictions and constraints on their female characters that did not altogether comport with the nuptial liberties of their contemporary readers. Egger's theory is dependent on the idea that romance plots do, indeed, reflect the marriage laws and attitudes of a culture.

One of the consequences of male bias in Greek romance was that it tended to prescribe a male-centered view of female virtue in love and marriage. This type of bias, one that restricts a woman's role in courtship and matrimony, shares affinities with some representations of women and marriage in Elizabethan and Jacobean reformist marriage literature: social subordination in wedlock acts as a metaphor for the type of patriarchal constraint that can be detected in Greek romance. A brief analysis will serve to illustrate this point. While many religious reformists and sixteenth- and seventeenth-century domestic writers, such as William Googe, Edmonde Tilnay, and William Whately, advocated the idea of the companionate marriage, conjugal affection, and the shared obligations of the spouses, they did not totally consider the wife as an equal to man: "They all agreed in regarding the wife as subordinate to the husband," a "second helper" or "servant."[53] In Tilnay's popular *A brief and pleasant discourse of duties in Marriage* (1568), the author provides a clear example of the importance at this time placed on the ideal of married love: "[f]or perfite love knitteth lovinge heartes, in an insoluble knot of amittie. Love indifferent serveth not, love fayned prospereth not. Wherfore it must be true, and perfite love, that maketh the *Flower of Friendship* betweene man and wyfe freshly to spring."[54] Despite this principle of conjugal affection and friendship, Tilnay prescribes the subservience of the wife in marriage. He commands the wife to obey her husband in all affairs, for the husband is far superior to his spouse in most everything: "[he] is, most apt for the soveraigntie being in government, not onely skill, and experience to be required, but also capacite to comprehend, wisedome to understand, strength to execute, solicitude to prosecute, pacience to suffer, meanes to sustaine, and above all, a great courage to accomplish, all which are commonly in a man, but in a woman very rare" (sig. Ei). Whereas Tilnay advises the husband to acquire such traits as eloquence, courtesy, and wisdom, one of the greatest attributes that a woman brings to her marriage remains matronly chastity: "For the happinesse of matrimonie, doth consist in a chaste matrone, so that if suche a woman bee conjoyned in true, and unfayned love, to hir beloved spouse, no doubt their lives shall be stable, easie, sweete, joyfull, and happie" (sig. Diiii). While Tilnay supports the idea of mutual love in marriage, a woman must remain true, chaste, and inferior in wedlock.

A similar view on love in marriage can be found in William Whately's *A Bride-Bush or A Wedding Sermon* (1617). Although Whately opines that love "is the life, the soule of marriage,"[55] he also recommends woman's subordination in wedlock: the wife is "to acknowledge her inferiority: the next, to carry her selfe as inferiour. First then the wives judgement must be convinced, that shee is not her husbands equall, yea that her husband is her better by farre; else there can bee no contentment, either in her heart, or in her house"(E4v). Whately expands on the requirement of the wife's inferiority: she is "a dutifull wife, when shee submits her-selfe with quietnesse cheerefully, even as a wel-broken horse turnes at the least turning, stands at the least check of the riders bridle, readily going and standing as he wishes that fits upon his backe" (sig. F4). Whately's statements suggest that mutual love in marriage does not correspond to equality in marriage. For example, Whately advocates the sharing of responsibilities in marital duties, but he privileges the husband's ability over the wife's: "the husband should bee most abundant, knowing that more of every grace is looked for in him, than from the weaker vessall." He continues to define the concept of mutuality in marriage duties: "Wee call them not therefore common or mutuall, because both should have a like quantity of them; but because both must have some of all, and the husband most of all" (sig. BIv). As these examples show, the idea of the companionate marriage, in which husband and wife participate lovingly in domestic obligations, did not indicate equality between man and woman. Likewise, male bias in Hellenistic romance, which both exploits and contains woman's erotic power, can be read as an analogy of patriarchal bias in these marriage pamphlets.

For its early modern audience, the love-leading-to-marriage plot of Greek romance invoked a version of romantic love that conformed to the Protestant ideal of wedded chastity and mutual affection in marriage. The problem of pre-marital sex represented, on the one hand, a temporary suspension in the hero's virtuous behavior to which he was quickly restored. On the other, the lapses in male chastity also added to the attraction of the story. Northrop Frye's theory that the fantasies of a culture can be revealed in the structure of romance applies to the trials of chastity in the romance plot.[56] The heroine, who is the epitome of feminine beauty and intelligence, repeatedly defends her virginity from various scoundrels in erotically-charged scenes of seduction and attempted rape. The hero, however, is allowed sexual intercourse in similar situations (e.g., Longus and Achilles Tatius). Inasmuch as the ultimate male fantasy is that a woman remain indisputably chaste while sacrificing her security and well-being for a potentially lawful marriage, the Greek romance love plot becomes increasingly patriarchal in its shape and scope. True, the virtuous and devoted romance hero, with his passion for love and romantic sentiments, was, in the most conventional sense, an engaging character. In fact, in sixteenth- and seventeenth-century England such popular fiction as Greek romance catered to a growing, and by no means exclusively, female readership whose members inclined toward the courtly.[57] We have seen that the romance heroine possessed a good deal of wit and moral excellence. But it is not perplexing that this audience valued the romantic plot and thematic features of the genre, especially given the potential for arranged marriages among the aristocracy.[58] Unlike some of their readers, the hero and heroine freely choose their martial partners, triumphing in trials of honor and virtue. Furthermore, because the primary couple resemble each other, their union in marriage affirms their social and economic homogeneity. Despite the couple's uniformity in love, the erotic suffering of the Greek romance hero differs in content and degree from the heroine's; it often lacks the sexual titillation and provocative suggestion that find repeated expression in the heroine's trials of chastity. This expression of female objectification demonstrates the story's interest in woman's eroticism. Thus, Egger's thesis applies especially here: "The price paid for women's erotic centrality [in the Greek romance] is their social containment in the realms of law and marriage, among others."[59] The fantasy of woman's erotic power, combined with the cultural and legal constraints imposed on her, may have contributed to the attraction of Greek romance as edifying and recreational literature for its Renaissance readership. The importance of readers envisioning that men and woman share equally in trials of fidelity and chastity (the *Aethiopica*), of female virginity and honor in love (*Leucippe and Clitophon*), and of imagining a pastoral world of sexual innocence and putiry (*Daphnis and Chloe*) is finally counterbalanced by a male-centered fantasy of woman's erotic power and its obsessive interest in female chastity.

In the next chapter, I show how the most influential prose romance of the Elizabethan and Jacobean era, Sidney's *Arcadia*, draws specifically on Greek romance. I argue that in the *New Arcadia* Sidney uses the Greek ideal of heroism as a model of female virtue. I examine how the idea of *erotika pathemata*, or erotic suffering, emerges as a key element in Sidney's construction of woman's heroism: suffering, fighting for sexual integrity, is a statement of valor.

------

[1] This essay will appear in the forthcoming book, *Prose Fiction and Early Modern Sexuality in England, 1580-1640*. It appears in this dissertation with the permission of Palgrave Macmillan. For a discussion of the plot affinities between the Greek novel and Elizabethan prose fiction and drama, see Samuel Lee Wolff, *The Greek Romances in Elizabethan Prose Fiction* (New York: Columbia University Press, 1912); see also Carol Gesner, *Shakespeare and the Greek Romance: A Study of Origins* (Lexington: University of Kentucky Press, 1970).

[2] John J. Winkler, "The Invention of Romance," in *The Search for the Ancient Novel*, ed. James Tatum (Baltimore: Johns Hopkins University Press, 1994), 23-38, 24. In Chariton and Xenophon, the primary lovers are already married before they separate.

[3] The romances of Xenophon and Chariton were not translated into English until the eighteenth century. For the approximate dates of the composition of the Greek romances, see E. L. Bowie "The Greek Novel," in *Oxford Readings in the Greek Novel*, ed. Simon Swain (Oxford: Oxford University Press, 1999), 39-59; and Niklas Holzberg, *The Ancient Novel: An Introduction*, trans. Christine Jackson-Holzberg (London: Routledge, 1995), 103-05.

[4] David Konstan, *Sexual Symmetry* (Princeton: Princeton University Press, 1994), 36. Konstan's central argument is that the Greek romances as a genre "portray *eros* as a fully reciprocal passion between equals" (33).

[5] Gesner writes that "In Greek romance the 'quest' usually is begun when a pair of youthful lovers--frequently married--are separated. Their desire for reunion usually motivates the journey." Gesner continues to explain the plot and its outcome: "Eventually the [heroine] is restored to the hero, most often at the conclusion of the romance in a triallike recognition scene in which all mysteries are explained and all loose threads are knitted up again" (*Shakespeare and The Greek Romance*, 4). For Frye's theory, see *Anatomy of Criticism: Four Essays* (Princeton: Princeton University Press, 1957), 186-206.

[6] Bruce R. Smith, *Homosexual Desire in Shakespeare's England* (Chicago: The University of Chicago Press, 1991), 126, 128, 122-23. Smith compares Achilles Tatius' romance to native English folk festival. In both contexts, male homosexual desire finds playful expression, enjoying a momentary refuge from the dominant heterosexual ideology. In Achilles Tatius, Clitophon's cousin Kleinias is involved in a homosexual

relationship with a young man, who tragically dies in a horse riding accident early on in the story. David Konstan argues persuasively that homosexual relationships in Greek romance, especially pederastic ones, often serve as a asymmetrical contrast to the symmetry of the heterosexual hero and heroine (*Sexual Symmetry*, 28).

[7] Mikhail Bakhtin, "Forms of Time and Chronotope in the Novel," in *The Dialogic Imagination*, ed. Michael Holquist and trans. Caryl Emerson and Michael Holquist (Austin: University of Texas Press, 1981), 84-258. Citations of Bakhtin's essay refer to this edition, and they will be cited parenthetically. For further information on Bakhtin's novelistic theory, see Katerina Clark and Michael Holquist, *Mikhail Bakhtin* (Cambridge, Mass.: Harvard University Press, 1984), 275-294.

[8] About the idea of the companionate marriage in Protestant doctrine, see Lawrence Stone, *The Family, Sex, and Marriage in England, 1500-1800* (London: Weidenfeld and Nicolson, 1977), 136. Stone's conclusions are often challenged. See note 14.

[9] James A. Brundage, *Sex, Law and Marriage in the Middle Ages* (Aldershot, Hampshire: Variorum, 1993), 364.

[10] James A. Brundage, *Law, Sex, and Christian Society in Medieval Europe* (Chicago: University of Chicago Press, date), 552.

[11] Eric Fuchs, *Sexual Desire and Love* (Cambridge: James Clarke; New York: Seabury Press, 1983), 157-63.

[12] Juliet Dusinberre, *Shakespeare and the Nature of Women*, 2nd edition (Houndsmills: Macmillan Press; New York: St. Martin's Press, 1996), 24.

[13] Merry E. Wiesner-Hanks, *Christianity and Sexuality in the Early Modern World* (London and New York: Routledge, 2000), 63.

[14] David Cressy, *Birth, Marriage & Death* (Oxford: Oxford University Press, 1997), 261. Cressy argues against Lawrence Stone's findings that marriage at this time lacked romantic intimacy. Cressy also points out that Puritans often advocated the idea of the "companionate marriage": the equal affection between a married couple "based on 'mutual society, help, and comfort'" (297).

[15] Consequently, Underdowne repeats several of his predecessor's mistakes. See Tomas Hägg, "The Renaissance of the Greek Novel," in *The Novel in Antiquity* (Berkeley and Los Angeles: University of California Press, 1983), 192-213. See also F. A. Wright's introduction to Underdowne's translation, *Heliodorus: An Aethiopian Romance* (London: Routledge, n.d.), 1-5.

[16] Sterg O'Dell, *A Chronological List of Prose Fiction in English Printed in England and Other Countries, 1475-1640* (Cambridge, Mass.: Technology Press of MIT, 1954), 39-98 passim.

[17] Carol Gesner gives a comprehensive listing of the publication dates and reprints of Greek romance in England and on the Continent (*Shakespeare and the Greek Romance*, 159-60).

[18] Thomas Underdowne, *An Aethiopian historie* (London, 1577), sig. iii. Citations of *An Aethiopian historie* refer to the 1577 edition unless indicated otherwise, and they will be cited parenthetically.

[19] Lodovicus Vives, *The office and duetie of an husband* (London, 1554), sig. O7v.

[20] For further discussion of the chivalric tradition, see C. S. Lewis, *The Allegory of Love* (Oxford: University of Oxford Press, 1936), 22-43.

[21] William Lisle, *The famous historie of Heliodorus* (London, 1638), sig. A2v.

[22] N.[ahum] Tate, *The Aethiopian History of Heliodorus* (London, 1686), sig. a5v. Further citations refer to this addition, and they will be cited parenthetically.

[23] Margaret Anne Doody states that the first printing of Heliodorus's romance was linked with the Protestant movement: "The first edition of the *Aithiopika* was published in 1534, in Basel, edited by Vincentus Obsopaeus, a humanist who translated some of Luther's works from German into Latin. Obsopaues' association with the new Lutheran movement may have made the novel the more appealing to new Protestants in northern countries" (*The True Story of the Novel* [London: Fontana Press, 1998], 233-34).

[24] *Daphnis and Chloe: The Elizabethan Version: From Amyot's Translation By Angel Day: Reprinted from the Unique Original*, ed., Joseph Jacobs (London: David Nutt, 1890), 1. Citations from *Daphnis and Chloe* refer to this reprint of the 1587 edition, and they will be cited parenthetically unless indicated otherwise.

[25] A. [nthony] H. [odges], *The Loves of Clitophon and Leucippe* (Oxford, 1638), title page. Further citations from Hodges's translation refer to this edition, and they will be cited parenthetically.

[26] Gosson, *Playes Confuted in Five Actions*, in *The English Stage: Attack and Defenses, 1577-1730*, ed. Arthur Freeman (New York: Garland, 1972), sig. D5v.

[27] Hallett Smith, *Shakespeare's Romances* (San Marino, Calif.: The Huntington Library, 1972), 9.

[28] Gertrude Marian Sibley, *The Lost Plays and Masques, 1500-1642* (Ithaca: Cornell University Press, 1933), 157-58.

[29] *The Loves of Clitophon and Leucippe. Translated from the Greek of Achilles Tatius by William Burton. Reprinted for the first time from a copy now unique by Thomas Creede in 1597*, eds. Stephen Gaselee and H. F. B. Brett-Smith (Oxford: B. Blackwell, 1923), sig. A4. Further citations of the romance refer to this reprint of the 1597 edition unless indicated otherwise, and they will be cited parenthetically.

[30] See note 3.

[31] David Konstan, *Sexual Symmetry*, 48.

[32] Marie H. Loughlin, *Hymeneutics* (Lewisburg: Bucknell University Press, 1997), 54.

[33] Ibid., 54.

[34] Francis Meres, *Gods Arithmeticke* (London, 1597), sig. A2v.

[35] Ibid., A2v.

[36] J. [ames] Sanford, *The Amorous and Tragicall Tales of Plutarch* (Ann Arbor, Mich.: University Microfilms, 1964), sig. D5, D5-D5v.

[37] R. B. Outhwaite, *Clandestine Marriage in England, 1500-1850* (London: The Hambledon Press, 1995), 1-17.

[38] Cressy, *Birth, Marriage & Death*, 267.

[39] Diana O'Hara, *Courtship and Constraint* (Manchester: Manchester University Press, 2000), 10-11. Jack Goody also explains the difference between present and future consent: "Consent alone, and not coitus, made a marriage valid, at least in terms of its 'present' form. With future consent, an indissoluble bond was created only by means of

sexual relations" (*The Development of the Family and Marriage in Europe* [Cambridge:

Cambridge University Press], 149).

[40] O'Hara, *Courtship and Constraint*, 149.

[41] Ruth Kelso, *Doctrine for the Lady of the Renaissance* (Urbana: University of Illinois

Press, 1956), 273.

[42] Abraham Fraunce, *The Countesse of Pembrokes Yuychurch* (London, 1591), sig. E3v.

Further citations refer to the 1591 edition, and they will be cited parenthetically.

[43] In Underdowne's translation, Chariclea states that she and Theagenes fought "to repell

the violence which was proffered to [her] virginitie" (*An Aethiopian historie*, sig. A3).

[44] Konstan writes: "The primary couple, invariably heterosexual, are either fellow citizens

or members of the same social class and are of more or less the same age--very young"

(*Sexual Symmetry*, 33).

[45] Whether Clitophon is actually a virgin or not appears to be unclear in the story; for

instance, John J. Winkler's modern translation does not mention the issue of the hero's

virginity. Clitophon merely says: "I have already taken a vow never to copulate in this

part of the world, where I lost Leukippe" (*Leucippe and Clitophon*, in *Collected Ancient

Greek Novels*, ed. B. P. Reardon [Berkeley and Los Angeles: University of California

Press, 1989], 239).

[46] Compare Winkler's modern translation to Burton's. His provides a different

interpretation of the passage, one that suggests that Clitophon is less than eager to marry

Melite: "On the next day we had agreed to meet at Isis's temple to speak further and to

exchange vows with the goddess as our witness. Menelaos and Kleinias accompanied us.

I pledged to cherish her without guile; she pledged to name me her husband and declare

me master of all her properties" (*Leucippe and Clitophon*, 240).

[47] The scene in which Chloe watches Daphnis bathe does not occur in Daye's translation.

For the controversy surrounding this lost passage, see Joseph Jacob's discussion in

*Daphnis and Chloe: The Elizabethan Version from Amyot's Translation*, xviii-xxv.

[48] It is important to note that in *Daphnis and Chloe* the hero and heroine never leave their

country for any substantial time; adventure comes to the lovers rather than vice-versa. For

a discussion of the generic differences in *Daphnis and Chloe*, see Bakhtin, *The Dialogic

Imagination*, 103.

[49] In the Elizabethan translation, Burton calls Gnatho an "unnaturall beast" who acts

"against nature" (*Daphnis and Chloe*, T2v). Such revilement does not occur in Longus's

story.

[50] I cite from Christopher Gill's translation of *Daphnis and Chloe*, in *Collected Ancient

Greek Novels*, ed. B. P. Reardon (Berkeley and Los Angeles: University of California

Press, 1989), 325. Further citations of this modern translation refer to this edition, and

they will be cited parenthetically.

[51] Brigitte Egger, "Women and Marriage in the Greek Novels," in *The Search for the

Ancient Novel*, ed. James Tatum (Baltimore: The Johns Hopkins University Press, 1994),

260-80, 266.

[52] Ibid, 267.

[53] Stone, *The Family, Sex and Marriage*, 136. Stone argues that the tenets of

Protestantism, which gave fathers and husbands, not the Church, power over the family unit, reinforced the authority of patriarchy (esp. 151-218). For further discussion of the concept and problems of equity in marriage in the early modern period, see Constance Jordan, *Renaissance Feminism* (Ithaca: Cornell University Press, 1990), esp. 21-64 and Ralph A. Houlbrook, *The English Family, 1450-1700* (London: Longman, 1984), 96-105. For a theory of marital relationships in the early modern period that challenges the notion of the absolute supremacy of the husband, see Keith Wrightson, *English Society, 1580-1680* (London: Routledge, 1982), 89-104.

[54] Edmonde Tilnay, *A brief and Pleasant discourse of duties in Marriage* (London, 1568), sig. Biiii. Citations refer to the 1568 edition, and they will be cited in the text parenthetically.

[55] William Whately, *A Bride-Bush* (London, 1617), sig. B2. Additional citations will refer to the 1617 edition, and they will be cited parenthetically.

[56] Frye writes: "The romance is the nearest of all literary forms to the wish-fulfilment dream, and for that reason it has socially a curiously paradoxical role. In every age the ruling social or intellectual class tends to project its ideals in some form of romance, where the virtuous heroes and beautiful heroines represent the ideals and the villains the threats to their ascendancy"(*Anatomy of Criticism*, 186).

[57] For an account of the rise of a female readership in recreational literature, see Suzanne Hull, *Chaste, Silent and Obedient* (San Marino, Calif.: The Huntington Library, 1982), 71-90. See also Caroline Lucas, *Writing for Women* (Milton Keynes: Open University Press, 1989), 48. Lucas argues that the Greek romance and its Elizabethan offshoots were directed toward both a female and a courtly audience.

[58] On the complex subject of the arranged marriage among the sixteenth- and seventeenth-century upper class, Keith Wrightson writes: "It is clear that even in the higher social ranks where families had most to lose by an imprudent match, the situation was far from monolithic when it came to the selection of future spouses. The 'arranged' match, initiated by parents, which left the child with nothing more than a right of veto was undoubtedly a reality throughout our period. But even among the social élite it presents a picture which is too stark unless accompanied by considerable qualification" (*English Society, 1580-1680*, 74). Recently, Diana O'Hara has explored the critical assertion that the poor and middle levels of society experienced greater freedom in choice of marriage partners and in courtship (*Courtship and Constraint*, 30-56).

[59] Egger, "Women and Marriage in the Greek Novels," 273. Egger contends that the patriarchal fantasy of woman's eroticism appeals to readers today in such books as the Harlequin romance.

# CHAPTER 3

## Sir Philip Sidney and Female Heroism:

## Erotic Suffering in the *New Arcadia*

Bring on the instruments of torture: the wheel--here, take my arms and stretch them; the whips--here is my back, lash away; the hot irons--here is my body for burning; bring the axe as well--here is my neck, slice through! Watch a new contest: a single woman competes with all the engines of torture and wins every round.--*Leucippe and Clitophon*

In his well-known statement, the Elizabethan John Hoskins names the textual sources of Sir Philip Sidney's *The Countess of Pembroke's Arcadia* as "Heliodorus in greeke, Sannazarus Arcadia in Itallian, and Diana de Montemaior in spanish."[1] It is generally agreed that these popular texts, along with the chivalric romance *Amadís de Gaula*, furnished Sidney with a rich supply of primary material from which he shaped the storyline and incidents of the *Old* and unfinished *New Arcadia*.[2] Critics speculate that Sidney, intending to create a more heroic epic, modeled his *New Arcadia* revision more exclusively on the episodic adventure structure of Greek romance, especially on Heliodorus's *Aethiopica*. According to Samuel Lee Wolff, Sidney "deliberately recasts" the *New Arcadia* "in the Heliodorian mould of narrative structure."[3] As Paul Salzman explains, "the revival of interest in Greek romance, particularly Heliodorus's *Aethiopica* which Sidney praises in the *Defence of Poetry* [as a heroic poem], was a more immediate influence on the structure of the *New Arcadia*" than medieval romance.[4] He continues: "Sidney uses the *in medias res* opening, with its retrospective narrative method, derived from the structure of the epic."[5] Likewise, Victor Skretkowicz argues that Sidney favors the *in medias res* narrative form of the Heliodorian heroic in his revision; yet, he also maintains, more interestingly, that Sidney looks to its chaste and faithful heroes, Theagenes and Chariclea, for ethical characterization.[6] Concerning this characterization, A.C. Hamilton writes: "He [Sidney] would be drawn particularly to Heliodorus by the exemplary nature of his characters and his variety of wonder-evoking episodes which test a character's inner worth."[7] Indeed, in *A Defence of Poetry* Sidney commends both Heliodorus "in his sugared invention of that picture of love in Theagenes and Cariclea" and the love-stricken Theagenes as "so true a lover."[8] Sidney's heroes prove chaste in the *New Arcadia* when Musidorus's attempted rape of Pamela and Pyrocles' seduction of Philoclea are expunged from the revision.[9] About this erasure, Jean Robertson notes that "Sidney did come to wish his heroes and heroines to emulate the chastity of Theagenes and Chariclea."[10] In the process of revising the *Arcadia* on a heroic model, Sidney not only turned to Heliodorus's *Aethiopica* for epic structure, but he also saw in it an idealized portrait of integrity in young love.

It has been well documented that Sidney employs Heliodorian narrative technique and characterization in the *New Arcadia*. I, however, broaden this argument by contending that Sidney utilizes a key thematic pattern of Greek romance, a pattern that enabled him to conceptualize a new brand of female heroism. According to Arthur Heiserman, the Greek romances of the Roman Imperial period (Heliodorus's *Aethiopica*,

Achilles Tatius's *Leucippe and Clitophon*, Longus's *Daphnis and Chloe*, Chariton's *Chaereas and Callirrhoe*, and Xenophon's *Ephesiaca*) were often referred to as *erotika pathemata*. The term denotes a kind of story "in which admirable characters survive the perils caused by love, fortune, and their own fidelity [ . . . ]."[11] Even though stories of erotic suffering, *erotika pathemata*, were widespread in Hellenic literature, the Greek romances of Hellenism shared a specific pattern, as we have seen in Chapter One: "[all] bring their admirable lovers through terrible perils--separation, captivity, torture, even burial--to a 'striking consummation' that saves and reconciles."[12] This thematic pattern finds its most elevated expression in Heliodorus's romance, but it would have also been known to Sidney in *Leucippe and Clitophon*--which has also been identified as a probable source[13]--and quite possibly in *Daphnis and Chloe*, which Amyot had translated into French by 1559. In the *New Arcadia*, Sidney incorporates a similar pattern of erotic suffering. Because the revision is unfinished, the reader does not see the "striking consummation" that most likely would have concluded the romance, as the second oracle suggests.[14] In the Captivity Episode of Book Three, Sidney's lovers are separated and imprisoned (except Musidorus); Pamela and Philoclea are badgered, beaten, threatened, and allegedly executed. What is particularly noteworthy about Sidney's use of erotic suffering is the degree and emphasis placed on the heroines' suffering. It has been suggested that Sidney invokes a Cyropaedeic model of heroism to depict male virtue in Book Two, a book that recounts the martial exploits of Musidorus and Pyrocles as they overthrow unjust governments in Asia Minor.[15] Victorious in arms, the princes gain notoriety though knightly combats. This study posits, however, that Sidney discovers in the Greek romance theme of erotic suffering an appropriate, even novel, expression of female heroism. This heroism is distinguished from heroic chivalry in that battles of virtue are won by means of willful resistance. As Margaret Anne Doody observes, "Resistance--framed as resistance to sexual violence--is recognized as heroic in the [Greek] novels."[16] The same may be said for Sidney's romance.

Like Sidney's heroines, the Greek romance heroine usually suffers physical and psychological torments for her belief in the ideals of romantic fidelity and sexual constancy. This heroism, one based on *erotika pathemata*, corresponds to what Doody views in Greek romance as "The *woman* enduring torture *for a cause* . . . ."[17] According to Doody, the suffering virgin of romance emerges as a heroic figure in Hellenistic literature precisely because she suffers for sovereignty over her sexuality. Her heroism consists in resisting forms of authority that impose control over her body, and the root of this authority can be found in the precepts of Roman civic law:

> The laws that affect the sexual and private life of every individual are designed to sustain the power of *paterfamilias* and to prevent *turbatio sanguinis* (confusion of the bloodline). Into this world comes the extraordinary novel with its emphasis on sexuality--including female sexuality--as a matter of individual choice and personal control.[18]

In defiance of laws that regulate sexuality, the romance heroine chooses the man she wants to marry and pledges her chastity to him, a trait that is especially evident in the stories of Heliodorus and Achilles Tatius. The heroine's adherence to chastity in the face of adversity does not necessarily indicate her obedience to societal mores. Rather, it demonstrates her desire to govern her body in a manner that suits her romantic standards. Even under torture, the romance heroine fights to keep herself pure until wedlock, and, if she is unable to preserve her maidenhead, she at least strives to remain loyal to her lover

(see *Chaereas and Callirrhoe*). In the *New Arcadia*, Pamela and Philoclea withstand

assaults upon their virginity, enduring not only sexual degradation but also attacks on

their self-worth and dignity. Throughout their ordeals, the princesses are determined to

procure sexual autonomy despite their father Basilius's constraints on them and primarily

despite Cecropia's subjugation of them.

In the *New Arcadia*, the romantic subplot of Argalus and Parthenia has

traditionally been read as the framing episode of the revision. It constitutes "a standard,"

according to Clare Kinney, "against which the behavior of all the other lovers and

questers in Arcadia may be measured."[19] This tale of heroic love, which does not appear

in the *Old Arcadia*, closely follows the romance pattern of *erotika pathemata*. As an early

example of erotic suffering, it provides an essential starting point from which to analyze

Sidney's conception of female heroism. The first segment of the story, told to Musidorus

by Kalander's servant in Book One, invokes the conventional love-leading-to-marriage

plot structure of Greek romance. Argalus, cousin to Gynecia, King Basilius's young wife,

falls in love with Parthenia, who is niece to the noble Kalander. After a set of trials that

tests Parthenia's constancy and Argalus's steadfast fidelity, including Argalus's hard

labor, Parthenia's temporary deformity, and the lovers' separation, the couple solemnizes

their marriage "with all conceits that might deliver delight to men's fancies" (48).[20] While

Argalus and Parthenia enjoy the blessing of a joyous and balanced union, in which

"likeness of manners" combines with shared "affection" (28), the conventions of the

Greek romance genre necessitate that the hero and heroine prevail in trials of virtue

before lawful matrimony. For Argalus and Parthenia, these ordeals occur as soon as the lovers exchange vows of mutual affection: "her heart hath vowed her to Argalus-- with so grateful a receipt in mutual affection that, if she desired above all things to have Argalus, Argalus feared nothing but to miss Parthenia" (28-29). The lovers' reversal of fortune occurs when Parthenia's mother arranges for her daughter to marry the wealthy and powerful Demagoras, but, fearing her daughter's unflagging devotion to Argalus, she uses the hero in "many dangerous enterprises" in order to eliminate him as a suitor (29). Parthenia's refusal to wed Demagoras initiates the couple's heroic suffering.

Tellingly, the type of suffering each undergoes takes on markedly different forms. At first, the lovers' suffering appears to reflect conventional modes of gendered behavior: Argalus is active in his perilous labors, while Parthenia is passive in her sufferance. The narrator states: "[B]ut it was hard to judge whether he in doing or she in suffering showed greater constancy of affection; for, as to Argalus the world sooner wanted occasions than he valour to go through them, so to Parthenia malice sooner ceased than her unchanged patience" (29). Unlike Parthenia's trial of patience, Argalus's chores are likened to those of "the famous Hercules" (29), and this comparison links Argalus with the mythical hero who succeeds in deeds that test strength, endurance, and courage. (Not surprisingly, Edmund Spenser in Book 5 of *The Faerie Queene* describes the "kingly powre" of Hercules as an example of virtue in justice.[21]) In fact, the more valiant Argalus proves himself in his tasks, the more Parthenia's mother redoubles her efforts to impede his success, so that "the more his virtue was tried, the more pure it grew" (29). Argalus's heroism consists in the fortitude to overcome the demands of an implacable enemy-parent. By contrast, Parthenia's heroism resides in her womanly "unchanged patience," a passive state of waiting and enduring. Despite this example of patience in suffering,

Parthenia's heroism assumes greater complexity throughout the romance. Parthenia vigorously resists the torments of her mother who "used all extremities possible upon her fair daughter to make her give over herself to her direction" (29). It is this active resistance to authority, interestingly a woman's authority, that makes Parthenia's erotic suffering unequivocally heroic: "with words of resolute refusal," she informed her mother that "she would first be bedded in her grave than wedded to Demagoras" (29). Yet the heroine is not unruly in her disobedience: "with tears showing she was sorry," she laments her insubordination (29). Nevertheless, Parthenia would rather die a virgin, "bedded in her grave," than marry a man she does not love.

Parthenia's resistance to imposed sexuality recalls Doody's description of heroines in Greek romance who "ignore or override legal and social ordinances in fulfillment of their own desires--which may be desires for chastity."[22] Although Parthenia is a fictional Greek pagan, Elizabethan readers may have recognized in her situation the doctrinal problem of parental consent in marriage, a prominent issue in reformists' writings on matrimony.[23] In the popular and much reprinted *The Christen state of Matrimonye*, translated by Miles Coverdale (1543), the Swiss reformist Heinrich Bullinger views parental approval in wedlock as a central aspect of the marital contract: "laws both natural (dyvyne specially) & cyvile, require the parentes consent to [the] childrens marriage."[24] According to his reasoning, children lack the discretion and experience necessary to choose an adequate spouse; they may be persuaded into an undesirable match by flattery, drunkenness, rewards, or promises. But although Bullinger condemns a son's or daughter's disobedience in marriage, he equally condemns parents who force children into loveless unions:

> The parents ought not to constrayne their children to matrimonye nether to
> marry them a fore ther tyme. In this poynt also ought not the parentes to
> take to much upon them selves because of their autorite nether to abuse it
> or to compell their child eyther because of filthy advauntage or
> lothsomnesse . . . .[25]

By Bullinger's standard, Parthenia's mother is guilty of abuse of authority and "filthy advauntage." Justifiably, the heroine overrides her mother's choice of husband by selecting a man who is more worthy of her love: "Parthenia had learned both liking and misliking, loving and loathing, and out of passion began to take the authority of judgement" (29). Similar to her romance prototype, Parthenia relies on both passion and judgment in her choice of husband, opting for a spouse who equals her in nobility, stature, and fidelity. As do some parents in Arcadia, parents in Greek romance usually do not sanction their children's proposed marital unions, partly because parental approval in marriage constitutes an integral aspect of the romance plot's denouement and happy resolution. Ultimately, the mother's death from "spiteful grief" grants Parthenia the freedom to marry Argalus, and the heroine's chastity is, consequently, safeguarded (30).

Parthenia successfully withstands the affronts of her mother and an unwanted suitor, but she is made to pay for her sexual autonomy with even greater suffering: the body is the site where the heroine's defiance, her refusal to wed Demagoras, is finally punished. When Demagoras learns that Parthenia "was her own," that she would never consent to his proposal of marriage now that her mother is dead, he ravages the heroine with a horrific substance: "the wicked Demagoras . . . with unmerciful force (her weak arms in vain resisting) rubbed all over her face a most horrible poison, the effect whereof was such that never leper looked more ugly than she did" (30). The narrative voice is at pains to emphasize the ferocity of the attack and its grotesque disfigurement of Parthenia's face. Because the villain mutilates the heroine's countenance, her "transgression" is visually marked as a sign of filial and sexual disobedience. As such, Demagoras's cruelty becomes a gendered crime, geared specifically toward debilitating the heroine's decorum and self-esteem, particularly since Parthenia is renowned in Arcadia for her "fairness" among other conventionalized attributes (28).

Parthenia's deformity and abasement at the hands of a jealous suitor lead her to withdraw from society, despite Argalus's protests of unchanged love. Myron Turner interprets Parthenia's disfigured face and subsequent retirement as part of a larger symbolic motif of alienation in the romance: "Parthenia's withdrawal prefigures a basic psychological pattern: the need to withdraw--if only temporarily--from 'all companie' in order to be alone with the shame or despair (usually both) arising out of some disfigurement of nature, some act or emotion felt to be unnatural--in violation of reason, virtue, nature."[26] Turner points out that Parthenia's seclusion exposes to the reader her silent suffering in shame and despair, her sense of hopelessness and loss of heroic resolve. In essence, it is the moment when the heroine's virtue fails her. Yet despite her sense of alienation, Parthenia's refusal to marry Argalus also demonstrates, I would suggest, her own peculiar brand of heroism: her drive to control her sexuality. In keeping with her resistance to imposed sexuality, Parthenia decides when and how Argalus will interact with her, even if it means losing him: "for truth is that so in her heart she loved him as she could not find in her heart he should be tied to what was unworthy of his presence" (31). In a twist of logic, Parthenia determines not to marry Argalus; she will not be wedded out of pity and self-sacrifice. Argalus, though, expresses his heroism differently. Even though Argalus suffers mental anguish, evincing compassion and selflessness in his love for the heroine, his erotic suffering eventually manifests itself in action and bloodshed. Argalus seeks to avenge Demagoras, and he enacts the role of heroic combatant by mortally wounding the impious Helot leader. Parthenia's suffering is painfully acted out on her body.

True to romance fashion, Parthenia's face is magically restored to its original beauty by Queen Helen of Corinth's physicians. Nonetheless, Sidney dramatically departs from romance convention by altering the story's fairytale ending. In Book Three, after the couple's marriage, Basilius summons Argalus, famed for chivalry and honor, to take up and redeem his quarrel with Amphialus. Amphialus, as we know, is complicit in his mother's imprisonment of the princesses Pamela and Philoclea. The importance of this scene lies in the extreme consequences of Parthenia's erotic suffering. She understands that Argalus's call to duty, which brings to mind his zealous call to action in his previous hard labors, will result in her own pain and eventual death: "'Parthenia shall be in the battle of your fight! Parthenia shall smart in your pain, and your blood must be bled by Parthenia!'" (502-03). (Incidentally, when the King's messenger arrives, Argalus is reading from a book that contains the stories of Hercules.) Whereas Parthenia has previously endured physical and psychological torment on account of her love for Argalus, now she will shed blood for him in death. In fulfillment of her prophecy, Parthenia turns into a male persona, the Knight of the Tomb, a symbolic embodiment of her demise. If Argalus had before won battles due to his knightly valor and gallant bravery, Parthenia looks to avenge her husband's slaying by becoming a reflection of this valor and bravery. Her heroism progresses from triumphant resistance to active revenge in combat, and Sidney underscores this change by having Parthenia change from a woman to a man.

The death wound that Amphialus inflicts on the Knight of the Tomb's neck, however, draws the reader's attention specifically to the femininity of her person, rather than to the masculinity that defines her deed and bearing. The author gives over a considerable amount of descriptive narrative-time in order to delineate Parthenia's unique beauty in death:

> her beauty then, even in despite of the past sorrow, or coming death, assuring all beholders that it was nothing short of perfection: for her exceeding fair eyes having with continual weeping gotten a little redness about them; her roundly sweetly swelling lips a little trembling, as though they kissed their neighbour death; in her cheeks the whiteness striving by little and little to get upon the roisness of them; her neck (a neck indeed of alabaster) displaying the wound, which with most dainty blood laboured to drown his own beauties, so as here was a river of purest red, there, an island of perfittest white, each giving lustre to the other--with the sweet countenance, God knows, full of an unaffected languishing.  (397)

The death blow illustrates the delicate and sensual attractiveness of Parthenia's warrior-like role, as "dainty blood" gathers on her exquisite "alabaster" neck. The gory wound transmogrifies into an aesthetic picture of the female body, so that it "apparell[ed] beauty in a new fashion" (397). Unlike the graphic depiction of the heroine's injury, Argalus's death wounds are described in terms of metaphor: the blood from the hero's lacerations causes his armor to "blush" (376), which externalizes Argalus's inward shame of defeat in combat. By contrast, the heroine is objectified and eroticized in the throes of death: Parthenia's "sweetly swelling lips" tremble, her cheeks grow pale, her "fair eyes" have grown a tender red "with continual weeping." Parthenia's face, her "sweet countenance," is the focal point of a man's brutality once again. If she had been made ugly before, now her wound reveals a pulchritude that transcends even death, "death being able to divide the soul, but not the beauty from that body" (398). The elegance of Parthenia's afflicted body stands for, in some sense, the beauty of her virtue and nobility of spirit, her exalted love of Argalus. However so, Parthenia's courageous death is counterbalanced by a narrative perspective that views the heroine as "full of unaffected languishing," a fragile female whose body suffers the consequences of manly valor.

The love story of Argalus and Parthenia lays the ground work for the development of Pamela's and Philoclea's heroism in Book Three. Like Parthenia, the Arcadian princesses experience the vicissitudes of erotic suffering, and their heroism lies in the ability to resist forms of power that seek to impose restrictions on their sexuality. Unlike Parthenia, the heroines do not adopt a male identity (as far as the unfinished version goes), so that their virtue does not align itself with knightly prowess. Nor do the sisters perish in their ordeals. In Book Three, Cecropia abducts and confines Pamela and Philoclea, along with Pyrocles, disguised as the Amazon Zelmane, in order to remove "these good inheritrixes of Arcadia" from succession (319). Since her son, Amphialus, has fallen in love with Philoclea, Cecropia elects to incarcerate, not murder, her nieces, hoping to forge a dynastic marriage between Amphialus and one of the princesses. At first glance, it seems that Pamela and Philoclea portray typified modes of feminine behavior as they patiently endure the confinement of captivity. Such conduct in the *New Arcadia* leads Anne Shaver to assert that "[t]he revising of Pamela and Philoclea allows them the kind of heroism available to the current male ideal of womanhood--patience within the constraints of gender--but no more."[27] But this view of the princesses' suffering, their patience in adversity, does not address the full nature of their heroism. Although Pamela and Philoclea do patiently suffer, they also actively oppose threats to their persons, chastity, and romantic ideals. In the Captivity Episode, Cecropia attempts to undermine Pamela's faith in a divine Creator and, by extension, her fidelity to Musidorus. She also attempts to weaken Philoclea's resolve, in this case her steadfast love for Pyrocles. Pamela and Philoclea withstand mental anguish and physical torments, and it is their suffering bodies that indicate the depth of their resistance in the face of Cecropia's ever-increasing cruelty and force. Importantly, because Pyrocles has adopted a female identity, "she," like the sisters, suffers imprisonment. Yet "her" heroism corresponds to a more masculine vision of virtue, one that is based on a chivalric code of honor in arms.

The Captivity Episode begins with the violent kidnapping of Pamela and Philoclea and their separation from Musidorus and Pyrocles.[28] This act instigates a series of trials that test the heroines' resistance to the will of Cecropia. Captured by twenty armed men, the sisters arrive at Cecropia's castle, a castle situated "in the midst of a great lake, upon a high rock" (316-17). The castle's apparent impenetrability intensifies the princesses' sense of seclusion and terror. This imprisonment also serves as a metaphor for Pamela's and Philoclea's impervious chastity. In order to gain control over the sisters, Cecropia isolates the women even further by shutting them away in separate rooms, chambers "so vaulted of strong and thickly built stone as one could no way hear the other" (425). The women are unable to hear, see, or communicate with each other:

> Each of these chambers had a little window to look into the hall, but because the sisters should not have so much comfort as to look out to another, there was of the outsides curtains drawn, which they could not reach with their hands, so barring the reach of their sight.  (425)

Pyrocles as Zelmane has been locked away in a chamber above Pamela's, while Philoclea's room stands "one story from the ground" across from her sister's (425). By separating the women, Cecropia believes that she can more easily persuade one of them to wed her son. Commentating on the effects of this separation, Cecropia states: "'Company confirms resolutions, and loneliness breeds a weariness of one's thoughts, and so, a sooner consenting to reasonable proffers'" (321). Cecropia understands the psychological implications of isolation: it weakens an individual's resolution by diminishing confidence in one's personal conviction and judgment. Even the narrator comments on the severity of this confinement: "[t]he poor ladies indeed not suffered either to meet together, or to have conference with any other but such as Cecropia had already framed to sing all her songs to their tune" (354). The confinement exacerbates the heroines' suffering, and Cecropia takes this opportunity--the sisters' separation from each other and from their lovers--to coerce them into submission.

Unable to escape captivity, Pamela and Philoclea rely on other means of resistance to oppose Cecropia's assaults on their sexual autonomy. Both use a method of dissimulation that veils their true intent. Philoclea admits this deceit to Pyrocles: "For dissimulation--my Pyrocles, my simplicity is such that I have hardly been able to keep a straight way" (430). Philoclea, however, does manage to keep a straight way. It is the misery of imposed isolation that she finds disagreeable, and she applies the argument of liberty versus constraint as a mask to counter solicitations for her love. For example, when Amphialus pleads his perpetual devotion to Philoclea, she rebukes him by reminding him of her confinement and his hypocrisy: "'[ . . . ] while you say I am mistress of your life, I am not mistress of mine own; you entitle yourself my slave--but I am sure I am yours. If then violence, injury, terror, and depriving of that which is more dear than life itself, liberty, be fit orators for affection, you may expect that I will be easily persuaded'" (322). The dissimilation is that Philoclea, set free, would never be persuaded by Amphialus's pledge of affection. She is in love with the Macedonian hero. As she later acknowledges to Pyrocles: "I confess the love of thee is herein my chiefest virtue" (430). To Amphialus, she says otherwise. Philoclea maintains that the problem of his unrequited love is a theoretical one: without liberty, she cannot exercise her freedom; she cannot freely choose his love. Interestingly, this logic is not dissimilar to late seventeenth- and early eighteenth-century philosophical discussions on the relationship between suffering and personal liberty. In her study, *Tortured Subjects*, Lisa Silverman examines how Enlightenment thinkers began to question the validity of legal torture as a justifiable means of persuasion or truth-seeking. Like Philoclea, these philosophers claimed that personal agency could not exist in a body under duress, for torture seeks to efface selfhood by impairing the rational process or the composure of the mind.[29] Although she does not yet suffer the intense physical pain of torture, Philoclea contends that, while under the constraint of Cecropia and her son, she cannot effectively exert her will. Philoclea's dissimulation operates on two levels: she forestalls a union with

Amphialus by reasoning her inability to consent to marriage while simultaneously beguiling her oppressor with hope.

As Philoclea mentions, Amphialus turns the rationale of Philoclea's captivity on its head. Rather than acknowledge his role as captor, Amphialus insists that it is the princess who has captured him: "she being indeed the mistress of his life, and he, her eternal slave" (322).[30] Amphialus even appropriates and inverts Philoclea's rhetoric on her loss of liberty. In his grueling duel with the Forsaken Knight (Musidorus), Amphialus asks, "since I lost my liberty, have I lost my courage?" (409). Needless to say, the juxtaposition between actual imprisonment and imaginative enslavement reveals the extent to which Amphialus has fallen victim to his own delusions. As Amphialus pines away for the unobtainable princess, he emerges as a picture of Petrarchan dejection. Neglected by the object of his adoration, he feels helpless, attenuates, becomes desolate and desperate. His only consolation abides in hope, the possibility of Philoclea's acceptance. On the other hand, his self-delusion also corresponds to a generic trope of Greek romance: the Greek romance heroine is so divinely beautiful that her captor believes she has caused her own erotic suffering.[31] Similarly, Amphialus maintains that Philoclea's own attractiveness has incarcerated her: "'It is you yourself that imprison yourself! It is your beauty which makes these castle walls embrace you!'" (323). The problem with this logic is that Amphialus wields absolute physical power over his prisoner, and his need to satisfy "'love's vehemency'" leaves Philoclea "quaking" in fear (323). Even though Amphialus promises not "to conquer her affection" by force, the threat of violence envelops Philoclea, so that she must live with the terror of ravishment (324). Sidney draws our attention to the unequal relationship between captor and captive,

Amphialus and Philoclea, in a suggestive comparison. Amphialus is likened to a poor, hungry woman who must sacrifice her beloved doe (Philoclea) in order to survive: "[m]any a pitiful look doth she cast upon it, and many a time doth she draw back her hand before she can give the stroke" (323). Emasculated by love, Amphialus feels profound compassion and tenderness for the princess regardless of his ultimate dominion over her.

We recall that Philoclea circumvents the sexual affronts of Amphialus through dissimulation. In her rhetoric against constraint, Philoclea evades marriage with a man she does not love, in addition to mollifying her tormentor. The princess escapes the evil stratagems of Cecropia through a similar technique. Realizing that her son, Amphialus, has been unsuccessful in his bid for Philoclea's heart, Cecropia accosts the heroine with "poison distilled in sweet liquor," the poison being arguments directed toward destabilizing Philoclea's self-possession and purposefulness (329). Thus, Cecropia tries to undermine the heroine's personhood by attacking her celebrated beauty, urging the princess to cease her incessant weeping as it will blemish the composure of her face and body: "'Shall tears take away the beauty of that complexion which the women of Arcadia wish for, and the men long after? Fie of this peevish sadness! In sooth, it is untimely for your age. Look upon your own body, and see whether it deserve to pine away with sorrow'" (330). There is the suggestion that Philoclea's "peevish sorrow" or stubbornness, her refusal to wed Amphialus, will transform into a symbol of her disobedience, just as Parthenia's deformed face becomes a sign of sexual disobedience-- her rejection of the ignoble Demagoras. Incidentally, Philoclea's face does suffer the ill effects of her imprisonment. When Pyrocles later sees Philoclea after their separation in the castle, the narrator records that "her face [was] not without tokens that beauty had been by many miseries cruelly battered; and yet showed it most the perfection of that beauty which could remain unoverthrown, by such enemies" (429). Instead of marring her beauty, Philoclea's "cruelly battered" visage is a symbolic indication of her resistance to the wills of Cecropia and Amphialus, an affirmation of her personhood. The threat of disfigurement in captivity does not deter Philoclea's determination to eschew a marriage with Amphialus. Even so, the princess pleads with Cecropia for her liberty, so that "grief" and "fear" are not her "unappointed executioners" (330). In response, Cecropia falsely argues that, rather than provoking grief or fear, Philoclea's captivity protects and safeguards her liberty, her freedom from unknown dangers.

Like her son, Cecropia distorts Philoclea's rhetoric on liberty, though she is more calculating and manipulative in her methodology. In response, Philoclea repeats her strategy of dissimulation. When Cecropia realizes that she cannot lure Philoclea into wedlock by appealing to her personal vanity, her sense of beauty, Cecropia develops her tactics. She turns the concept of liberty into a commodity, a gift that only she and Amphialus can bestow on the princess; the stipulation is that Philoclea marry her son: "'[Amphialus] doth by me present unto you the full enjoying of your liberty--so as, with this gift, you will accept a greater (which is this castle, with all the rest which you know he hath in honourable quantity), and will confirm his gift, and your receipt of both, with accepting him to be you yours'" (331). Philoclea's dissimulation--she deceptively claims that she cannot accept Amphialus's gift of marriage because she wants to remain a virgin--should not be viewed as a sign of moral lassitude. Quite the opposite, dissimulation is an integral aspect of the heroine's virtue. "'But my heart is already set,'" says Philoclea, "and staying a while on that word, she brought forth afterwards, 'to lead a virgin's life to my death, for such a vow I have in myself devoutly made'" (332). Naturally, Philoclea fabricates this statement in order to stay true to Pyrocles. This method of dissimulation harks back to situations in Greek romance in which the suffering heroine uses deception as a way to remain faithful to the hero, an occurrence that is especially notable in the *Aethiopica*: one is reminded of Chariclea's falsehood to the captor Thyamis and to the pirate Trachinos, both of whom hunger for the heroine as their lover and spouse.[32] Following in the path of Chariclea, Philoclea resorts to falsehood precisely because she is compelled to protect her chastity, as well as her freedom to choose a husband, from an overpowering adversary.

This dissimulation does not go unnoticed by Cecropia. Philoclea's tormentor deftly switches her argument from the gift of liberty in marriage to the joys of motherhood and wedded life: if Philoclea will not be persuaded by the prospect of an advantageous union with her son, then she will be persuaded, Cecropia suspects, by the sentimental value of conjugal affection and duty. Thus, Cecropia relates to Philoclea the standard early modern views on the benefits of married life: motherhood, mutual companionship, and solace.[33] Cecropia counters what Philoclea cunningly calls the "burdenous yoke" of marriage by conjuring up Philoclea's earlier rhetoric on liberty (332). According to Cecropia, it is single life that is an undesirable "liberty" and marriage a desirable restraint, just like "rose-water kept in a crystal glass" (333). Cecropia's metaphor, however, of the "crystalline marriage," one in which wedlock is compared to a prison of glass, does little to promote the mutual benefits of wedded life, one in which "you have a yoke-fellow to help to draw through the cloddy cumbers of this world"

(333). In her quest for power, Cecropia uncovers power-based relationships in her very attempt to promote companionship in marriage; as her metaphor insinuates, the husband represents the crystal glass that restrains the rose-water, his wife. Whereas Cecropia searches for an artful argument that will coerce the princess into marriage, Philoclea dissimulates in order to defend herself from the verbal assaults of her enemy. Hence, her deception serves, figuratively speaking, as a protective armor that resists Cecropia's rhetorical affronts. The narrator elucidates Philoclea's tactic:

> Therefore, listing not to dispute in a matter whereof herself was resolved, and desired not to inform the other, she only told her that whilst she was so captived she could not conceive of any such persuasions (though never so reasonable) any otherwise than as constraints; and as constraints, must needs even in nature abhor them, which at her liberty, in their own force of reason might more prevail with her; and so, fain would have returned the strength of Cecropia's persuasions, to have procured freedom. (334)

Concealing her real feelings by pretense, Philoclea repeats the argument against constraint that she had earlier delivered to Amphialus. Essentially, Philoclea suggests that, while imprisoned, she cannot exert her will or reasoning to choose a husband freely.

This form of deception, saying one thing but meaning another, resurfaces in Cecropia's dealings with Pamela. Although Amphialus does not love Pamela, Cecropia harasses both sisters in a similar manner in order to appease her love-sick son. Cecropia endeavors to make Pamela vulnerable by playing to her sense of vanity, a ploy that is similar to Cecropia's earlier attack on Philoclea. Like her sister's, Pamela's *modus operandi* is dissimulation. When Cecropia urges the princess to put her beauty to use by marrying her son, Pamela repudiates this request on grounds of filial duty: "'But as I have often answered you, so resolutely I say unto you that he must get my parent's consent, and then he shall know further of my mind; for, without that I know I should offend God'" (357). Pamela prevaricates in order to combat Cecropia's rhetorical subterfuge, and what sets her situation apart from her sister's ordeal is that Pamela adopts the argument of parental obedience as the ultimate grounds for refusal. It can be further deduced that Pamela dissimulates at this moment as she later uses the exact same argument to discourage another unwanted suitor, the warrior Anaxius: "[ . . . ] Pamela forced herself to make answer to Anaxius that, if her father gave his consent, she would make herself believe that such was the heavenly determination, since she had no means to avoid it' (456). Hidden behind Pamela's words lies her strong affection for Musidorus, revealed in such outbursts as "'Live long, my Musidorus" or in such wishes as "the virtuous joining themselves together" (422).

As pointed out in the Argalus and Parthenia episode, the issue of parental consent in marriage would have been perceived by an Elizabethan and Jacobean audience as a fundamental aspect of the marriage process, especially for an aristocratic pairing. According to such an authority on marriage as Lodovicus Vives, "the younge man shuld leave the care of this election to his parentes, the which have better judgement & are more free from the agitations and motions of al affections, then they are."[84] In the *Old Arcadia*, Pamela and Musidorus disregard the issue of parental consent in matrimony when they elope, as if in direct defiance of Basilius's wishes: "there was the general opinion grown the duke would grant his daughters in marriage to nobody."[85] In the *New Arcadia*, parental disobedience in marriage exists as a remote possibility as Cecropia reminds the heroine of her father's "peevish thoughts," his refusal to allow his daughters suitors (358).[36] Pointedly, Pamela even later admits to Pyrocles that her own "parents are content to be tyrants" (455). Yet responding with deference, not vanity or disrespect, Pamela's answer to Cecropia reveals the limits of her tolerance to her aunt's sophistry: "'If he be peevish,' said Pamela, 'yet is he my father; and how beautiful soever I be, I am his daughter, so as God claims at my hands obedience, and makes me no judge of his imperfections'" (358). Despite her tendency toward deception in this episode, Pamela's prerogative is to remain obedient to her father, and thus to God's ordinance. This ushers in Cecropia's famous assault on the existence of a divine Creator and Pamela's more powerful and sincere defense.

Cecropia understands that her rhetorical maneuvering has not compelled either Philoclea or Pamela to marry Amphialus. As a result, she decides upon a more intense course of physical violence and psychological terror that will break the resolve of the heroines. She hopes that "weary of their bodies, they should be content to bestow them at her appointment" (423). The weakened body, Cecropia imagines, will be the key to the sisters' yielding to her force. As Elizabeth Dipple argues, the degree to which Pamela and Philoclea stand up for their romantic ideals in the Captivity Episode marks a turning point in Sidney's overall conception of the revised *Arcadia*: unlike the *Old Arcadia*, in which the function of Book 3 had been "the exposure of sexual sin in the major characters," which "necessitated the trial and its tragic possibilities," Book 3 in the *New Arcadia* veers in the opposite direction. According to Dipple, "after the extended philosophical passages about love, virginity, and sex, it is obviously impossible to revert back to the idea of sexual guilt."[37] More than defending their sexual virtue, Pamela and Philoclea withstand bodily and mental torture aimed at hindering their resistance to Cecropia. If Cecropia's guile, coupled with enforced isolation, cannot impel the sisters to wed Amphialus, then the next tool of persuasion is pain. At this point in the episode, a noticeable distinction arises between the suffering body and the will of the mind: the heroines' bodies must give in to and bear the experience of pain, but their resolution and fortitude to resist Cecropia remain unassailable. Although their bodies suffer defilement, the strength of their conviction and sexual autonomy illustrate a form of heroism predicated on the principles of fidelity and chastity, standards that grow from a quasi-spiritual devotion to the princesses' romantic partners, Musidorus and Pyrocles.

Cecropia embarks upon a systematic plan of torture that progresses in intensity and cruelty from deprivation, to beatings, to the threat of execution. Although Pamela and Philoclea maintain their integrity in imprisonment, Cecropia aims to vex them with the torment of additional hardship. She withholds "all comfort both of servants and service from them" (419). Besides denying the Arcadian princesses their liberty, a privation that mirrors, to some extent, Basilius's sequestering of his own daughters, Cecropia increases their discomfort by disallowing them the social comforts of their class, for they "had been used unto, [servants] even at home" (419). Moreover, she takes her ruthlessness to a new level by "dishonourably using them both in diet and lodging" in order to "pull down their thoughts to yielding" (419). Like an experienced torturer, Cecropia uses deprivation to inflict physical and inward pain and fracture the sisters' firmness of purpose. Yet it is exactly their defiance of such hardship that toughens the heroines' resolution, making their endurance of suffering an active, heroic act: "[Pamela and Philoclea] found in themselves how much good the hardness of education doth to the resistance of misery"

(419). This resistance to misery includes braving the hardship of privation: lack of proper food, lodging, comfort, and sensory experience.

Cecropia methodically introduces the Arcadian princesses to new kinds of torture in her scheme to subdue their wills. She moves beyond deprivation to psychological terror, scaring them "with noises of horror, sometimes with sudden frightings in the night, when the solitary darkness therof might easier astonish the disarmed senses" (419). By catching them off guard, Cecropia endeavors to beleaguer their intellectual bearing and stability. This cruel mind game has roots in Cecropia's earlier scare tactics when she entreats the princesses with either "gifts" or "threatenings," depending on the probability for success (418). Similar to abused creatures, the heroines do not know whether they will be coddled or punished, and the experience of such psychological terror causes a general anxiety, an uneasiness about not knowing what will happen and when. No matter how much Cecropia terrorizes Pamela and Philoclea, however, the narrator concludes that "but to all, virtue and love resisted, strengthened one by the other when each found itself over-vehemently assaulted" (419). Pamela and Philoclea, represented here as allegories of Virtue and Love respectively, refuse to commit their persons to the shifts of Cecropia.

After Cecropia comprehends that neither deprivation nor terror can alter the heroines' constancy, she descends into an "abominable rage" (420). In her fury, she is perhaps cognizant that the experience of violent pain negatively affects a person's selfhood. As David Morris writes in *The Culture of Pain*, "To be in pain is often to be in a state of crisis. It is a state in which we experience far more than physical discomfort. Pain has not simply interrupted our normal feeling of health. It has opened a huge fault or fissure in our world."[38] By wickedly beating the princesses, Cecropia tries to break the heroines' resistance and to forge a "fault" or "fissure" in their belief systems. Philoclea is first violated in this manner. Not only does Cecropia lash her with a rod, but she adds the extra horror of having evil tormentors thrash the heroine as well, hags who "flew to the sweet Philoclea, as if so many kites should come about a white dove." Equaling that villainy, Cecropia "fell to scourge that most beautiful body," an act that reverberates back to the eroticized violence of Parthenia's death (420). The dichotomy between the suffering body and the inviolable will comes into sharp focus; for, despite Philoclea's resignation to this gruesome scourging, one perversely orchestrated by her very own aunt, the princess stays faithful to her dedication to Pyrocles / Zelmane: "[A]nd that was the only worldly thing wereon Philoclea rested her mind--that she knew she should die beloved of Zelmane, and should die rather than be false to Zelmane" (421). Of course, the beating does not kill or drive Philoclea to marry Amphialus, though the flogging brings about "tearful eyes" and a "sobbing breast" (420).

Philoclea begs her aunt to cease her cruelty for the sake of humanity and common decency. Not only does Cecropia deny her, but she also unleashes "hellish monsters," the hags, to torment the heroine once again (421). Crucially, this attack on Philoclea calls attention to a vital concept in the construction of both Philoclea's and Pamela's heroism. While Philoclea withstands the deleterious action of her adversaries, Sidney describes her valor in a simile that equates her long-suffering to "a fair, gorgeous armour." This association recalls the Pauline metaphor of protective armor: "Put on the whole armor of God, so that you may be able to stand against the wiles of the devil" (Ephesians 6:11).

Just as armor guards the body from the blows of an enemy, so too does Philoclea's

courage safeguard her from an inimical force:

> [S]o that with silence and patience, like a fair gorgeous armour hammered
>
> upon by an ill-favoured smith, she abode their pitiless dealing with her, till
>
> rather reserving her for more than meaning to end, they left her to an
>
> uncomfortable leisure, to consider with herself her fortune . . . . (421)

It is the heroine's resistance, her "gorgeous armour," that effectively protects her from

the blows of Cecropia, the "ill-favoured smith." This comparison suggests that Philoclea

does not suffer passively, though she is indeed patient; nor does she merely accept her

fate; she fights, albeit defensively. Philoclea stands her ground through a determination to

dispose of her person as she privately wishes. Likewise, Pamela, who receives a similar

beating at the hands of her aunt, is forced to yield to bodily punishment, and as in

Philoclea's case, her opponents cannot impose their will on her: "for when reason taught

her there was not resistance, for to just resistance first her heart was inclined, then with so

heavenly a quietness and so graceful a calmness did she suffer the divers kinds of

torments they used to her that, while they vexed her fair body, it seemed that she rather

directed than obeyed the vexation" (421-22). Notwithstanding beatings, threats, and

terrors, Pamela will not subjugate herself to her aunt's authority. To Cecropia, Pamela

insists that "'Thou mayest well wreck this silly body, but me thou canst never

overthrow'" (422). Pamela's body is made to suffer under the various torments that

Cecropia devises, but her opposition to imposed sexuality has not been quelled.

In fact, the body in pain takes on new meaning for the heroines. Far from

passively accepting their hostile situation, Pamela and Philoclea view suffering as a powerful weapon of defiance. Because they have not been emotionally enfeebled by physical distress, the sisters believe that enduring pain is a singular virtue. Suffering urges them on to even greater forbearance, so that their resistance, like Philoclea's imagined armor, figures forth as a protective covering in their warfare:

> so these princesses, second to none (and far from any second, only to be matched by themselves), with the use of suffering their minds got the habit of suffering, so as all fears and terrors were to them but summons to a battle whereof they knew beforehand they should be victorious, and which in the suffering was painful, being suffered, was a trophy to itself. (423)

The experience of pain is conceptualized like a battle in which the sisters know they will be triumphant. Predictably, Cecropia misinterprets this protective armor as an "armour of obstinacy," rather than as one of virtuous resistance (423). For Pamela and Philoclea, suffering becomes an extension of their valor and virtue; yet, unlike Parthenia, who actually engages in a bloody duel in order to avenge Argalus's honor, the sisters intellectualize their conflict. Pain is the defining, abstract embodiment of victory.

The final act of torture reifies the dichotomy between the suffering body and the willful intellect. When Cecropia learns that she has not prevailed over her nieces, since they have not succumbed to her torments, she subjects them to a macabre ritual of pain and humiliation. Pamela and Philoclea must watch one another's faked execution, so that each thinks that the other has been murdered. These staged executions actualize the literal split between head and torso, mind and body. When Philoclea describes her beheading to Pyrocles, she tells how the executioners thrust her head through a hole in the scaffold: "'they did put about my poor neck a dish of gold whereout they had beaten the bottom, so as, having set blood in it, you saw how I played the part of death'" (436). Even though the execution is a sham, Philoclea still feels the effects of physical anguish during the event: "'and so had they set me that I reached but on tiptoes to the ground, so as scarcely I could breathe, much less speak. And truly, if they had kept me there any whit longer, they had strangled me instead of beheading me'" (436-37). In this spectacle, the head (will) is symbolically dissevered from the body (site of suffering), as if Cecropia acknowledged the power of the heroine's will to intellectualize and thereby overcome affliction. Moreover, the simulated beheading functions as a gesture symbolizing Philoclea's severed maidenhead, the threat of which Cecropia continually hopes to uphold. This staged scene causes Pyrocles, who sees the deflowering of Philoclea as his destiny, to bemoan her demise. Upon witnessing what he believes to be her decapitation, he mawkishly decries the separation of Philoclea's head from her body: "'Alas! why should they divide such a head from such a body? No other body is worthy of that head; no other head is worthy of that body'" (433). The heroine's head is even more precious than the gold that encircles it: "'I saw your head--the head indeed, and chief part of all nature's works--standing in a dish of gold, too mean a shrine, Got wot, for such a relic'" (436). An object of adoration, Philoclea's head sits ceremoniously gilded in blood. The head is regarded as the seat of reason or the human will and, as the ambiguity of the term "Nature's works" suggests, the seat of beauty as well. Pyrocles' words sustain the view of the suffering female whose body, like Parthenia's, is oddly resplendent in death. The image of the decapitated heroine paints a picture of her virtue that is erotic in its aesthetic objectification.[39]

Unbeknownst to Philoclea and Pyrocles, Pamela does not enter the stage of execution. Instead, Cecropia apparels the lady Artesia in Pamela's clothes, putting the imposter, not the princess, to death. Artesia, who was once Cecropia's handmaid, one who helped her entrap the princesses, has double-crossed Cecropia by conspiring to assassinate Amphialus. Thus, Artesia ends her life in a vile and debased fashion, indicating that mode of death parallels the depravity of her deed. She approaches the scaffold with "hands bound before her" and with "her eyes to her lips muffled with a fair handkerchief" (425). Artesia kneels down about to speak but,

> before the unfortunate lady could pronounce three words, the executioner cut off the one's speech and the other's attention with making his sword do his cruel office upon that beautiful neck. Yet the pitiless sword had such pity of so precious an object that at first it did but hit flatlong--but little availed that, since the lady falling down astonished withal, the cruel villain forced the sword with another blow to divorce the fair marriage of the head and body.  (426)

If Pamela and Philoclea each prevails over Cecropia by keeping her betrothal intact, by keeping the "marriage" of head and body, Artesia's punishment in defeat is the separation ("divorce") of head from body. Artesia, who had previously been defended by the knight Phalantus as the fairest in the land (Book 1), now meets with the ugly blow of the sword. The narrative voice describes the event through the eyes of Philoclea and Pyrocles, spectators who mistakenly recognize the "rare whiteness" of this neck as belonging to Pamela (425). Like Pamela, Artesia has physical beauty, but her actions have not. As a result of her villainy, Artesia encounters a botched death, taking a second hit to the neck in order to sever it from the body. While the horror of the incident serves to heighten

Philoclea's and Pyrocles' pain as they watch what they think is Pamela's execution, it

also emphasizes Artesia's moral and intellectual depravity. About her beheading,

Philoclea later asserts: "'Truly I am sorry for the poor gentlewoman, though justly she be

punished for her double falsehood'" (436). Artesia's execution provides an example of

the anti-heroine, a woman who suffers for no cause other than for vainglory. Fittingly,

Cecropia's unnatural death, later in the story, is also a reflection of her iniquity: falling

from the castle leads, Cecropia "with hellish agony" must watch her son stab himself as

she slowly dies, sprawled on the castle ground (440).

Pyrocles confronts the trial of imprisonment in Cecropia's castle in a strikingly

diverse manner. Unlike the princesses, who envision bodily suffering as a liberating

force, Pyrocles / Zelmane undertakes to liberate the sisters in actual combat: "Zelmane

for her part desired no more but to have armour and weapons brought into her chamber,

not doubting therewith to perform anything, how impossible soever, which longing love

can persuade and invincible valour dare promise" (388). Yearning for the accouterments

of private warfare, Pyrocles falls back on a familiar notion of valor-in-arms. Mark Rose,

in his book *Heroic Love*, suggests that, through his adversity, Pyrocles aspires to a new

code of male virtue: "Pyrocles regards his love for Philoclea as a new manifestation of

heroism."[40] This erotic heroism, it can be said, draws from the thematic plot pattern of

Greek romance, in which the hero faces dangerous obstacles all in the name of fidelity in

love; that model of heroism requires virtuous conduct in perilous trials of faith and

constancy. As Rose states: "To pursue virtuous desire in an imperfect world, however, is

to enter upon a state as fraught with peril as any battle or campaign." He continues: "on the one hand the lover must avoid the danger of melancholic despair and, on the other, lies the threat that, the distant goal forgotten, his passion may degenerate into lust."[41] Pyrocles must navigate the psychological perils of despair or lust in his quest for virtuous love. Nonetheless, his erotic suffering is infused with a martial sense of urgency, which parallels his role of Amazon warrior. His heroism still retains elements of conventional chivalric valor. Several passages underline this point. Pyrocles / Zelmane,

> only wished but to come by a sword, not doubting then to destroy them all and deliver Philoclea, so little did both the men and their forces seem in her eyes, looking down upon them from the high top of affection's tower. (428)

Or Pyrocles / Zelmane exudes so much violence in captivity that:

> she was the true image of overmastered courage, and of spite that sees no remedy--for her breast swelled withal; the blood burst out at her nose; and she looked paler than accustomed, with her eyes cast on the ground with such a grace as if she were fallen out with the heavens for suffering such an injury. (415)

And:

> Zelmane's heart was rent in pieces with rage of the injury and disdain of her fortune. (316)

Unable to rescue the princesses by arms, Pyrocles, overcome with frustration, only prays that Musidorus can save them (459). By chance, Pyrocles acquires the sword of Zoilus, an ally of Amphialus, killing him and his brother, Lycurgus, and he is about to slay their elder brother, Anaxius, as the *New Arcadia* abruptly ends in mid sentence.

What can be seen, then, from Sidney's use of the romance pattern of erotic suffering in the *New Arcadia* is, as Doody argues, that "Chastity becomes an oddly active virtue, and characters become heroines--and heroes--of chastity."[142] Like the Greek romance heroine, the Arcadian heroine suffers in order to protect her chastity, her desire to commit her person and sexuality to whom she chooses. The Arcadian heroine shows her courage and independence by spurning the sexual or romantic advances of an unwanted suitor. These admirers generally share a similar social and economic background with the heroine; hence, she does not repulse these suitors for lack of aristocratic advantage or monetary gain but for lack of desirability. The heroine possesses an unwavering will to marry the man who has won her heart: Parthenia rejects a marriage arrangement with the affluent Demagoras; Philoclea denies the affection of her dauntless cousin Amphialus; Pamela deflects Cecropia's demand that she marry her son; both Pamela and Philoclea reject the "proud wooers," Anaxius and Lycurgus (456).

Pamela and Philoclea enlarge upon the trial of suffering by transforming pain into a weapon of resistance. This victory over pain is figured as a battlefield in which the princesses emerge triumphant. What Sidney also adds to this romance motif is a greater concern for the dichotomy between the body and the human will: the female body is assaulted, but her mind remains steadfast. Pamela and Philoclea survive the degradation of the staged executions, but the trauma of the ordeal, combined with their long imprisonment, proves too much for their bodies. Exhausted from emotional turmoil and corporeal torture, their constitutions can no longer bear the pain. Yet Cecropia, like an experienced torturer, does not seek really the princesses' death, only psychological intimidation. As Philoclea explains to Pyrocles:

And finding both of us even given over, not like to live many hours
longer, and my sister Pamela rather worse than myself (the strength of her
heart worse bearing those indignities), the good woman, Cecropia, with
the same pity as folks keep fowl when they are not fat enough for their
eating, made us know her deceit, and let us come one to another.  (437)

Because Pamela believes her sister has been murdered, she openly defies Cecropia
further by refusing to eat; this resistance, her denial of nourishment, illustrates, yet again,
the division between the debilitated body and the strength and independence of the
heroine's mind. For Pamela and Philoclea, the consequence of autonomy and private
desire is the destruction of the body.

This characterization of suffering-in-love finally evokes the pain of the heroine
Zelmane, Pyrocles' namesake and Philoclea's look alike. Unable to withstand the torment
of her unrequited passion for Pyrocles, Zelmane's "dainty body" simply expires (266).
Her body gives out, falling into "deadly swoundings" (266), though her allegiance and
immutable love remain firm. Zelmane does not fit into the Greek romance paradigm of
female heroism because she literally dies for love, while the ideal romance heroine
survives the obstacles that confront her. When Zelmane disguises herself as Pyrocles'
page, her cross-dressing does not translate into resourcefulness, only death. Furthermore,
Pyrocles' admiration of Zelmane lacks the intensity of passion love that takes hold of him
with Philoclea. What Zelmane imparts to Pyrocles is the "female" aspect of erotic
suffering. By adopting her name, Pyrocles shares in Philoclea's and Pamela's experience
of vulnerability and imprisonment.

This figure of the powerless female body has a critical link with the idea of a hierarchy of gender. One the one hand, the heroine has a vigorous determination to control her sexuality: to remain faithful to her beloved and to her private vow of honor. On the other hand, the erotic suffering of Pamela and Philoclea also reveals the limitations Sidney places on female heroism: it is a conception of female valor that regards the heroine as integrally bound to the realm of the body. Ironically, the heroine suffers the consequences of defending her sexuality with her very physical being: her body is the place where her self-empowerment is made manifest, whether it be by visual scars or by the signs of stress from deprivation. Not all of Sidney's female heroes can survive the perils of love. But as the *New Arcadia* stands in its incompleteness, one sees that a central aspect of Pamela's and Philoclea's heroism is fulfilled in their ability to triumph boldly in erotic suffering.

In the next chapter, I examine how Shakespeare applies the idea of erotic suffering to *Pericles.* As will be shown, the play has an intricate source history that relates back to the tradition of Greek romance. *Pericles*, however, begins with an irregular plot line that introduces the theme of father-daughter incest. To rectify this irregularity, Shakespeare overlays the Greek theme of romantic symmetry with the story of Antioch's unnatural lust. The pairing of the hero and heroine, who suffer for love, follows a romance pattern of adventure and separation. Heroism in this play is not only defined by fortitude in suffering, but it is also demonstrated by forbearance. In *Pericles*, Shakespeare combines the romance / comedic structure of triumphing in adversity with the psychological model of growth through suffering: the hero learns to reconsider his error in order to transcend the obstacles that blind him.

---

[1] Quoted in R. W. Zandvoort, *Sidney's Arcadia: A Comparison between the Two Versions* (1929; Amsterdam: N. V. Swets and Zeitlinger 1966), 189.

[2] Zandvoort, as well as contemporary scholarship, adds *Amadís de Gaula* as primary source material. For a more recent discussion of this chivalric romance as source, see John J. O'Connor, *Amadis de Gaule and its Influence on Elizabethan Literature* (New Brunswick, New Jersey: Rutgers University Press, 1970), 183-201. For a more general discussion of Sidney's primary and secondary sources in both the old and revised versions of the *Arcadia*, see the General Introductions in Jean Robertson, ed., *The Countess of Pembroke's Arcadia: The Old Arcadia* (Oxford: Clarendon Press, 1973), xix-xxix; Katherine Duncan-Jones, ed., *Sir Philip Sidney, The Old Arcadia* (Oxford: Oxford University Press, 1985), vii-xvi. Maurice Evans, ed., *The Countess of Pembroke's Arcadia* (Harmondsworth: Penguin, 1977), 19-27; A. Ringler, Jr., ed., *The Poems of Sir Philip Sidney* (Oxford: Clarendon Press, 1962), xxiv; Victor Skretkowicz, Jr., ed., *The Countess of Pembroke's Arcadia: The New Arcadia* (Oxford: Clarendon Press, 1987), xvii-xxiv.

[3] Samuel Lee Wolff, *The Greek Romances in Elizabethan Prose Fiction* (New York: Columbia University Press, 1912), 353. For a further account of the influence of Heliodorus's narrative technique on Sidney, see Arthur Kinney, *Humanist Poetics: Thought, Rhetoric, and Fiction in Sixteenth-Century England* (Amherst: University of Massachusetts Press, 1986): "Heliodorus was the first of the great romancers to interweave multiple plot; the first to invert chronology; the first to begin with an oracle

and end with a prophecy; the first to open visually with a ghastly *tableau vivant*.
Prophecy, magic, destiny, character, and human will are all--once we know enough--seen
as correlative in Heliodorus as in Sidney" (247).

[4] Paul Salzman, *English Prose Fiction, 1558-1700: A Critical History* (Oxford: Clarendon
Press, 1985), 4. See also Robert W. Parker, "Terentian Structure and Sidney's Original
*Arcadia*," *English Literary Renaissance* 2 (1972): 61-78. Parker argues that in the *Old
Arcadia* Sidney frames his story on the unified five-act structure of Terentian comedy,
based on the dramatic principles of "protasis," "epitasis," and "catastrophe"; yet, in his
revision Sidney turns his attention to the more digressive and looser construction of epic
and heroic romance.

[5] Salzman, *English Prose Fiction*, 4.

[6] Victor Skretkowicz, "Sidney and Amyot: Heliodorus in the Structure and Ethos of the
*New Arcadia*," *Review of English Studies: A Quarterly Journal of English Literature and
the English Language* 27 (1976): 170-74. Skretkowicz contends that Sidney took the idea
for his epic structure and characterization from Amyot's Proem to his translation of
Heliodorus.

[7] A. C. Hamilton, "Sidney's *Arcadia* as Prose Fiction: Its Relation to Its Sources," *English
Literary Renaissance*, 2 (1972): 29-60, 42. Hamilton points out that in the *New Arcadia*
"Heroic characters who evoke our amazement and wonder displace the pastoral
characters whose very human responses serve rather to delight us" (52).

[8] Sir Philip Sidney, *Miscellaneous Prose of Sir Philip Sidney*, eds. Katherine Duncan-
Jones and Jan Van Dorsten (Oxford: Clarendon Press, 1973), 79, 81.

[9] Recent criticism has challenged the hypothesis that Sidney's sister Mary, the Countess of Pembroke, bowdlerized the illicit love stories of Musidorus and Pamela, Pyrocles and Philoclea. See William Leigh Godshalk, "Sidney's Revision of the *Arcadia*, Books III-V," *Essential Articles for the Study of Sir Philip Sidney*, ed. Arthur F. Kinney (Hamden, Conn: Archon, 1986), 311-26. For Mary Sidney's role in the creation and publication of the *Arcadia*, see also Margaret P. Hannay, "Sister unto Astrofell," in *Philip's Phoenix* (New York and Oxford: Oxford University Press, 1990), 59-83, esp. 69-78.

[10] Robertson, *Old Arcadia*, lxii, note 2. Quoted in Skretkowicz, "Sidney and Amyot: Heliodorus in the Structure and Ethos of the *New Arcadia*," 174, note 3.

[11] Arthur Heiserman, *The Novel before the Novel: Essays and Discussions about the Beginnings of Prose Fiction in the West* (Chicago: University of Chicago Press, 1977), 6.

[12] Ibid, 9.

[13] Maurice Evans, *The Countess of Pembroke's Arcadia*, 19. See also Duncan-Jones, *The Old Arcadia*, xi.

[14] Skretkowicz writes: "This change from the tragic to the benevolent oracle indicates Sidney's intention to have the princes marry Basilius' daughters" ("Sidney and Amyot," 172).

[15] Edwin A. Greenlaw, "Sidney's *Arcadia* as an Example of Elizabethan Allegory," *Essential Articles for the Study of Sir Philip Sidney*, 271-85. Greenlaw uses the term "Cyropaedia" to distinguish Pyrocles' and Musidorus' first set of adventures from the second set that deals with "sins against love" (275).

[16] Margaret Anne Doody, *The True Story of the Novel* (Hammersmith: Fontana Press, 1997), 76.

[17] [17] Ibid, 75.

[18] Ibid, 71.

[19] Clare R. Kinney, "Chivalry Unmasked: Courtly Spectacle and the Abuses of Romance in Sidney's *New Arcadia*," *Studies in English Literature, 1500-1900*, 35 (1995): 35-52, 37. See also Jon S. Lawry, *Sidney's Two Arcadias: Pattern and Proceeding* (Ithaca: Cornell University Press, 1972). Lawry writes: "Book I aligns Arcadian action with a 'procession' of Corinthian models of heroic love. They scale down in a triad from the perfect love but dangerously 'perfect' honor of Argalus and Parthenia (*troublous; virginal*), through a middle relationship between Amphialus and Helen (*at sea; torch*) that is wracked by misunderstanding but in the end seems destined to flourish, to the completely negative example of two unloving egoists, Phalantus and Artesia (*line of battle; hanger-on*). These 'pictures' and the internal or direct narrative that speak for them inform and guide the young Arcadian princes and princesses as they fall in love" (164).

[20] Citations from the *New Arcadia* refer to Skretkowicz's edition, and page numbers will be indicated by parentheses.

[21] Edmund Spenser, *The Faerie Queene*, ed. Thomas P. Roche, Jr. (Harmondsworth: Penguin, 1978), 5.2.9. Hercules also represents the idea of "patience in adversity" for the Roman Stoics; in addition, he becomes a "model of Christ-like patience" in some

Christian writings (Robert J. Lenardon and Mark P. O. Morford, *A Companion to Classical Mythology* [White Plains, N.Y.: Longman, 1997], 160).

[22] Doody, *The True Story of the Novel*, 80.

[23].See James A. Brundage, *Law, Sex, and Christian Society in Medieval Europe* (Chicago: University of Chicago Press, 1987), 562-64.

[24] Heinrich Bullinger, *The Christen state of Matrimony*, trans. Miles Coverdale (London, 1541), sig. Biiiv.

[25] Ibid, sig. Bvii.

[26] Myron Turner, "The Disfigured Face of Nature: Image and Metaphor in the Revised *Arcadia*," *English Literary Renaissance* 2 (1972): 116-35, 126.

[27] Anne Shaver, "Women's Place in the *New Arcadia*," *Sidney Newsletter & Journal* 10 (1989-1990): 3-15, 15.

[28] It is true that Philoclea and Pyrocles have been separated before. In Book One, Basilius and Gynecia have fallen comically in love with Pyrocles-Zelmane; consequently, both parents desperately try to keep their beautiful daughter away from the Amazon. Likewise, Pamela and Musidorus have been previously kept apart on account of Basilius. The king, fearing the pronouncement of the Athenian oracle, has removed Pamela from suitors, enlisting help from his family of rustics, Dametas, Miso, and Mopsa.

[29] Lisa Silverman, *Tortured Subjects: Pain, Truth, and the Body in Early Modern France* (Chicago: University of Chicago Press, 2001). Silverman studies the changing attitudes toward judicial torture in early modern France, from Christian theology to Enlightenment ethics: "Torture inflicted pain as a means of achieving the spontaneous truth of the body

rather than the composed truth of the mind. Torture sought the evidence of an animate body that could not dissimulate. And it was precisely this attempt to destroy human will through pain as a means of achieving truth that aroused the objections of the philosophes" (9).

[30] Compare the characterization of Pyrocles in the *Old Arcadia* and the imagery of constraint used to describe his love for Philoclea: "when each thing he saw seemed to figure out some part of his passions, and that he heard no word spoken but that he imagined it carried the sound of Philoclea's name; then did poor Pyrocles yield to the burden, finding himself prisoner before he had leisure to arm himself, and that he might well, like the spaniel, gnaw upon the chain that ties him, but he should sooner mar his teeth than procure liberty" (Duncan-Jones, 11).

[31] See Heiserman, *The Novel before the Novel*, 75-93.

[32] In both instances, Chariclea's captors, taken by her beauty, urgently desire the heroine for their bride. Chariclea manages to avoid an immediate marriage with Thyamis by feigning the necessity to lay aside her priesthood at a shrine of Apollo before matrimony. Moreover, Chariclea, lying, demands proof of Trachinos's affection before marriage: she asks that her "brother," Theagenes, and "father," Kalasiris, not be separated from her. See *An Ethiopian Story*, trans. J. R. Morgan, in *Collected Ancient Greek Novels*, ed. B. P. Reardon (Berkeley: University of California Press, 1989), 353-79, 445-72.

[33] See, for instance, William Harrington's *Commendations of Matrimony* (London, 1515). Harrington argues that marriage should be entered into for the following reasons: to beget children; to avoid fornication; to provide help and solace (sig. Aiiiv-Aiiii).

34 Lodovicus Vives, *The office and duetie of an husband* (London, 1554), sig. D4v.

35 *Old Arcadia*, ed. Duncan-Jones, 11.

36 The reality of filial disobedience in marriage remains a shadow possibility in the story. If the sisters were to elope in the *New Arcadia*, their actions would perhaps receive the moral approbation of the Arcadians. The scene in which Basilius considers whether to besiege Cecropia's castle is a good example of parental fatuity and reader sympathy: "[Basilius] would have proceeded on, when Gynecia came running in, amazed for her daughter Pamela but mad for Zelmane; and falling at Basilius' feet, besought him to make no delay, using such gestures of compassion instead of stopped words that Basilius (otherwise enough tender-minded) easily granted to raise the siege, which he saw dangerous to his daughters; but indeed more careful for Zelmane, by whose besieged person the poor old man was straitly besieged" (549).

37 Elizabeth Dipple, "The Captivity Episode and the *New Arcadia*," *Journal of English and Germanic Philology* 70 (1971): 418-31, 423.

38 David B. Morris, *The Culture of Pain* (Berkeley: University of California Press, 1991), 31.

39 Elizabeth Bronfen notes that Freud construed decapitation as symbolic castration. Applying this idea to the myth of Medusa, she finds that decapitation represents the female genitalia that threatens man's castration: "It enacts a killing of the metonymy for other sexuality, for feminine genitalia, which have been culturally construed as a signifier of castration" (*Over Her Dead Body: Death, Femininity, and the Aesthetic* [Manchester: University of Manchester Press, 1992), 70.

---

[40] Mark Rose, *Heroic Love* (Cambridge, Mass.: Harvard University Press, 1968), 55.

[41] Ibid.

[42] Doody, *The True Story of the Novel*, 72.

CHAPTER 4

Romantic Symmetry in Shakespeare's *Pericles*


No doubt some mouldy tale,

Like *Pericles*--Ben Jonson


Despite its exclusion from the First Folio of 1623, *Pericles* was one of

Shakespeare's most successful plays on the early modern stage.[1] One seventeenth-century

compiler of English drama notes that it "was much admired in the Author's Life time and

published before his Death."[2] Indeed, by 1611 *Pericles* had appeared in three individual

quartos as "The Late and Much admired play, called Pericles, Prince of Tyre," with two

of these editions bearing the impress 1609 and issued within a year of the play's first

performance at the Globe theater.[3] Capitalizing on its success, George Wilkins's 1608

*The Painfull Adventures of Pericles Prince of Tyre* reports to be "the true History of the

Play of Pericles" in the form of a prose romance.[4] Although it is impossible to determine

with any certainty the reason behind its appeal, Ben Jonson's often quoted reference to

*Pericles* as "some mouldy tale" links the drama suggestively with its narrative sources in

the anonymous *The Story of Apollonius King of Tyre*, a well-known tale that existed in

numerous early modern versions and translations both in England and on the Continent.[5]

Old and much recycled, *The Story of Apollonius King of Tyre* first appeared in

Latin manuscripts of the fifth century as *Historia Apollonii Regis Tyri*. Evidence of the

*Historia*'s extraordinary popularity exists in the survival of over a hundred of these Latin manuscripts.[6] Significantly, the *Historia* has clear roots in Greek prose romance; Xenophon's *Ephesiaca* or *Habrocomes and Anthia* (2nd century AD) provides a close analogue.[7] In both works, a young heroine is sold into a brothel, suffers adversity, defends her chastity, and finds redemption in Ephesus. As a matter of course, it has been conjectured that *The Story of Apollonius King of Tyre* derives ultimately from a lost Greek original.[8] The story's long-standing popularity and readership in England finds proof in surviving fragments of an Old English version that dates from the eleventh century.[9] By the fourteenth century, it had been retold in John Gower's *Confessio Amantis* (Book 8), a rendering itself based on a metrical tale in Godfrey of Viterbo's twelfth-century *Pantheon*. While a version of the story makes an appearance in the late medieval *Gesta Romanorum*, it also resurfaces in Robert Copland's 1510 English translation of the French *la cronique et hystorie d Appolin roy de thir* and famously in Laurence Twine's *The Patterne of Painefull Adventures*, registered in 1576 and printed in 1595 and 1607. As scholarship has well established, Twine's Elizabethan prose romance and Gower's *Confessio Amantis* served as the principal sources from which Shakespeare and his coauthor scripted the dramatic text for the King's Men's repertoire.[10] In *Pericles*, Shakespeare conjoins Gower's and Twine's versions of *The Story of Apollonius King of Tyre*. According to Geoffrey Bullough, this antiquated story "probably sprang from a Greek romance."[11]

True to Greek romance fashion, *Pericles* exhibits the familiar plot pattern of "adventure, long separation, and tearful reunion."[12] It also embraces the usual stock conventions of the genre: tempests and shipwrecks, abductions and attempted rapes, supernatural and rare events, distant journeys and revelatory dreams, lost children and miraculous scenes of recognition. In *Pericles*, Shakespeare draws on the separation plot of *The Story of Apollonius King of Tyre*, but this "mouldy tale" presents a thematic anomaly in the ancient romance pattern of love, loss, and restoration. Whereas the extant Greek romances of antiquity (by Chariton, Xenophon, Longus, Achilles Tatius, and Heliodorus) recount the equal and often instantaneous love between a young pair of lovers, *The Story of Apollonius King of Tyre* shifts noticeably from this paradigm. This is the variation proposed by the classicist David Konstan, who argues that the "symmetrical" passion or "reciprocal enamorment" that is characteristic of the hero and heroine in Greek romance is supplanted in the fifth-century Apollonius story by an "asymmetrical or transitive attachment." Konstan further states:

> *Apollonius King of Tyre* appropriates the general form of the Greek novel, involving the separation and reunion of a primary couple, in the service of a distinct problematic in which conjugal love is de-eroticized and passionate infatuation or *eros* is charged with anxiety over incest.[13]

As the passage indicates, the mutual rapture that defines the amorous coupling of the lovers in Greek romance gives way here to a vision of romantic love that is at once asymmetrical and de-eroticized. Certainly, Apollonius's initial wish to marry Antiochus's daughter dissolves instantly upon learning of her involvement in paternal incest. Moreover, Apollonius's courtship with his wife displays none of the incendiary passion that enkindles a young man's ardor in Hellenistic romance. His own daughter, too, is silently handed over in wedlock to an aristocratic ruler, forever joined to a man she had only recently converted to purity in a seedy brothel. Added to all this, Apollonius's interest in a pretty maiden (his own daughter) belies an unorthodox attraction to his child just prior to the disclosure of their identities.[14] This divergent picture of amatory relations, with its emphasis on incest and uneven passion, yields a view of erotic desire that is both potentially destructive and sexually degenerate.

Criticism of Shakespeare's *Pericles* has addressed how the play works toward rectifying the tale's motif of degenerate sexuality. C. L. Barber, for example, elegantly observes that the playwright negates the story's "threat of sexual degradation" by recovering--in the structure of separation, loss, and reunion--a benevolent feminine power in the restitution of mother and daughter: "The play as a whole moves from the sexual degradation of family relationships in incest to [a] beautifully moving restoration of relationship through the new generation."[15] From a psychoanalytical perspective, Coppélia Kahn suggests that, by overcoming "the providential tempest," Pericles breaks free from a detrimental Oedipal crisis: "Shakespeare resolves this crisis through the father-daughter relationship, using the daughter's chaste sexuality and capacity to produce heirs as a bride to the hero's new identity as father."[16] Cyrus Hoy points out that the play's participation in the romance quest aims at "the revelation of a radiant young woman," who brings "[ . . . ] light to the darkness in which fathers are plunged as a consequence of the world's evil or their own folly or both."[17] In addition, Charles Frey maintains that the chaste daughter's journey "outward through time and space" is the solution for "patriarchal overcontrol and quasi-incestuous inwardness."[18] These interpretations emphasize the redemptive role of woman, especially the daughter: she redresses the error of the father and thus ends the play's pattern of painful adventures.

Readings of *Pericles* have argued for the importance of female chastity in the resolution of the play; in turn, these readings have increased our awareness of the theme of regenerative sexuality in Shakespeare's retelling of the story. This essay builds on these interpretations by turning the critical focus away from the regenerative ideal of female chastity back to the Greek romance ideal of romantic symmetry, a concept derived from Michel Foucault's analysis of male and female sexuality in the late Hellenic romances of antiquity. According to Foucault, these romances introduced a new ideal of sexual love, which diverged sharply from the classical pederastic model: "This new erotics organizes itself around the symmetrical and reciprocal relationship of a man and a woman, around the high value attributed to virginity, and around the complete union in which it finds perfection."[19] In the play, Shakespeare looks back to a similar organizing principle of reciprocal attraction, one that is based on the valorization of heterosexual love with its fulfillment in marriage. Although this model of erotic desire calls for the chastity of the heroine, it also demands the physical integrity of the hero, even though the hero is allowed minor lapses in judgment (see the romances of Achilles Tatius [Book 5] and Longus [Book 3]). In order to implement a pattern of romantic symmetry that resembles the ancient romance pattern, the playwright changes key aspects of *The Story of Apollonius King of Tyre*--as retold in Gower and Twine--to suppress the troublesome asymmetry that characterizes the Apollonius narrative. In *Pericles*, regenerative sexuality is suggested by a reciprocal amatory fidelity, initiated by a sudden desire or emotive force. Ideally, this erotic energy is tempered by physical constancy. One of the essential components of reciprocal attachment in Hellenistic romance and in *Pericles* pertains to the first meeting of the primary hero and heroine. The first meeting establishes mutual love between the protagonists, a powerful attraction often that occurs at first sight. Before turning to an analysis of symmetrical love in *Pericles*, it will be helpful to consider briefly the convention of love-at-first-sight in Greek romance.

At a crucial point in the story, the romance hero and heroine unexpectedly encounter each other and fall in love (except in Longus's romance in which the lovers know each other from childhood). As Mikhail Bakhtin writes, "A sudden and instantaneous passion flares up between them that is irresistible as fate, like an incurable disease."[20] This sudden lovesickness drives the pair to embark on their initial adventure, often because the lovers want to remain together despite parental objection or the machinations of evildoers ( see especially Heliodorus's *Aethiopica* [Book 4]; Achilles Tatius's *Leucippe and Clitophon* [Book Two]; Chariton's *Chaereas and Callirhoe* [Book One]). From their elopement proceed heroic defenses of chastity, tests of loyalty, and shows of bravery, all of which come to fruition in the couple's lawful joining or renewal of fidelity. If one takes into account the early modern influence of Greek romance, especially Heliodorus's *Aethiopica*, one sees that the ancient romance convention of love-at-first-sight holds importance for two central reasons, among others. First, it exhibits to the reader the reciprocal nature of the attraction between the hero and heroine; the sweethearts fall in love at the exact same time with an equal amount of fervor. For example, when Heliodorus's hero and heroine first lay eyes on one another, the narrator describes the overpowering magnetism that unites them: "For at that moment when they set eyes on one another, the young pair fell in love, as if the soul recognized its kin at the very first encounter and sped to meet that which was worthily its own. For a brief second full of emotion they stood motionless."[21] Thomas Underdowne's 1577 translation reads:

"For they looked one upon an other as though the minde knew first that, which was like to itselfe, and did approche neare to that, which both in excellencie, and dignitie was of affinitie to it. At the firste therefore they stoode still soudainely, as though they had been amazed."[22] This attraction differs from the intellectual idea of physical love in Renaissance Neoplatonism, which also propounds that sensual desire possesses the lover through his eyes; such desire may be reciprocated, but it is "the lowest rung on the ladder by which we can ascend to true love."[23] Hutton explains the dissemination of Neoplatonism in Britain, or Ficino's brand of it: "In English circles the most influential of these treatises [on Plato's *Symposium*] was Baldasar Castiglione's *Il cortegiano* (*The Courtier*). The Latin translation by the Englishman Batholomew Clerke, *De curiali sive aulico libri quatuor* (1571), was more widely known in England than Thomas Hoby's English version, *The Courtyer* (1561), which is more famous today."[24] By comparison, the ennobling love between the ancient romance hero and heroine remains firmly connected to their erotic desire for one another.[25] When the lovers Habrocomes and Anthia see each other for the first time in Xenophon's *Ephesiaca*, their physical attraction is so potent that they fall head-over-heels in love: "[Habrocomes] kept looking at the girl and in spite of himself could not take his eyes off her . . . And Anthia too was in a bad way, as she let his appearance sink in, with rapt attention and eyes wide open."[26] The strength of this ocular and all-consuming passion binds the pair together, and it remains wholly intact at the completion of their manifold adventures.

Secondly, the attraction between the romance hero and heroine, particularly the Heliodorian lovers, grows into an a solid commitment, one that springs from the protagonists' esprit de corps. Well before the trials that test their love, the hero and heroine already recognize a lasting kinship. Consequently, the youths prevail in trials of unexpected hardship that test their affection; they prove that their unforseen passion for each other develops into a valorous and spiritual sentiment, moving beyond juvenile obsession or puerile infatuation. As Foucault explains, "the two lovers have to preserve their physical integrity, but also their purity of heart, until the moment of their union, which is to be understood in the physical but also the spiritual sense."[27] These trials fortify the veracity of an already instinctive attachment; hence, the immediate attraction that binds the romance hero and heroine points to their infrangible and homogenous pairing, despite the cruel vicissitudes of fortune that mar the relationship.

The Greek romance motif of love-at-first-sight, which signals the robust and equal attraction between two people, is reduced at the beginning of the fifth-century *The Story of Apollonius King of Tyre* to the theme of perilous conquest: either the suitor solves King Antiochus's riddle of incest and wins the prize, his daughter, or he dies in the venture. Take, for instance, the first meeting between Apollonius and Antiochus's daughter in two of the tale's offshoots, Gower's *Confessio Amantis* and Twine's *The Patterne of Painefull Adventures*. (The purpose in referring to these texts is not to conflate Shakespeare's source materials, but to bring into sharper focus the play's modifications and treatment of romantic symmetry.) Just as King Antiochus abuses his paternal authority in incest, Apollonius treats his supposed bride-to-be as an object to possess, one intended for his use in marriage. These relationships are not only constructed on a conception of male hierarchy, but they also indicate that this hierarchy encourages mastery over the woman, not her shared love. Antiochus's daughter, who is given no name, has neither choice nor opinion regarding her future husband; she is a thing, a commodity on which suitors, like Apollonius, journey far and wide to lay hold.

Both of Shakespeare's references underscore this point. Twine pens: "Now, when Fame had blowen abroade the possibilitie to obtaine this Ladie, such was the singular report of her surpassing beautie, that many kings and men of great nobility repaired hither." Likewise, Gower's narrator says: "But fame, which goeth every weye / To sondry reignes all aboute, / The greate beautee telleth oute / Of such a mayde of hie parage. / So that for love of mariage / The worthie princes come . . . ."[28] As an object of conquest, Antiochus's daughter is a simulacrum of the riddle itself: like the father who has "unlosed the knot of her virginitie" in rape (Twine 426), Apollonius must undo the "knot" of the riddle of incest in order to sever, at least theoretically, the princess's maidenhead in matrimony. Apollonius's relationship with Antiochus's daughter is unequal and his interest in her temporary.[29]

Shakespeare's *Pericles*, however, shows a subtle reworking of the theme of male conquest and asymmetrical pairing that begins the source narratives. The encounter between Pericles and Antiochus's daughter develops this idea further. In the play's Prologue, the chorus declares that Pericles has sailed to Antioch "To seek her [the princess] as a bed-fellow, / In marriage-pleasures play-fellow" (Prologue, 33-34). Incited by the report of King Antiochus's pretty daughter, Pericles attempts to answer the riddle in order to acquire the princess as a reward, a connubial partner to use and enjoy in marriage. Although the playwright follows Gower and Twine up until this point, an important alteration takes place in this scene. Like standard romance lovers, Pericles and Antiochus's daughter appear suddenly to fall in love with each other. At their first encounter, Pericles is enthralled by the princess, and this bewitchment carries all the dramatic force of a love-at-first-sight. Struck by the daughter's comeliness--"Her face the book of praises" (1.1.16)--Pericles apostrophizes to the heavenly powers his new-found feelings of intoxication:

> You gods, that made me man, and sway in love,
>
> That have inflam'd desire in my breast
>
> To taste the fruit of yon celestial tree
>
> Or die in the adventure, be my helps,
>
> As I am son and servant to your will,
>
> To compass such a boundless happiness!  (1.1.20-25)

Even though Pericles envisions the daughter as "fruit" to satiate his appetite, and even though she is configured as an object of male possession or consumption, Pericles is smitten and conquered by the daughter's "celestial" form. Moreover, his attraction to the princess also involves a degree of gallantry and courtly chivalry. Pericles imagines himself as a knight who, when called to defend his lady, makes himself ready for the challenge: "Like a bold champion I assume the lists, / Nor ask advice of any other thought / But faithfulness and courage" (1.1.62-64). More interestingly, the daughter seems to reciprocate this attraction. When Pericles proclaims to her his chaste "unspotted fire of love" (1.1.54), she responds with distinct approbation. "Of all, 'say'd yet, may'st thou prove prosperous! / Of all 'say'd yet, I wish thee happiness" (1.1.60-61). These words, albeit few, show that the daughter's attraction to Pericles is far more than her desire for the other suitors, who "Drawn by report, advent'rous by desire . . . stand martyrs slain in Cupids' wars" (1.1.36-38).[30]

The mutual adoration between Pericles and Antiochus's daughter does not occur in either Gower or Twine. Its incidence in *Pericles* demonstrates that Shakespeare infuses their first encounter with a heightened sense of amatory attraction and reciprocal desire. Significantly, this reciprocity arises with even greater intensity in Wilkins's *The Painefull Adventures of Pericles Prince of Tyre*. As noted earlier, Wilkins's prose romance purports to be "the true History of the Play of *Pericles*"; because this romance is apparently based on Shakespeare's stage play, Wilkins's rendering may provide further evidence for the theme of symmetrical love in this scene. Just as Pericles admires "so glorious a beauty as was inthroned in his [Antiochus's] princely daughter"(498), the princess in Wilkins's romance expresses a comparable sentiment. As Pericles studies the riddle or "darke Engima," the princess is overcome with emotion:

> Desire flew in a robe of glowing blushes into her cheekes, and love inforced her to deliver thus much from hir own tongue, that he was sole soveraigne of all her wishes, and the gentleman (of all her eies had ever yet behelde) to whome shee wished a thriving happinesse. (498-99)

In an instant, the daughter glows with longing for Pericles, and her visceral reaction is stirred by a visual impression that corresponds to love-at-first-sight. This sensory response, one in which a woman's romantic desire is personified, accentuates the daughter's feelings of passion and her choice of husband. As in the play, the princess hopes for Pericles' victory, hinting that his "thriving happiness" will also become her happiness in their nuptial joining.

If the sudden love that ignites passion in the lovers of ancient romance functions as a paradigm of ideal love, it is largely because the intensity of the protagonists' mutual feelings spurs the hero and heroine on to heroic and virtuous conduct. The attraction between Pericles and Antiochus's daughter gives the impression of true love. Despite the gesture of portraying a mutual attraction between the pair, Pericles soon learns that his feelings are grounded on false perception. Simply, Pericles' sojourn in Antioch teaches him to see the danger of false perception, for the sudden and reciprocal love that erupts between the hero and the princess is tainted by the problem of incest. This episode does not necessarily condemn the headlong rashness of love-at-first-sight; rather, it implies that romantic desire, the kind that strikes a pair of lovers suddenly, should have the capacity to elevate the couple to virtue. Therefore, the cluster of images that concern eyesight / vision in the first scene shows that Pericles, blinded by the loveliness of the princess, is badly mistaken concerning her purity. It is worthwhile to consider this imagery. When Pericles first beholds the daughter, he exclaims: "See, where she comes apparell'd like the spring, / Graces her subjects, and her thoughts the king / Of every virtue gives renown to men!" (1.1.13-15). Pericles compares the daughter's outward form with "spring," a symbol of her burgeoning sexuality and maiden innocence; from this innocence flourishes "every virtue" that men celebrate. In addition to this adulation, Pericles discerns virtue in "Her face the book of praises," where he reads "curious pleasures" that are antithetical to sorrow and "testy wrath" (1.1.16-19). Although Pericles imbues the figure of the princess with an exquisite sensuality, her visage of "curious pleasures" forebodes a darker sexuality, the secret of incest. However so, Pericles perceives the daughter's honor in her face, so much so that he "would be son to great Antiochus" (1.1.27). Even Antiochus intimates that such blind passion can breed destruction. Recalling the metaphor that associates the daughter with a "celestial tree," and recalling the biblical image of forbidden fruit, Antiochus discourages Pericles from his daughter, "this fair Hesperides, / With golden fruit, but dangerous to be touch'd" (1.1.28-29). He adds:

> Her face, like heaven, enticeth thee to view
>
> Her countless glory, which desert must gain;
>
> And which, without desert because thine eye
>
> Presumes to reach, all the whole heap must die.  (1.1.31-34)

Ruth Nevo observes that the princess, or "the golden apples of the Hesperides," is equated with the scriptural fruit, "whose eating is the source and origin in Genesis of sexual guilt, and of death."[31] To be sure, Antiochus forewarns Pericles of imminent danger: his daughter has enticed the prince down a perilous path, precisely because his "eye" has stood in judgment, not his "desert." As it happens, Pericles picks up and repeats the language of false perception. After unraveling the meaning of the riddle, Pericles remonstrates against blind love: "O you powers / That gives heaven countless eyes to view men's acts: Why cloud they not their sights perpetually" (1.1.73-75). He continues: " Fair glass of light, I lov'd you, and could still" (1.1.77). The daughter, the "Fair glass of light," transmutes into an instrument of visual deception; as a mirror, she refracts and reflects a counterfeit image. Pericles no longer reciprocates her love. Moreover, the hero applies the image of visual deception to the King's sin of incest. This image recurs in several places. Antiochus's vice resembles the "wand'ring wind" that "Blows dust in others' eyes, to spread itself," even though truth prevails in the end. As Pericles sums up, "And yet the end of all is brought thus dear, / The breath is gone, and the sore eyes see clear" (1.1.97-100). Just a few lines later, Pericles also comprehends

"How courtesy would seem to cover sin, / When what is done is like an hypocrite, / The which is good in nothing but sight!" (1.1.122-24), and how "wisdom sees, those men / Blush not in actions blacker than the night, / Will shew no course to keep them from the light" (1.1.135-37).

The encounter between the hero and Antiochus's daughter incorporates the exchange of sexual energy; however much so, the play indicates that without the constraint of chastity and other attendant virtues, this energy has the capability to turn "as black as incest." Back at Tyre, Pericles has absorbed the lesson of artful deception:

> I sought the purchase of a glorious beauty,
>
> From whence an issue I might propagate,
>
> Are arms to princes and bring joys to subjects.
>
> Her face was to mine eye beyond all wonder;
>
> The rest, hark in thine ear, as black as incest.  (1.2.72-76)

Having learned to re-see the daughter, Pericles can distinguish between her interior and exterior decorum: her figure dazzles his eyes "beyond all wonder," while her virginal integrity is darkened and damaged by incest. Earlier, Pericles' sensual appetite, his yearning for the "fruit of yon celestial tree" (1.1.22), indicated a voluptuous, almost illicit, interest in the daughter. Now, he pictures this same sexual attachment as if it were channeled into lawful procreation: a Prince's duty, if not the duty of marriage, requires the propagation of heirs. Sullied by unlawful sex, the daughter is no longer suitable as a wife. Furthermore, in the Prologue the play had enlarged upon the daughter's role in the incestuous affair with her father. Unlike the source stories, which stress her victimization,[32] the playwright increases the daughter's willful participation in incest.

Shakespeare's Gower says: "Bad child, worse father, to entice his own / To evil should be done by none. / But custom what they did begin / Was with long use account'd no sin" (1.27-30). In the framework of ancient romance, in which symmetrical and chaste partners are privileged and even exalted, the irregular and unchaste union between Antiochus and his daughter engenders merely their base death. As eyesores, "they so stunk, / That all those eyes ador'd them ere their fall / Scorn now their hand should give them burial" (2.4.10-12). Pericles falls in love with the princess only to see through her unspeakable sin: the pairing between the hero and Antiochus's daughter finally reveals an asymmetrical and inglorious alliance.

Soon after Pericles solves the riddle of Antioch, he flees to Tyre. Fearing the wrath of Antiochus, Pericles leaves his kingdom and sets sail for the city of Tharsus. Here, he delivers the citizens from imminent starvation. I find that the events in Tharsus become a political version of the romance convention of love-at-first-sight; for, the hero's interaction with Cleon and Dionyza, the city's governors, reiterates the axiomatic lesson Pericles had painfully learned in Antioch: plainly, appearance can be deceptive if it is not supported by honest conduct. Pericles' love ache for Antiochus's daughter has left him vulnerable, and his kindness and empathy for Tharsus's indigent populace only terminates in trickery and deceit: fourteen years later Cleon and Dionyza have their hands dirtied in the attempted murder of Pericles' daughter, Marina. As the Gower chorus interjects, "See how belief may suffer by foul show!" (4.4.23). The imagery that deals with eyesight / vision in this section spells out the danger that accompanies false perception, and appropriately this imagery coincides with the "descr[ying]" (1.4.60) of Pericles' fleet on the neighboring shores of Tharsus: "for by the semblance / Of their white flags display'd, they bring us peace" (1.4.71-72). Driven by the mistrust of others, Cleon casts doubt on the verity of Tyre's "white flags" of peace. He comments, "Who makes the fairest show means most deceit" (1.4.75). Just the same, Pericles proves his sincerity when his intention of peace is bolstered by a bona fide determination to help the poverty-stricken city. His ships laden with corn, Pericles urges Cleon, saying, "Let not our ships and number of our men / Be like a beacon fir'd t'amaze your eyes . . . Nor come we to add sorrow to your tears / But to relieve them of their heavy load" (1.4.86-90). Similar to the deceptive appearance of Antiochus's daughter, who seemed to be a "Fair glass of light" (1.1.77), the city of Tharsus operates like a distorted glass that gives back to Pericles a false picture. Earlier, Cleon had used the metaphor of glass to describe the city's prosperity. About its former riches, Cleon remembers how

> strangers ne'er beheld but wond'red at;
>
> Whose men and dames so jetted and adorn'd,
>
> Like one another's glass to trim them by--
>
> Their tables were stor'd full to glad the sight,
>
> And not so much to feed on as delight. (1.4.25-29)

As if reflecting the duplicity of its rulers, the affluence of the city and the decadent extravagance of its citizens vanish. "But see what heaven can do by this our change," laments Cleon after enumerating the atrocities of starvation (1.4.33). Dionyza affirms with "Our cheeks and hollow eyes do witness it" (1.4.51), deploring how their grief is "seen with mischief's [misfortune's] eyes" (1.4.8). The imagery continues. Cleon anticipates that ingratitude to Pericles "shall ne'er be seen" (1.4.105), while the statue erected to immortalize the hero's generosity, the statue being a visual memento of gratitude, ultimately puts into sharp relief the murderous dishonesty of Cleon and Dionyza: "such a piece of slaughter / The sun and moon ne'er look'd upon!" (4.3.2-3). The repeated language of semblance and illusion in the Tharsus episodes serves to highlight the true portrayal of love that manifests itself on the shores of Pentapolis.

After sailing from Tharsus, Pericles is shipwrecked at Pentapolis, where he marries King Simonides' daughter, the princess Thaisa. In Gower and Twine, the pair do not form an immediate and mutual love match; in fact, these authors describe an awkward courtship between the two, one that stems from Apollonius's diffidence and intellectual remove from the daughter. As will be shown, Shakespeare ameliorates this imbalance by replacing the awkward courtship with a greater sense of symmetry between Pericles and Thaisa. Furthermore, unlike Pericles' attraction to Antiochus's daughter, which is rooted in false perception, the sudden attraction between Pericles and Thaisa transcends the seduction of appearance. What emerges as important in their union is the commitment between the two and the suffering that attests to this commitment: the blind passion of Pericles' former attachment to Antiochus's daughter transforms into an all-encompassing devotion, one in which the couple's dedication is revealed after many years of separation. The complex cluster of eyesight / vision imagery that had suggested deception in Act 1 is now used to indicate a deep-rooted fidelity and allegiance in conjugal relations. This conjugal love, enriched by time, still remains as passionate as it had been at their propitious encounter. To appreciate this aspect of Shakespeare's modifications of his sources, it will be necessary to recreate summarily the context of Pericles and Thaisa's first meeting as it develops from the playwright's two principal versions of the story.

In Twine's *The Patterne of Paineful Adventures*, the courtship between the hero and heroine retains the basic pattern of asymmetry, a pattern that extends all the way back to its proto-source in the fifth-century *Historia*. (Twine uses the name "Lucina" for Thaisa, "Altistrates" for Simonides and, of course, "Apollonius" for Pericles). It will be helpful to review the levels of this asymmetry. At their initial encounter, Apollonius and Lucina are, in a superficial sense, externally dissimilar despite their shared nobility. While Lucina stands out as "a singular beautifull ladie" (436), Apollonius, shipwrecked, is ashamed to enter King Altistrates' presence "by reason of his base aray," even though fishermen have earlier "beheld the comlinesse and beautie of the yoong Gentleman" (434, 436). While Lucina comfortably takes her position at her father, the King's, royal table, Apollonius sits uneasily in the place of honor with "the golde, silver, and other kingly furniture, whereof there was great plentie"; such magnificence recalls his lost property and friends (436). Altistrates even hopes that his daughter will take pity on the sea-wracked man; he hopes that she is "mooved with compassion" upon learning of his adventure (437). On the other hand, a more significant incongruity arises between the pair, and this time it exposes Apollonius's artistic superiority: it becomes apparent that he far excels the skills of Lucina in music. Indeed, when Lucina entertains her father's banquet guests on the harp, Apollonius minimizes and demeans her talent: "The lady Lucina your daughter is pretily entred, but she is not yet come to perfection in musike" (438). Lucina's imperfection simply brings to the fore Apollonius's own artistic expertise: "he seemed rather to be Apollo then Apollonius, and the kings guests confessed that in al their lives they never heard the like before" (438). Apollonius's superiority as a harpist raises him to the position of schoolmaster; for, he instructs Lucina in the "Art of Musicke, and other good qualities, wherein hee is skilfull" (439). Lucina eventually "matche[s], or rather surpasse[s] her maister" in musical preeminence (439); yet, the hierarchy that is intrinsic to a schoolmaster-student relationship features largely in the design of their courtship.

In Twine, the schoolmaster-student courtship begins after Lucina falls in love with Apollonius, but the hero does not seem to reciprocate this passion. Part of the asymmetry that constitutes this courtship resides in Apollonius's alarming detachment: whether or not he fears displeasing Altistrates, or whether he remains disquieted by his narrow escape in Antioch, Apollonius avoids expressing any perceptible interest in his beautiful and very available student, "a maiden now of ripe yeeres for marriage" (436). When Lucina asks her "welbeloved Schoolemaister" whether, hypothetically speaking, he would grieve if she married another, Apollonius responds, "No madame it greeveth not me." He adds coolly, "whatsoever shall be for your honour, shall be unto me profitable" (440). Conversely, Lucina can hardly contain her crush. Her passion for Apollonius blossoms after he overpowers Lucina with his exceptional musical talent. When asked to perform on the harp, Apollonius receives the acclamation of the entire banquet hall: "But when Lucina had heard and seene what was done she felt hir selfe sodainely mooved within, and was sharpelie surprised with the love of Apollonius" (438). Interestingly, Lucina's sharp pains of love do not flare up at first sight; rather, she is "sodainely mooved" by hearing and viewing Apollonius's artistry, notwithstanding the fact that she had earlier observed his "grace and comliness" and had "already in hir heart professed to doe him good" (437). In effect, Lucina is enamored of Apollonius's musical mastery and experience, over and beyond his physical attributes.

Lucina's love pangs uncover a further division between the two as she grows increasingly despondent from love over her schoolmaster: "Lucina laie unquitely tumbling in her bed, alwaies thinking upon Apollonius, and could not sleep" (439). At lessons, she burns with "fervent love of Apolonius" until "she fell sicke and became weaker everie day than other" (439-40). Apollonius does not reveal such feelings. Meanwhile, forced by three suitors to choose a husband, Lucina decides upon Apollonius in a letter to her father. It is only after Altistrates happily bestows Lucina to Apollonius that he candidly expresses any sentiment akin to twinges of love. To the King, Apollonius swears the following: "to remain both loyall and constant to you, and your daughter, whom above all creatures, both for birth and beauty and good qualities, I love and honour most intirely" (443). Even though this vow lacks the zeal of romantic passion, and even though it is addressed to Altistrates, not his daughter, Apollonius reveals his "love and honour" for Lucina, while demonstrating his respect to her father. In the end, the asymmetry of the schoolmaster-student courtship redeems itself in the fairy tale of matrimony.

Gower follows a similar pattern of asymmetry in his version of the courtship. Like Shakespeare's *Pericles*, the hero and heroine come together at a tournament; Gower, however, does not make the two fall in love instantly, for the daughter (given no name here) only slowly acknowledges Apollonius's overall suitability and attractiveness, though the narrator had earlier declared that there "Was none so semely of persone, / Of visage, and of limmes bothe" (387). A familiar story takes shape (Gower uses the name "Appolinus" for Apollonius and "Artestrates" for Altistrates). After the daughter hears Appolinus play the harp and sing, she confesses that "he is of great gentilnesse" (389), and next requests Appolinus for her teacher. Later, when Appolinus "taught hir, till she was certeyne / Of harpe, citole and of riote" (391), the daughter succumbs to the delirium of lovesickness: "Hir herte is hote as any fyre, / And otherwhile it is a cale. / Now is she redde, nowe is she pale" (391). Her condition worsens: "she hath lost all appetite / Of mete and drynke, of nightes rest" (391). Despite instructing the daughter in the arts, Appolinus does not show any special regard for her until King Artestrates announces, much to the consternation of other suitors, that his daughter has designated Appolinus to be her husband. Appolinus accepts the marriage proposal: "With good herte and with good corage, / Of full love and full mariage / The kinge and he be hole accorded" (393).

At this point, the daughter reverses the asymmetry of the courtship by single-handedly electing Appolinus as her wedded partner. This union does not produce the same galvanizing results as the ancient romance convention of love-at-first-sight, in which the equal passion of a pair of lovers manifests itself all at once; nor do we see trials of fidelity that strengthen an existing bond between the two. Instead, the master-student relationship becomes a vehicle for gradually testing the honesty and purity of the pairing. Twine's narrative elucidates this point in particular. King Altistrates praises Apollonius for his restraint during Lucina's education: the intimacy that private instruction affords might otherwise have given rise to unchecked opportunity. The King states: "Apollonius, the vertue which I have seene in thee, I have testified by my liberalitie towards thee, and thy trustinesse is prooved by committing mine onelie childe and daughter to thine instruction" (442). Likewise, it seems that the daughter constrains herself from unchaste conduct during her instruction with Appolinus: "She wolde hir good name kepe / For fere of womannyshe shame" (Gower, 391). The self-control that underpins the nature of this courtship, although the daughter evinces much more enthusiasm than Appolinus, establishes the mutual integrity and worthiness of the couple, as well as the parental trust for their marital union.

In *Pericles*, the playwright does not incorporate the schoolmaster-student courtship into the drama, even though it is alluded to in the play (2.3.17, 2.5.38-39). In place of that irregular courtship, a more distinct pattern of romantic symmetry is created between Pericles and Thaisa. As pointed out in the first chapter, this symmetry can be seen as homologous to the concept of mutuality in marriage. Just as the convention of love-at-first-sight is often a component in the formation of erotic love in Greek romance, the spectacle of the birthday tournament provides the backdrop for the occurrence of love between Thaisa and Pericles: after Pericles wins Thaisa's heart through his superior showmanship in jousting and after Thaisa secures Pericles' affection at the very same ceremony, her birthday games, the two are betrothed as "Man and wife" (2.5.83). Before analyzing the pair's first encounter more closely, it will be useful to place Pericles and Thaisa's meeting in the generic context of ancient romance. As Bakhtin points out, in Greek romance the hero and heroine usually chance upon one another and fall in love at a public festival or holiday (see notably Heliodorus [Book 3]; Chariton [Book 1]; Xenophon [Book 1]).[33] This public gathering, I believe, attests to the appropriateness and symmetry of the pairing: not only do the couple capture each other's attention at this event, but they also gain the admiration and reverence of the community. Beautiful, valiant, and statuesque, the lovers visually stand out from all the rest in handsomeness and stature. Heliodorus provides the reader with a representative example of this romance convention. When the Greek lovers Theagenes and Chariclea first make eye contact at the

Pythian tournament, the narrator describes the eye-catching pair as "universally admired" and "universally acclaimed": "Men lost their hearts to Charikleia, and women theirs to Theagenes" (413). Underdowne's Elizabethan translation also emphasizes the pair's universal appeal: "So faire and so happie were they as menne had felicitie inough, if they were like him, and women if they were like her." He continues: "For they counted it an immortall thinge to be such a couple. Although the people of that countrie rather praised the yong man, the Thessalians, the maide, bothe praising that wonderfully which they never sawe before."[34] Together, the two notables light the game's ceremonial torch, the hero being the captain of the Thessalians and the heroine the votaress of Artemis or Diana. In that dramatic moment, the pair not only lose their hearts to each other, but they are also portrayed as spectacles of universal admiration, extolled for exceptional beauty and dignity.

In a similar way, Pericles and Thaisa meet at a public celebration, the princess's birthday tournament. The First Fisherman apprizes Pericles of the tourney: "And I tell you, he [King Simonides] hath a fair daughter, and to-morrow is her birthday; and there are princes and knights come from all parts of the world to joust and tourney for her love" (2.1.105-09). At the tournament, Thaisa and Pericles surpass all others in attractiveness and valor, despite the fact that the shipwrecked Pericles "comes / To an honour'd triumph strangely furnished" (2.2.51-52): "For by his rusty outside he appears / To have practis'd more the whipstock than the lance" (2.2.47-50). Thaisa crowns Pericles "king of this day's happiness"; symmetrically, Thaisa is regaled as "queen o'th' feast" (2.3.11, 2.3.17). Comparable to conventional romance lovers, the two are presented as spectacles of admiration within the larger ceremonial display of the tournament. For instance, in the gallery above the lists Simonides describes Thaisa in language that evokes an image of the princess as a wondrous spectacle; she sits like "Beauty's child" at whom many will look and marvel:

> and our daughter,
>
> In honour of whose birth these triumphs are,
>
> Sits here like Beauty's child, whom Nature gat
>
> For men to see, and seeing wonder at. (2.2.4-7)

Simonides highlights his daughter's visual appeal: "men" will "see" Thaisa and, amazed by her natural beauty, will "wonder" at such rarity. Indeed, Pericles echoes the words of the King when he later calls the princess "wondrous fair" (2.5. 36). When Thaisa modestly opposes her father's declaration of her "commendations great" (2.2.9), Simonides conjures up a visual metaphor to remind his daughter that princes of renown should shine in all their divine illustriousness: "princes are / A model which heaven make like to itself: / As jewels lose their glory if neglected, / So princes their renowns if not respected" (2.1.10-13). Pericles mirrors Thaisa's modesty by imagining, with a good deal of self-deprecation and melancholy, that he shines "like a glow-worm in the night, / The which hath fire in darkness, none in light" (2.3.43-44). In spite of his exemplary showmanship at the evening's banquet, Pericles quietly deplores his homeless and luckless state. The depiction of Thaisa as an entity "For men to see," however, is complicated by her role in the processional triumph. As the spectator of honor, it is Thaisa who surveys and appraises the knightly suitors, admirers who eagerly "present themselves" for the princess and the King to behold (2.2.3). Correspondingly, when Pericles imagines that he will enter the tiltings dressed in his father's armor, so that he may "appear a gentleman" (2.1.140), he conceptualizes his presentation in terms of a

spectacle. To the three fishermen, who had earlier caught the hero's armor "through the

rough seams of the waters" (2.1.148-49), Pericles illustrates his gratitude and

resourcefulness:

> By your furtherance I am cloth'd in steel;
>
> And spite of all the rapture of the sea
>
> This jewel holds his building on my arm.
>
> Unto thy value I will mount myself
>
> Upon a courser, whose delightful steps
>
> Shall make the gazer joy to see him tread. (2.1.153-58)

Pericles visualizes that his garment of steel, along with the newly-acquired horse, will

beckon the spectator to view him as a "gentleman," regardless of the rusty condition of

his armor: at Simonides' court the "gazer," joyous, will take notice of the "delightful

steps" of the courser and, by extension, its dexterous rider. Pericles does present an image

of himself at court that is beyond the ordinary: "To me he seems like diamond to glass,"

says Thaisa (2.3.36). Not surprisingly, Wilkins's prose version of the play, *The Painfull

Adventures of Pericles Prince of Tyre*, reinforces the image of Pericles as a spectacle of

universal admiration: "[the knights] went forward to the triumph, in which noble exercise

they came almost all as short of Pericles perfections, as a body dying, of a life

flourishing. To be short, both of Court and Commons, the praises of none were spoken

of, but of the meane Knights" (509). So too in *Pericles*, "the mean Knight," excelling in

the art of jousting, dons the "wreath of victory" (2.3.10). Although the editor F. D.

Hoeniger reminds us that several of the play's episodes "affect us as 'pictures more than drama,'" the use of spectacle in the above scene enhances the congruity between Pericles and Thaisa as recipients of widespread commendation and respect.[35]

The first meeting of Pericles and Thaisa attracts the gaze of the court: at the tourney, Pericles stands out as the only knight to make direct (eye) contact with Thaisa. When each of the knights delivers his heraldic emblem, that knight's squire or page presents the device, with motto, to the princess. Because, however, Pericles loses his assistants and accouterments in the shipwreck, he hands his device to Thaisa herself--face to face; the stage direction reads: *"Pericles, passes in rusty Armour, without Shield, and unaccompanied. He presents his Device directly to Thaisa"* (2.2). Simonides directs the court's attention to this unique action: "And what's the sixth and last, the which the knight himself / With such a graceful courtesy deliver'd?" (2.1.39-40). Unrivaled in his presentation, Pericles is singled out as the chosen knight; this reading gains currency when one considers that the hero's device, which consists of "A wither'd branch, that's only green at top; / The motto, *In hac spe vivo*" (In that hope I live) (2.2.42-43), strongly invokes the pictorial iconography of St. Joseph at the Betrothal of the Virgin; Joseph, the only suitor who carries a rod with a top that flowers, holds a visible sign of his preferment.[36] (We can also see a connection between the Christian iconography of the Virgin's betrothal and Thaisa's pagan association with the goddess Diana, the protectress of virginity and chastity).[37] The ceremony of the devices spotlights Pericles in the position of a nonpareil, regardless of his battered exterior. As Simonides expounds, "Opinion's but a fool, that makes us scan / The outward habit by the inward man" (2.5.55-56). The King's statement, regarding Pericles' "outward habit," reverses the notion that outward show hides an inner perversity, an idea that occurs with prominence in the Antioch and

Tharsus episodes. As Annette C. Flower claims, "Pericles, Simonides, and Thaisa are all adept at seeing through surface appearance to the true worth that lies within."[38] As such, Thaisa regards Pericles as her most distinguished suitor. Simonides agrees: "'Tis well, mistress; your choice agrees with mine. . . .Well, I do commend her choice" (2.5.18-21).[39]

Over and above the allusion to the Virgin's betrothal, the playwright suffuses the post-tournament activities with the suggestion of Pericles and Thaisa's providential union, if not sudden love; this is symbolically indicated when the two are paired off in a courtly dance, which takes place after the knight-in-arms' "soldier's dance" (2.3.95).[40] Once again, the hero and heroine emerge as spectacles of admiration, especially when King Simonides labels Pericles as "the best" in his performance with Thaisa (2.3.108). Earlier in the scene, orchestrating the evening's entertainment, Simonides had escorted Pericles to Thaisa, saying: "Come, sir, here's a lady that wants breathing too; / And I have heard, you knights of Tyre / Are excellent in making ladies trip, / And that their measures are as excellent" (2.3.100-03). Despite the strange sexual innuendos in the passage, which will be discussed next, the staging of this dance spectacle represents the harmonious conjoining of lovers, a conventional analogy in medieval and Renaissance correspondence theory. As William A. McIntosh writes, "The actual dance of Pericles and Thaisa is emblematic of their lawful sexual union that is to follow and contrasts sharply with the 'uncomely claspings' of Antiochus and his daughter."[41] The asymmetry that typifies the pair's first meeting in Gower and Twine, particularly the hero's musical superiority over the princess, is replaced in this scene with the rhythm and balance of the two coupled in dance. Befittingly, Pericles' musical expertise in the source versions diminishes to mere references in the play: he is "music's master" (2.5.30), and his "sweet music" produces "delightful pleasing harmony" (2.5.26-28), but apropos there are no directions in the blemished 1609 Quarto to indicate that Pericles plays an instrument on stage or that his musical talent surpasses that of Thaisa. One must look to Wilkins's prose romance, copied partly from Shakespeare's play, to discover that Pericles withdraws into his bedchamber that night with "some delightfull Instrument," and that the King "rejoyced to be awakened by it" (513). This version of events sheds light on the reason why Shakespeare has Simonides praise Pericles' musical talent the very next day: "I am beholding to you / For your sweet music this last night. I do / Protest my ears were never better fed / With such delightful pleasing harmony" (2.5.25-28). It also embellishes the overall symbolism in the play of music and its providential harmony.[42]

The love between Pericles and Thaisa works because it follows the thematic pattern of romantic symmetry. Not only do the pair make a peerless match, but their shared excellence unites them in virtue, and their erotic attachment has its foundation in moral scrupulousness. When Thaisa expresses a sexual, if not carnal, attraction to Pericles, she does so by couching her sentiment in the moral language of marriage: "By Juno, that is queen of marriage, / All viands that I eat do seem unsavoury, / Wishing him my meat" (2.3.30-32). Equally, King Simonides' sexual innuendoes, which touch upon his daughter's marital eligibility, do not categorically give offense because they go hand in hand with an insistence on Thaisa's stalwart chastity. Phrases such as, "Princes, it is too late to talk of love / And that's the mark I know you level at" (2.3.112-13) or "I will see you wed; / And then, with what haste you can, get you to bed" (2.5.91-92), are counterbalanced by the King's celebration of Thaisa's "virgin honour": "she'll wear Diana's livery; / This by the eye of Cynthia hath she vow'd, / And on her virgin honour will not break it" (2.5.10-12). In this scene, Simonides falsely tells the suitor-knights that

Thaisa will not wed for another year, concealing the fact that she has her eye on Pericles,

or "never more to view nor day nor light" (2.5.17). But the description of Thaisa's

maiden pledge, "by the eye of Cynthia," does more than just pinpoint the princess's

watchful chastity; it also encapsulates an idea central to the romance ideal of romantic

symmetry: that erotic love be sustained by chastity and rewarded in fidelity and marriage.

Thus, the mock trial that Simonides conducts to verify the sexual virtue of Pericles and

Thaisa does not so much as test their virtue as much as it does confirm it. Pericles is able

to substantiate his sexual integrity by avowing that his "actions are as noble as [his]

thoughts / That never relish'd of a base descent" (2.5.58-60), and that he "came unto [the

King's] court for honour's cause, / And not to be a rebel to [Thaisa's] state (2.5.60-61).

Pericles calls on Thaisa to bear witness to his own honor because she is "as virtuous as

fair" (2.5.66).

It is important to mention that in Act 2 Shakespeare interweaves the love-leading-

to-marriage ethos of ancient Hellenic romance with the chivalric romance convention of

courtly knighthood. As stated, the hero and heroine's first meeting takes place at Thaisa's

birthday celebration, where suitors tourney for the privilege of the princess's love.

Importantly, "tournaments were," according to the historian Maurice Keen, "public tests

of individual prowess in which prizes and renown could be won"; in addition, "they

helped to gain currency and respect for the role of the knight errant, the wanderer urged

forward by love, enterprise and inherent virtue to seek the opportunity to win honour."[143]

Although the shipwrecked Pericles has good reason to improve his estate by displaying

martial prowess, his participation in the tournament entails more than an individual quest for reputation and honor. Pericles' knightly expertise and chivalric courtesy lead him to a marital union that is also founded on the romance ideal of symmetrical love. Broadly considered, this paradigm of amour differs from the chivalric and courtly model; in the latter, a knight is traditionally spurred on to martial virtue by his adoration of a noble lady, who is usually the knight's spiritual superior and "source of excellence."[144] The Greek romance ideal of romantic love, however, depends upon the lovers' freedom to marry the person whom fate has destined as their unmistakable equal, the consummate partner. As Foucault explains, "[e]verything that happens to the one has its counterpart in the changes of fortune the other is made to undergo, which allows them to show the same courage, the same endurance, the same fidelity."[145] This symmetry also involves the separation and trials of both the hero and heroine in tests of their shared commitment to reunite with their loyalty unscathed or in the attainment of lawful marriage.

If the Apollonius source narratives portray an asymmetrical attraction between the hero and his future wife, Shakespeare introduces into the well-known storyline a greater equality between Pericles and Thaisa, especially with regard to their volition to wed. Like Antiochus's daughter, Thaisa is renowned for beauty, and knights "from all parts of the world" seek her favor (2.1.108); perhaps, the report of Thaisa's charm has enticed Pericles even before their first meeting. When the First Fisherman speaks of Thaisa's birthday tournament, Pericles remarks: "Were my fortunes equal to my desires, I could wish to make one there" (2.1.110-11). "Desires" refers either to Pericles' wish to gain the admiration of a fair maid, or to flaunt his jousting technique, or to take away game prizes, or to all of the above. Although his words suggest a measure of self-interest and opportunism, especially when he says, "This day I'll rise, or else add ill to ill" (2.1.165), they express an equal amount of ingenuous expectation and hope: "I'll show the virtue I have borne in arms," responds Pericles to the First Fisherman's question: "Why, wilt thou tourney for the lady?" (2.1.143-44). Moreover, when Pericles delivers to Thaisa his heraldic device, King Simonides interprets the emblem as a symbol of chivalrous hope and inspiration: "From the dejected state wherein he is, / He hopes by you [Thaisa] his fortunes yet may flourish" (2.2.44-45). In effect, Pericles is motivated by private "desires"; his aspirations, romantic or otherwise, progress beyond acquiescence or happenstance. Comparatively, Thaisa is not a mere object of male possession like Antiochus's daughter, who remains under the peremptory authority of an abusive father; unlike Antiochus's daughter, Thaisa chooses Pericles as her marital partner, a choice initiated by heartfelt sensations of erotic love. Thaisa's willful determination to marry Pericles does not deviate from the portrayal of her willfulness in the source narratives: although suitors endeavor to "win" Thaisa--not by solving a riddle but through chivalric skill--it is the princess who ultimately selects for marriage the knight with whom she has fallen directly in love. Thaisa's letter to her father reinforces her resolution: "She tells me here, she'll wed the stranger knight . . . how absolute she's in't, / Not minding whether I dislike or no!" (2.5.16-20). Even though Pericles, the "stranger knight," refrains from revealing as much ebullience as Thaisa, his circumspection does allow him to corroborate King Simonides' conviction that Thaisa is a "most virtuous princess" and fair as "a fair day in summer" (2.5.34-36).

The joyous solemnization of the couple's wedding turns tragic when the newlyweds are separated on account of an offshore tempest and the mistaken belief that Thaisa dies in childbirth. In its generic scope, the physical attraction that first brings together the ideal romance pair, like Pericles and Thaisa, carries with it the seed for

virtuous growth through perils and suffering. In *Pericles*, Shakespeare conveys the idea

of growth through suffering by creating transcendent images that pertain to eyesight and

vision: in the process of surmounting their travails, Pericles and Thaisa, now referred to

as King and Queen, begin to see anew by refocusing their vision inward, and this inner

vision dovetails with a temporary relinquishment of earthly pleasures. For example, it is

remarkable that when the physician Cerimon revives Thaisa after she appears dead--

"look how fresh she looks!" (3.2.81)--he observes, in rich and elegant detail, the vital

signs of life animated in the Queen's eyes:

> Behold, her eyelids, cases to those
>
> Heavenly jewels which Pericles hath lost,
>
> Begin to part their fringes of bright gold.
>
> The diamonds of a most praised water
>
> Doth appear to make the world twice rich.  (3.2.100-04)

The metaphor that links Thaisa's eyes with precious jewels, gems that emanate with

angelic light, poeticizes the Queen's sublime beauty, a material essence that arrests the

onlooker; yet, the eyelids or lashes "of bright gold," which surround the eyes, resemble

something nonmaterial, a luminous halo. This image does not mean that Thaisa, saint

like, awakes to a renunciation of sensual love or to a denial of the physical world. On the

contrary. She is still deeply tied to Pericles, asking: "O dear Diana, / Where am I?

Where's my lord? What world is this?"(3.2.106-07). As the Queen's eyes open, Cerimon

detects that tears have begun to gather around them, like "diamonds of a most praised

water," foreshadowing the years of sorrow that Thaisa will spend at the temple of Diana in Ephesus. Because Thaisa supposes that the sea storm has parted her from Pericles, so that she will never see her "wedded lord" again, she turns her attention inward to the self-abnegation of chastity: "But since King Pericles, / My wedded lord, I ne'er shall see again, / A vestal livery will I take me to, / And never more have joy" (3.4.7-10). Suffering, in this case self-abnegation, is a choice Thaisa courageously makes, not because she has chosen a life of virginity, but because, married, she wants no other man except Pericles.

Pericles' self-abnegation takes on a different form. Believing that his wife and child are dead, he "swears / Never to wash his face, nor cut his hairs. / He puts on sackcloth, and to sea" (4.4.27-29). As noted earlier, Pericles travels to Tharsus, leaving his new-born daughter, Marina, under the guardianship of Cleon and Dionyza. Marina survives a murderous attack by Dionyza, is captured by pirates, sold into prostitution in Mytilene, all the while managing to preserve her virginity. The final scenes of the play dramatize the wondrous recognition and reunion of Pericles and Marina, as well as Thaisa, whose whereabouts have been revealed in a prophetic vision. A crucial aspect of the play's resolution hinges on Pericles' ability to see, from the depth of his suffering, the world from a wiser and enlightened perspective. It is striking that, during the recognition scene with Marina, Pericles makes repeated references to vision and seeing: "Pray you, turn your eyes upon me"(5.1.101); "for thou look'st / Modest as Justice, and thou seem'st a palace / For the crown'd Truth to dwell in" (5.1.120-22); "for thou look'st / Like one I lov'd indeed" (5.1.124-25); "I am wild in my beholding" (5.1.221). Instead of gazing at Marina as an otherworldly object--she herself says, "I am a maid, / My lord, that ne'er before invited eyes, / But have been gaz'd on like a comet" (5.1.85-86)--Pericles sees her with the eyes of compassion, as one who can decipher in another's face the indignities of hardship and misery: "yet thou dost look / Like Patience gazing on kings' graves, and smiling / Extremity out of act" (5.1.137-39). About the regenerative nature of this unexpected meeting with Marina, Frank Brownlow writes that "[t]he simple miracle of the coincidental meeting blends in the king's mind with the wonder of her beauty to give him a sense of life's beginning again."[46] The ability to recognize suffering, in this case Marina's patience in distress, newly raises Pericles from despair to hope, as he envisions the afflicted body of his dead wife in the very body of Marina, a young woman once called "this piece / Of [Pericles'] dead queen" (3.1.17-18). Unaware that Marina is his daughter, Pericles goes on to compare her to the memory of his "dead queen," projecting the shadow image of Thaisa onto Marina:

> My dearest wife
>
> Was a maide, and such a one
>
> My daughter might have been: my queen's square brows;
>
> Her statue to an inch; as wand-like straight;
>
> As silver-voic'd; her eyes as jewel-like
>
> And cas'd as richly; in pace another Juno.  (5.1.106-111)

This passage can be interpreted as a return to the incest motif that had beleaguered Pericles in the Antioch episode: the father sees in his daughter a seductive version of his wife. In fact, in Gower and Twine the encounter between Pericles and Marina results in a ritualistic and symbolic repetition of father-daughter incest, the violence Antiochus had enacted upon his daughter.[47] Far from indicating a purely sexual attraction to his daughter, however, Pericles' candid pronouncement of Marina's beauty facilitates one of the highest tributes to conjugal love: Pericles sees the same loveliness in his daughter that he had cherished in his wife. He remembers Thaisa's physical presence, her eyes, eyebrows, voice, and height. In his lyrical depiction, Pericles borrows the metaphor that Cerimon had used in Act 3, which likens Thaisa's eyes to jewels and her eyelids to riches, in order to paint a verbal picture of Marina, a picture that leaves Pericles thinking, tenderly, of the majesty of Thaisa. The physical correlation between Marina and Thaisa does not appear in either Gower, Twine, or Wilkins, thus suggesting the unique emphasis given to idealized love in Shakespeare's conception of the story.

Immediately after his reunion with Marina, Pericles hears the enchanting sound of music, a celestial harmony that lulls him into a deep sleep: "It nips me unto list'ning, and thick slumber / Hangs upon mine eye; let me rest" (5.1.232-33). Having been poignantly reminded of the figure of Thaisa through Marina, Pericles enters into a dreamscape where he "sees" a theophanic vision, a manifestation of Thaisa's allegiance to married chastity. Diana, the "goddess argentine," appears to his inward eye, guiding him to Thaisa (5.1.248). Bidding Pericles to journey to her temple at Ephesus, Diana says, "reveal how thou at sea didst lose thy wife" (5.1.242). To regain Thaisa, Pericles must put into words what his mind's eye has seen. "Awake and tell thy dream," the goddess commands (5.1.247). Pericles and Thaisa's love has gone from youthful attachment to weathered fidelity; struggle, triumphing in painful adventures, is the element that reunites Pericles with Thaisa, Marina with her family. Upon recognizing Thaisa, Pericles wishes to disappear in a figurative sexual union: "That touching of her lips I may melt and no more be seen " (5.3.42-43). Such a metaphysical kiss, which dissolves the two into an indivisible one, harks back to the passionate embrace that had years before sealed the couple's engagement by "hands and lips" (2.5.84). In Ephesus, the two are knitted together again as husband and wife, father and mother, King and Queen. As Pericles rejoices, "Pure Dian / I bless thee for thy vision" (5.3.68-69).

In an effort to remold *Pericles* according to the thematic pattern of romantic symmetry, Shakespeare radically downplays the governor Lysimachus's visitations to the brothel where Marina has been virtually imprisoned. The playwright substantially rewrites the brothel episode in order to suppress Lysimachus's darker attraction to the young heroine. Because Gower's version does not include the governor at the brothel, one must consult Twine's romance in order to illuminate Shakespeare's alterations. In Twine, before Marina (called Tharsia) is sold into prostitution, Lysimachus (called Athanagoras) tries to purchase the heroine only to be outbid by a bawd. Undaunted, Athanagoras plans to deflower the virgin nonetheless (456). When Athanagoras secretly enters the brothel, Tharsia begs the prince to take pity on her, recounting the horrific events that have brought her to the house of prostitution (457). Anthanagoras feels sorry for the young girl, in part because she reminds him of his own daughter (456). Pretending to leave the brothel, Anthanagoras, as a voyeur, spies on Tharsia, and he takes pleasure in seeing her plead to other men for her virginity (458).[48] Nowhere in Shakespeare's *Pericles* does Lysimachus find in Marina a substitute for his daughter; moreover, there is no mention that he even has a daughter. It is true that Lysimachus enters the brothel disguised (4.5.15), but he is quickly repulsed when learning of Marina's virtue: "Thou are a piece of virtue, and I doubt not / But thy training hath been noble, hold" (4.4.111-12). Lysimachus does not stay to spy on Marina, for the implication is that he trusts in her purity. Although the play's happy ending requires that Marina marry Lysimachus, the marriage, which matches a brothel-going governor with an innocent maiden, seems ill-suited and ultimately asymmetrical.[49] But, after all, Marina does not really fit the paradigm of the ideal romance heroine, even though her singular complexion "did steal / The eyes of young and old" and causes all "to cast their gazes on Marina's face" (4.1.40-41, 4.3.33). Marina does not fall wildly in love, and her extreme chastity, or "virginal fencing" (4.4.56), is cultivated for her own sense of integrity, not for the benefit of any one man. More than that, Marina never fully transitions into a conventional romance heroine because she is, first and foremost, a daughter, even in marriage. "Our son and daughter shall in Tyrus reign," declares Pericles at the conclusion (5.3.82). In the play's epilogue, Shakespeare's Gower brings the story to a close in a final tableau of father, mother, and daughter, a tableau of familial renewal. This regeneration issues from the principle of romantic symmetry: erotic love has prevailed over the tyranny of unforseen perils on through to the next generation. As Gower says,

> In Pericles, his queen and daughter, seen,
>
> Although assail'd with fortune fierce and keen,
>
> Virtue preserv'd from fell destruction's blast,
>
> Led on by heaven, and crown'd with joy at last.  (3-6)

*Pericles* departs from the Greek romance pattern by introducing the plot irregularity of father-daughter incest. This irregularity is ameliorated by the foregrounding of the symmetrical relationship between Pericles and Thaisa. The couple's separation at sea initiates their erotic suffering: Thaisa's presumed death in childbirth leads to Pericles' wanderings and affliction. What Shakespeare adds to this pattern of adventure romance is a concern with spiritual growth: suffering for romantic love enables the protagonists, especially the hero, to recognize the suffering in others. This recognition happens when Pericles shows compassion for Marina's hardship. While Marina does not suffer for erotic love, she is the agent that restores the conjugal union of Pericles and Thaisa. Her marriage to Lysimachus is, in a sense, a sacrifice, the factor that redeems the family and ensures its generation. Moreover, the trials of sexual integrity are displaced onto the young heroine. Her heroic defenses of chastity in the brothel measure courage and steadfastness. As we will see in the next chapter, the heroine's suffering becomes a greater part of the dramatic focus. In *The Winter's Tale*, female suffering unsettles male tyranny and creates a new model of sexual relations based on ideal love.

---

[1] The question of authorship in *Pericles* is still under debate. Most critics agree that the play shows signs of two authors. The debate centers around two possibilities: that Shakespeare rewrote parts of an existent play, or that he collaborated (the first two acts) with a minor playwright(s). George Wilkins has been considered the most likely second author, especially since his prose romance, *The Painfull Adventures of Pericles Prince of Tyre*, was based directly on the stage play. Wilkins also had written a popular play, *The Miseries of Enforced Marriage* (1607), which was composed in the same approximate time frame as *Pericles* and performed by the King's Men. See Stanley Wells and Gary Taylor, eds. *The Oxford Shakespeare* (Oxford, Clarendon Press, 1998), 1037. See also Stephen Greenblatt, ed., *The Norton Shakespeare* (New York and London: W. W. Norton & Company, 1997), 2715-17. Other candidates for collaboration are Rowley, Heywood, and John Day. For a discussion of these authors as candidates for collaboration, see F. D. Hoeniger, ed., *Pericles*, The Arden Shakespeare (1962; London: Methuen & Co., 2000),

lii-lxiii. For a study that explores the controversery surrounding Shakespearean authorship, see Brian Vickers, *'Counterfeiting' Shakespeare* (Cambridge: Cambridge University Press, 2002). Citations of the play refer to the Arden edition, and they will be cited parenthetically.

[2] Charles Gildon, *The Lives and Characters of the English Dramatick Poets* (London: 1698), 126-29.

[3] Charles Praetorius, ed., *Pericles: By William Shakespere and Others. The First Quarto 1609, A Facsimile* (London: 1886).

[4] Tycho Mommsen, ed., *Pericles Prince of Tyre. A Novel by George Wilkins. Printed in 1608 and Founded upon Shakespeare's Play* (London: 1857), xxix.

[5] Gildon, *The Lives and Characters*, 510.

[6] Gerald N. Sandy, trans., *The Story of Apollonius King of Tyre, in Collected Ancient Greek Novels*, ed. B. P Reardon (Berkeley: University of California Press, 1989), 736-72, 736-37.

[7] Ibid, 737. Incidentally, the first English translation of Xenophon's romance appears in 1727. Angelo Poliziano, however, translates a fragment of the romance in Latin as early as 1489 (Carol Gesner, *Shakespeare and The Greek Romance* [Lexington: The University Press of Kentucky, 1970], 162).

[8] B. P. Reardon, ed., *Collected Ancient Greek Novel*, 4.

[9] Peter Goolden, ed. *The Old English Apollonius of Tyre* (Oxford: Oxford University Press, 1958), xii.

[10] For comprehensive discussions of the sources and their relationship to *Pericles*, see Geoffrey Bullough, *Narrative and Dramatic Sources of Shakespeare*, vol. 6 (London: Routledge, 1966); F. D. Hoeniger, ed., *Pericles*, The Arden Shakespeare (1962; reprint, London: Methuen & Co., 2000), xiii-xix; Doreen Delvecchio and Anthony Hammond, eds., *Pericles, Prince of Tyre*, The New Cambridge Shakespeare (Cambridge: Cambridge University Press, 1998), 1-8.

[11] Bullough, *Narrative and Dramatic Sources of Shakespeare*, 6:351.

[12] David Bevington et al., ed., *The Late Romances: Pericles, Cymbeline, The Winter's Tale, The Tempest* (Toronto: Bantam Books, 1980), xxv. Bevington makes a useful distinction between the influence of Greek romance in Romances and the influence of its counterpart, tragicomedy. While Greek romance deals with fantastic events--"shipwreck, capture by pirates, riddling prophecies, children set adrift in boats or abandoned on foreign shores, the illusion of death and subsequent restoration to life, the revelation of the identity of long-lost children by birthmarks, and the like" (xxv)--tragicomedy refers to a play in which the protagonist "commits a seemingly fatal error or crime" or endures "an extraordinarily adverse fortune"; as a result, the protagonist experiences "agonies of contrition and bereavement until he is providentially delivered from his tribulations" (xxv-xxvi).

[13] David Konstan, *Sexual Symmetry* (Princeton: Princeton University Press, 1994), 101-02, 111. Konstan argues that heterosexual love in the Apollonius narrative becomes associated with the threat of man's feminization.

[14] Ruth Nevo contends that the fear of incest haunts the hero throughout his adventures and in the final union scene with his daughter: "[ . . . ] the progress of the play is the haunting of Pericles by the Antiochus in himself, the incest fear which he must repress and from which he must flee" ("The Perils of Pericles," in *Shakespeare: The Last Plays*, Longman Critical Readers, ed. Kiernan Ryan [London: Longman, 1999]), 61-87, 69. See also W. B. Thorne, who discusses Pericles' fear of paternal incest (*"Pericles* and the 'Incest-Fertility' Opposition," *Shakespeare Quarterly* 22 (197): 43-56, 47.

[15] C. L. Barber and Richard Wheeler, "'The masked Neptune and / The gentlest winds of heaven': *Pericles* and the Transition from Tragedy to Romance," in *The Whole Journey: Shakespeare's Power of Development* (Berkeley and Los Angeles: University of California Press, 1986), 298-342, 310.

[16] Coppélia Kahn, *Man's Estate: Masculine Identity in Shakespeare* (Berkeley and Los Angeles: University of California Press, 1981), 196. About the psychological, male passage of "the providential tempest," Kahn writes: "This pattern is that of a journey [ . . . ] the tempest and shipwreck initiating the main action represent the violence, confusion, and even terror of passing from one stage of life to the next" (194). This salutary movement ushers in a reunion with the hero's family, "with a renewed sense of identity or 'rebirth' for its members" (194).

[17] Cyrus Hoy, "Fathers and Daughters in Shakespeare's Romances," in *Shakespeare's Romances Reconsidered*, eds. Carol McGinnis Kay and Henry E. Jacobs (Lincoln: The University of Nebraska Press, 1978), 77-90, 84. For other interpretations that discuss the way in which degenerate sexuality is corrected in the play, see W. B. Thorne, *"Pericles*

and the 'Incest Fertility' Opposition." Thorne bases his analysis on folk-drama or old festival plays with roots in morality drama, plays that commemorate the rebirth of spring after the desolation of winter: "the ritual of renewal replaces the ritual of death, and ritual asceticism gives way to the marriage festival" (54). See also Phyllis Gorfain, "Puzzle and Artifice: The Riddle as Metapoetry in 'Pericles,'" *Shakespeare Survey* 29 (1976): 11-20. Gorfain finds that the riddles in the play break cycles of destruction: "All three princesses employ either riddling or deceptive remarks. But the latter two use indirection to sanctify, not desecrate, bonds with fathers and lovers" (14).

[18] Charles Frey, "'O sacred, shadowy, cold, and constant queen': Shakespeare's Imperiled and Chastening Daughters of Romance," in *The Woman's Part: Feminist Criticism of Shakespeare*, eds. Carolyn Ruth Swift Lenz, Gayle Greene, and Carol Thomas Neely (Urbana: University of Illinois Press, 1983), 295-313, 300.

[19] Michel Foucault, *The Care of The Self*, trans. Robert Hurley, vol. 3 (London: Penguin Books, 1984), 231-32. Incidentally, it is David Konstan who appropriates the term "sexual symmetry" to explain "how a unique conception of *eros* or passionate love as a uniform and reciprocal emotion conditions the fundamental structure of the ancient Greek novels" (*Sexual Symmetry*, 14).

[20] M. M. Bakhtin, *The Dialogic Imagination*, ed. Michael Holquist, trans. Caryl Emerson and Michael Holquist (Austin: University of Texas Press, 1981), 87.

[21] J. R. Morgan, trans., An Ethiopian Story, in *Collected Ancient Greek Novels*, ed., B. P. Reardon (Berkeley: University of California Press, 1989), 349-588, 414. Modern

citations of Heliodorus's *Aethiopica* will refer to this translation, and they will be cited parenthetically.

[22] Thomas Underdowne, trans. *An Aethiopian historie* (London: Henrie Middleton, 1577), sig. F2. Early modern citations of Heliodorus's *Aethiopica* will refer to this translation, and they will be cited parenthetically.

[23] In Elizabethan England, knowledge of Neoplatonism derived largely from Castiglione's immensely popular *Il Cortegiano*, translated by Thomas Hoby in 1561 as "The Courtyer of Count Baldessar Castilio."

[24] "Plato and the Neoplatonists," in *Platonism and the English Imagination*, eds. Anna Baldwin and Sarah Hutton, 3-17 (Cambridge: Cambridge University Press, 1940), 10. Following Plato's lead in the *Phaedrus* and *Symposium*, Renaissance Neoplatonists present a developmental conception of love in which the progression of eros in the individual moves from the concrete and sensory to the abstract and ideal. For a full Renaissance account of the Neoplatonic theory of sensual and divine love, see Pietro Bembo's speech in *The Book of the Courtier*, trans. George Bull (London: Penguin Books, 1967), 322-45.

[25] Foucault points out that in Greek romance physical love is tied directly to spiritual love in the union of the primary couple: "the two lovers have to preserve their physical integrity, but also their purity of heart, until the moment of their union, which is to be understood in the physical but also the spiritual sense" (*The Care of the Self*, 232).

[26] *An Ephesian Tale*, trans. Graham Anderson, in *Collected Ancient Greek Novels*, ed. B. P. Reardon (Berkeley: University of California Press, 1989), 125-69, 130.

[27] Foucault, *The Care of the Self*, 231-32.

[28] Geoffrey Bullough, *Narrative and Dramatic Sources of Shakespeare*, 427, 378. Citations from Twine's *The Patterne of Painefull Adventures*, Gower's *Confessio Amantis*, and Wilkins's *The Painfull Adventures of Pericles Prince of Tyre* refer to Bullough's edition, and they will be cited parenthetically.

[29] For a discussion of the relationship between incest and the idea of property in early modern England, see Constance Jordan, "'Eating the Mother': Property and Propriety in *Pericles*," in *Creative Imitation: New Essays on Renaissance Literature in Honor of Thomas M. Greene*, ed. David Quint et. al., Medieval & Renaissance Texts and Studies, vol. 95 (Binghamton, New York: 1992), 331-53.

[30] Antiochus's daughter desires Pericles in a way that could be regarded as all-purpose licentiousness instead of high-minded love at first sigh. I would suggest that Shakespeare in this scene suppresses the daughter's darker attraction to Pericles.

[31] Ruth Nevo, "The Perils of *Pericles*," 65.

[32] While the play suggests the daughter's complicity in sin, both of Shakespeare's sources make it a point to emphasize her innocence. In Gower, for instance, the force that Antioch uses to rape his daughter cannot be withstood (377). Twine's version redoubles the intensity of Antioch's attack and the depth of his daughter's fear and shame (426). Not only does the daughter deeply mourn her violation in Twine's version, but she looks to death in hope of consolation. Incidentally, Wilkins follows Twine and describes the incestuous rape in similar terms: "[Antioch] throwing away all regard of his owne

honesty, hee unloosed the knotte of her virginitie, and so left this weeping braunch to wyther by the stocke that brought her forth" (496).

[33] Bakhtin, *The Dialogic Imagination*, 87.

[34] Underdowne, *An Aethiopian historie*, sig. F1.

[35] Hoeinger, *Pericles*, lxxvii. Hoeinger cites J. Arthos, "*Pericles, Prince of Tyre*: A Study in the Dramatic Use of Romantic Narrative," *Shakespeare Quarterly* 4 (1953): 257-70.

[36] I would like to thank Kalpen Trivedi for bringing to my attention the correlation between Pericles' heraldic device and the iconography of St. Joseph's flowering rod. For pictorial representations that incorporate the symbol of the flowering rod, see, most famously, paintings of the Betrothal of the Virgin by Giotto, Flémalle, and Raphael. As far as I know, there has been no written study on this correlation, although Mary Judith Dunbar analyzes the device's relationship to the Christian iconography of renewal. As Dunbar explains, "The dry and verdant tree or branch recur in classical and Christian iconography to relate natural (vegetative) reflowering and human renewal; in some instances, the image indicates the renascence of a noble family, despite death and time, through the growth of children" ("'To the Judgement of your Eye': Iconography and the Theatrical Art of *Pericles*," in *Shakespeare: Man of the Theater*, eds. Kenneth Muir, Jay L. Halio, and D. J. Palmer (Newark: University of Delaware Press; London: Associated University Presses, 1983), 86-97, 90.

[37] For a discussion of Diana and the Temple of Ephesus and its relation to Protestantism in early modern England, see Caroline Bicks, "Backsliding in Ephesus: Shakespeare's

Diana and the Churching of Women," in *Pericles: Critical Essays*, ed. David Skeele

(New York: Garland Publishing, 2000) 205-27.

[38] Annette C. Flower, "Disguise and Identity in *Pericles, Prince of Tyre*," *Shakespeare*

*Quarterly* 26 (1975): 30-41, 33.

[39] In Gower's version, Thaisa receives permission from her mother, as well as from her

father, for the impending marriage: "The quene is come; and whan she herde / Of this

mater, howe that it ferde, / She sigh debate, she sighe disease, / But if she wolde hir

doughter please, / And is therto assented ful, / Which is a dede wonderfull" (393).

Notably, there is no mother figure in Twine, Wilkins or Shakespeare. Interestingly, in

Wilkins's story Simonides shows wholehearted approval of Pericles, an approval that

boarders on homoerotic: "both King and daughter at one instant were so strucke in love

with the noblenesse of his woorth, that they could not spare so much time to satisfie

themselves with the delicacie of their viands, for talking of his prayses" (510).

[40] For a discussion of the knight's dance, see John P. Cutts, "Pericles in Rusty Armour,

and the Matachine Dance of the Competitive Knights at the Court of Simonides,"

*Yearbook of English Studies* 4 (1974): 49-51. Cutts writes: "[ . . . ] the dance the knights

perform in *Pericles* is a matachine dance, the ostensible purpose of which is to prove a

man's worth in honour of his lady" (50).

[41] William A. McIntosh, "Musical Design in *Pericles*," *English Language Notes* 11

(1973): 100-06, 102. See also John H. Long, "Laying the Ghosts in *Pericles*,"

*Shakespeare Quarterly* 8 (1956): 39-42. About the symbolic nature of this dance, Long

states that "Shakespeare followed the accepted Renaissance belief about love and dancing"; he cites Sir John Davies's poem *Orchestra* as an example: "Kind nature first doth cause all things to love; / Love makes them dance and in just order move" (42). Long argues that Pericles and Thaisa perform the second dance alone, as a duet; moreover, this dance forms part of a tripartite chivalric test, examining the skills of Pericles in courtly and chivalric love (41). This viewpoint is countered by the editorial remarks of Hoeniger, who believes that the pair are joined on the stage by other dancing couples, and that the dance is used for courtly entertainment, not for testing (n.106).

[42] For the role of music in *Pericles*, see the following studies: F. Elizabeth Hart, "Cerimon's 'Rough' Music in *Pericles*, 3.2.," *Shakespeare Quarterly* 51 (2000): 313-320; F. D. Hoeniger, "Musical Cures of Melancholy and Mania in Shakespeare," in *Mirror up to Shakespeare: Essays in Honour of G. R. Hibbard*, ed., J. C. Gray, 55-67 (Toronto: University of Toronto Press, 1984); William A. McIntosh, "Musical Design in *Pericles*," 100-06.

[43] Maurice Keen, *Chivalry* (New Haven: Yale University Press, 1984), 100.

[44] Maurice Keen, "Chivalry and Courtly Love," in *Nobles, Knights and Men-at-Arms in the Middle Ages* (London: The Hambledon Press, 1996), 23. Keen argues that medieval prose romance yokes together two amatory traditions: the courtly tradition in troubadour poetry--in which a noble and often superior woman inspires her young lover to acts of virtue--and the chivalry tradition, in which the knight errant performs great martial deeds: "In this context there was little difference, it should be noted, between the potency of adulterous love, such as that of Lancelot and Guinevere (or of Tristram and Iseult), and of the regulated love that hopes ultimately to make a bride of an adored woman" (25). For a

further discussion on chivalry and courtly love, see Keen's "The Historical Mythology of Chivalry," in *Chivalry*, 102-124; J. J Huizinga, "The Dream of Heroism and of Love," in *The Waning of the Middle Ages*, trans. F. Hopman (London: Penguin Books, 1990), 75-83. For a more recent discussion, see Larry D. Benson's "Courtly Love and Chivalry in the Later Middle Ages," in *Fifteenth-Century Studies: Recent Essays*, ed. Robert F. Yeager (Hamden Conn: Archon Books, *1984*), 237-57

[45] Foucault, *The Care of the Self*, 229.

[46] Frank Brownlow, *Two Shakespearean Sequences: Henry VI to Richard II and Pericles to Timon of Athens* (Pittsburgh: University of Pittsburgh, 1977), 130.

[47] In Twine, when Tharsia (Marina) embraces and begs Apollonius (Pericles) to snap out of his dreary melancholy, Apollonius, full of rage, "stroke the maiden on the face with his foote, so that shee fell to the ground, and the bloud gushed plentifully out of her cheekes (466-67). The blood that the father makes appear on his daughter's cheeks is a re-enactment of the blood that Antiochus causes his own daughter to shed, the "fresh bleeding of the greene wound" (Twine, 427). In Gower, after the daughter touches Apollonius, he "with his honde / He smote" (414), while in Wilkins story Pericles hits his daughter as well (543). In Shakespeare's version, it seems that Pericles pushes Marina away from him, although there are no stage directions to indicate further violence. See Hoeniger's editorial note (n. 83).

[48] Following Twine, Wilkins incorporates Lysimachus' voyeuristic activities at the brothel in his retelling of the story (536-37).

[49] For a discussion of Marina's uneven match with Lysimachus, of his disturbing association with syphilis, see Margaret Healy, "Pericles and the Pox," in *Shakespeare's Late Plays: New Readings*, eds. Jennifer Richards and James Knowles (Edinburgh: Edinburgh University Press, 1999), 92-107. For a comparison of the brothel scenes in Shakespeare and Twine, see Steven Mullaney, "'All That Monarchs Do': The Obscured Stages of Authority in *Pericles*," in *Shakespeare: The Last Plays*, ed. Kiernan Ryan (London and New York: Longman, 1999), 88-106. Mullaney argues that Shakespeare delimits the market aspect of the brothel house by having Marina preach instead of showing "a shrewder sense both of business and of theatre" (97). Mullaney's conclusion is that "*Pericles* reveals Shakespeare's systematic effort to dissociate his art from the marginal contexts and affiliations that had formerly served as the grounds of its possibility" (101).

# CHAPTER 5

"The casting forth to crows thy baby daughter":

Female Suffering and Child Abandonment in Shakespeare's *The Winter's Tale*

> thy untimely death must pay thy Mother's Debts, and her guiltless crime
>
> must be thy ghastly curse [ . . . ] what Father would be so cruell? Or what
>
> Gods will not revenge such rigor?
>
> Let me kiss thy lippes (sweet Infant) and wet thy tender cheekes with my
>
> teares, and put this chayne about thy little necke, that it fortune save thee,
>
> it may help to succour thee. Thus, since thou must goe to surge in the
>
> ghastful Seas, with a sorrowfull kisse I bid thee farewell, and I pray the
>
> Gods thou maiest fare well.
>
> --Bellaria to Fawnia in *Pandosto*

> the history of your sorrow and mine, written in the blood
>
> and tears shed for you by a mother whose first childbearing
>
> was the occasion of such grief.
>
> --Persinna to Chariclea in Heliodorus's *Aethiopica*.

In *Shakespear Illustrated* (1753-54), Charlotte Lennox had famously derided

Shakespeare's use of "the old paltry Story" of *Pandosto: The Triumph of Time* as the

primary source for the playwright's even more "absurd" and "ridiculous" *The Winter's*

*Tale*.[1] Despite such derision, Robert Greene's "old paltry" story (the running title reads

"The Historie of Dorastus and Fawnia") was enormously popular.[2] In the late Elizabethan and Jacobean periods, it had been printed and reissued in clear rapid succession: 1588, 1592, 1600, 1607, 1609, 1614.[3] Greene's fashionable story of jealous tyranny and Arcadian love belongs to a period in the writer's career that Walter Davis has classified as one of pastoral romance "strongly influenced by Greek romance (1588-89)."[4] Particularly, Greene draws on Longus's *Daphnis and Chloe,* a Hellenistic romance recently translated into English by Angell Daye in 1587, for its stock pastoral plot: an infant is abandoned and raised by rural shepherds; the revelation of the child's highborn identity restores the family, removing the obstacle to the hero and heroine's aristocratic marriage. Greene uses this antiquated plot line, but revises it in a significant manner. In *Daphnis and Chloe*, the titular hero and heroine partake of identical childhoods: both lovers are exposed as newborns, reared by shepherds, and restored to genteel parents. During adolescence, Daphnis attends to goats, Chloe to sheep. In *Pandosto* Greene modifies the symmetrical upbringing of the young lovers. He applies the pastoral device of the exposed child only to the heroine: the hero, prince Dorastus of Sicily, wins the heart of Fawnia, a shepherdess, who is really King Pandosto of Bohemia's abandoned daughter. Dorastus and Fawnia's asymmetrical courtship, one between prince and shepherdess, may have suited at this time Greene's artistic proclivity for Euphuism, a literary style that develops precisely from balanced antithesis and alliterative contrast.[5]

In *The Winter's Tale*, Shakespeare adapts Greene's story to the early seventeenth-century stage, a story indebted to the pastoral plot of Longus's *Daphnis and Chloe*. As Frank Kermode writes, the play derives "ultimately from the Greek novel, especially perhaps from *Daphnis and Chloe*."[6] This debt to Longus occurs with great effect in the play's bucolic second half, the sheepshearing episode of Act 4. Here the young lovers Florizel and Perdita (Dorastus and Fawnia) celebrate the seasonal holiday feast: the courtly hero is disguised as a country swain, the "poor lowly" heroine as the goddess Flora (4.4.09). It often has been noted that one of the prominent changes Shakespeare makes to Greene's story, a change that brings the play closer to Greek romance, deals with the thematic issue of mutual love. In Shakespeare's source, Greene's *Pandosto*, the asymmetrical courtship between prince and shepherdess encourages, in John Lawler's words, "the laboured exchanges of lovers"; these are verbal exchanges and monologues that stem from the protagonists' anxiety over entering into a socially unequal marital alliance.[7] J. H. P. Pafford writes that "[t]he preliminary wooing of Fawnia by Dorastus, long-drawn-out and tedious in Greene, is omitted by Shakespeare."[8] Indeed, the labored and tedious exchange of lovers does not figure largely into Shakespeare's dramatic adaptation. On the contrary, Florizel and Perdita have already affianced themselves prior to their introduction at the sheepshearing feast: offstage the pair have pledged a contract of true love, a "celebration of that nuptial which / [the] two have sworn shall come" (4.4.50-51). The nature of Florizel and Perdita's mutual love, one that declares itself from the very onset, plainly resembles the reciprocal and chaste passion of romance characters like Daphnis and Chloe; the model of eros in that Greek romance, alongside the others of the genre, is exactly one of equal and unwavering love. Just as Daphnis and Chloe swear to an oath of fidelity, Florizel and Perdita--the "turtles pair / That never mean to part" (4.4.154-55)--pledge their hearts in marriage.

The Greek romance ideal of symmetrical love is reestablished in the Florizel-Perdita story. As in *Pericles*, Shakespeare changes his source material in order to create a symmetrical relationship between the hero and heroine. Despite changes to emphasize equal love, however, Shakespeare retains the chief asymmetry of Greene's pastoral romance plot: the class divide between hero and heroine, prince and shepherdess. The apparent social divide between Florizel and Perdita, a "poor lowly maid" (4.4.09), conflicts with a fundamental narrative feature of Greek romance, what the classicist Massimo Fusillo terms "parallelism." The concept of parallelism applies to the overall similitude of the young hero and heroine as follows: "The couple comprises two young people of the same age, the same enviable social status, and divine beauty, going through identical adventures, always wishing to die in times of separation, and both victims of powerful rivals." Implicit in this description of parallelism resides the idea that the romance couple, who are of "the same enviable social status," suffer for love in equal proportion. Naturally, the ancient title of the genre, *erotika pathemata*, indicates the passionate, erotic suffering of both. All the same, Shakespeare, following Greene, places the burden of erotic suffering onto the play's maiden character, Perdita, a supposed "shepherd's daughter" (4.1.27). Even though Florizel, a "sceptre's heir" (4.4.420), risks losing the kingdom of Bohemia for his beloved, it is Perdita who is subjected to a series of ordeals that begin remarkably even from birth: her suffering is explicitly intertwined with the pastoral topos of the abandoned child.

An analysis of *The Winter's Tale* can profit considerably from looking at the way Shakespeare's romance plot determines the nature and intensity of female suffering. The dramatic action of the second half of the play consists partially in the movement away from an anti-parallel pattern, in which the young heroine is socially inferior to the hero, to one of parallelism--in which the heroine's true identity as princess of Sicily is revealed. The pastoral theme of the exposed child forms an essential basis for examining the anti-parallel movement in the play. It is because Perdita suffers abandonment that she is made inferior to Florizel, and it is through overcoming such adversity that she becomes parallel to the prince. In *The Winter's Tale*, female suffering heals and restores the wrongdoings of patriarchy: the young hero and heroine emerge as romantic equals when Perdita recovers her homeland and royal birth right from which she has been alienated.

Perdita's suffering begins prenatally with Hermione's arrest and false imprisonment. As one of the queen's ladies comments before her incarceration, "She is spread of late / Into a goodly bulk" (2.1.19-20). We know that Hermione's pregnancy, her "goodly bulk," arouses the suspicions of Leontes, who imagines his wife an adulteress with the "harlot king" Polixenes (2.3.04).[10] The very force of Leontes' jealousy, his abrupt mistrust of Hermione's hospitality to his boyhood friend, constitutes a large part of the cruelty that is inflicted upon Hermione and, by extension, her unborn daughter. The symmetrical relstionship of marriage is disrupted by the recurrence of the childhood symmetry of the homosocial friendship with Polixenes. Concerning Leontes' eruption of jealousy, Polixenes describes the emotion as nothing less than violent: "This jealousy / Is for a precious creature: as she's rare, / Must it be great; and, as his person's mighty, / Must it be violent" (1.2.451-54). Confounded by the king's oppressive anger, Polixenes surmises that the cause and magnitude of Leontes' resentment will culminate in bitter revenge, saying: "and, as he does conceive / He is dishonour'd by a man which ever / Profess'd to him; why, his revenges must / In that be made more bitter" (1.2.454-57). Perdita is born into a vindictive climate of mistrust, and her adversity dovetails with the misfortune of Hermione, a queen forced to relinquish her infant to the tyrannical whims of an enraged husband.

The hostile environment of Perdita's birth diverges from the idyllic Greek device of the exposed child raised by shepherds. A fundamental aspect of the anti-parallel pattern in *The Winter's Tale* concerns the violent context of Perdita's exposure. When this plot feature is juxtaposed to the prototype in *Daphnis and Chloe*, it becomes apparent that Perdita's abandonment unfolds in a radically different manner than the traditional paradigm in Greek romance. In Longus, the narrative feature of infant exposure pertains equally to the boy and girl child. It is based on the compassionate abandonment of the newborn and on the future promise of the child's recuperation. Alternatively, Leontes casts off his baby daughter to her presumed demise. In doing so, the king ruptures the tie between mother and daughter, husband and wife. Rather than a benevolent exposure, Perdita's fate is interlocked with the abuses of patriarchy, and these abuses result in the ruthless "casting forth to crows" of a baby daughter (3.2.191).

In the Renaissance, the standard plot feature of the exposed child reared by shepherds had literary precedent in many genres, including the prose romances of late antiquity. As previously mentioned, Angell Daye had translated Longus's pastoral romance *Daphnis and Chloe* (c. 3rd century AD) in the late 1580's, but it would have been well known to early modern readers in Jacques Amyot's stylish French version, *Les Amours pastorales de Daphnis et de Chloé* (1559, 1594, 1596, 1609).[11] In Book 6 of *The Faerie Queene*, Spenser draws on the ancient motif, using the idyll of the exposed child in his portrait of the shepherdess Pastorella.[12] The abandonment of Pastorella takes its structure from New Comedy and Greek romance: a *senex* figure blocks the union of

Claribell and Bellamour; their love child, Pastorella, is secreted away and reared by a shepherd. The abandonment of the heroine as a newborn also occurs in the Greek romance by Heliodorus, the *Aethiopica* (4th century AD). An Ethiopian queen, Persinna, deposits her light-skinned daughter, Chariclea, near a roadside because she fears accusations of adultery. Although the circumstances of Chariclea's pastoral childhood are only briefly alluded to in a narrative flashback (Book Two), the plot device establishes an important theme that arises with greater clarity in *Daphnis and Chloe*: benevolent exposure.

A comparison of the lost child in Daye's *Daphnis and Chloe* and in *The Winter's Tale* reveals that Shakespeare increases the level of cruelty that the natal father exerts on the female infant. In Daye, the motive behind the abandoning of the female child arises out of the family's financial hardship, not paternal jealousy. The aristocratic father of Chloe, who is identified as "Megacles a wealthie noble citizen," disposes of his newborn daughter because of a temporary crisis in fortune:

> I had then a daughter borne unto me by my wife Rhode, and forsomuch as my estate was at that instant so weake, as made me in great hazard how I might recover my losses and fortune againe, and yeelded me also some despaire how, or by what meanes I might afterwards live having so manie children.[13]

Having sustained commercial loss at sea, Megacles falls into despair, and his despondency is directly correlated with a sudden inability to support a large family. Therefore, with "great agonie of minde," he orders the exposure of the infant Chloe "to the protection and guidance of some better hap" (sig. X1).

Although the idea of infant abandonment seems cruel by modern day criteria, the Hellenistic figure of Megacles believes in the benevolent and auspicious prospect of his deed: his faith in the infant's "protection and guidance" implies the providential, happy outcome of the exposure. Furthermore, Megacles' lack of self-recrimination indicates that he thinks of child abandonment more optimistically than might otherwise be expected. In Christopher Gill's modern translation, Megacles even justifies the desertion of his babe on altruistic grounds: "Shrinking from bringing this child up in poverty, I fitted her up with these tokens and exposed her, knowing that many people are eager to become parents even by this means."[14] Megacles has no other children in this translation, nor does he suffer loss at sea; his lack of money is due to civic expenditures. The exposure, however, of Chloe in both versions does allow a childless family to acquire a daughter. When the shepherd Dryas chances upon Chloe as a foundling, his wife, Nape, showers the child with maternal warmth. Urged on by Dryas, she "began to imbrace and entertain the girle, deeming already that she became a mother unto it, by meere affection, her conceit grew tender over it, and with such fervant love, and continuall watching did she endevour to foster it" (Daye sig. C2). This abundant show of affection initiates Nape into the role of motherhood and the responsibility of guardianship. In fulfillment of Megacles' wish, Chloe receives the care and nurture she requires from her rustic foster parents, a nurture that is stereotyped by the importance of motherly devotion.

While Megacles opts to expose Chloe to "some better hap," there are few textual clues in the story to deduce how the birth mother, Rhode, feels about dispensing with her daughter (her only child in Longus). Furthermore, the details of Chloe's exposure are told from Megacles', the birth father's, perspective. Either Rhode's silence suggests her consent in the abandonment, or this silence suggests her certain exclusion from the decision; in the latter situation, the father, like Leontes, decrees the course of action, thereby abrogating the natural right of the natal mother to keep her child. Although the text remains ambiguous on the issue of the birth mother's silence, both Megacles and Rhode show overwhelming joy when they recover their lost daughter. This show of joy at the recovery of their child seems to imply the parents' mutual sorrow at the time of her abandonment. The natal parents of Daphnis display the same jubilant reaction at his recovery. In fact, Daphnis's childhood adheres to character parallelism since his exposure as a newborn and recovery as a young adult mirror the very experience of Chloe.[15] Like Rhode, Daphnis's birth mother does not express an opinion regarding her son's abandonment, for that event is recollected solely by the father. Despite the suppression of the birth mothers' voices, the plot feature of exposure in Longus exhibits redeeming characteristics: the abandonment permits a couple without offspring to parent a child; it furnishes hope for the child's better fortune; and it enables the design of providence to work for the good of all.

The suffering of the female child in *The Winter's Tale* is at variance with the pastoral romance model of infant abandonment. Even though the exposure of Perdita grants a rural family another child, and, even though it allows providence to assert its grace and beneficence, the play imposes a strong element of cruelty onto the female infant. The extreme conditions of Perdita's exposure are exacerbated by her birth father's suspicion of the female sex. Leontes' distrust of Hermione, "his tyrannous passion" (2.3.28), is suggestively displaced onto the daughter: the queen's alleged adultery becomes the inherited sin of womankind, passed from mother to daughter. In a state of paranoia, Leontes makes the universality of unruly women clear: "Should all despair /

That have revolted wives, the tenth of mankind / Would hang themselves" (1.2.198-200).

Earlier in the aside, Leontes had made the sexual nature of this revolt crudely plain:

"There have been, (Or I am much deceiv'd) cuckolds ere now, / And many a man there is

[ . . . ] holds his wife by th' arm, / That little thinks she has been sluic'd in 's absence"

(1.2.191-94). Perdita and Hermione are not only connected to each other through an

obvious mother-daughter bond, but they share, as daughters of Eve, the ill effects of their

wayward sex.

Hermione had playfully alluded to mankind's sexual fall from a prelapsarian

innocence in the first act. Cajoling Polixenes about his fall from "boy eternal" into the

"doctrine of ill-doing" (1.2.65, 70), Hermione jests that she, as well as Polixenes' queen,

must be "devils." As she-devils, they had first tempted their spouses into sexual relations:

"Th' offenses we have made you do, we'll answer, / If you first sinn'd with us, and that

with us / You did continue fault, and that you slipp'd not / With any but with us" (1.2.84-

86). Leontes' jealousy is instigated by the imagined carnal "offenses" of womankind, so

that Hermione's light-hearted banter forebodes Leontes' darker preoccupation and

obsession with fallen woman. Because Perdita's birth is aligned with post-Edenic

woman--who is as false as wind, water, and dice (1.2.131-33), or who is invariably

"fish'd" by neighbor "Sir Smile" (1.2.194-96)--Leontes transfers Hermione's sin of

adultery onto her daughter, condemning the innocent newborn to the doom of erring

woman, a witch's doom: "take it hence / And see it instantly consum'd with fire." Again,

"Go, take it to the fire." Yet again, "commit them to the fire!" (2.3.132-33, 2.3.140,

2.3.94-95). The threat of death by fire also falls to Perdita's protectress, Paulina, the "mankind witch," and the unidentified "them" of Leontes' commandment (2.3.68).

What's more, Leontes had earlier envisioned Hermione "given to the fire" before her trial

(2.3.08). In a historical context, Brian P. Levack documents that accused witches in

Shakespeare's period were usually burnt at the stake for their heretical association with

the devil, including copulation.[16] The accusation of perverse sexuality also coincided with

the witches' fallen state. As Marianne Hester contends, "women were perceived as more

likely to be sexually deviant than men because women were by definition (like Eve in the

Garden of Eden) sexually deviant."[17] According to Leontes, Perdita belongs by birth to

the "slippery" and deviant Hermione (1.2.273), and she belongs by sex, one can infer, to

the corruptibility of fallen woman.

In response to the court's entreaties, Leontes permits the infant Perdita to escape

execution only to suffer exposure: "let it live. / It shall not neither" (2.3.156). Her

exposure is intrinsically bound up with Leontes' psychological cruelty against Hermione,

his manic skepticism about her fidelity, as well as general distrust in female sexuality.

The king's irrationality creates part of the pattern of imbalance, or anti-parallelism, that

contributes to Perdita's adversity. Nevill Coghill maintains that Leontes' skepticism

gradually overwhelms him before Polixenes announces his departure from Sicily, and he

supports this position by pointing out that Leontes, brooding steadily with resentment,

interacts with his guest in a terse and edgy manner.[18] The sheer force, however, of

Leontes' hostility, his tirades against women and fear of cuckoldry, indicates a jealous

possessiveness that includes an explosive, frenetic quality. Charles Frey rightly argues

that Leontes' anger is both sudden and motivated by a repulsion of woman.[19] Indeed, the king's volatility, which causes him to reject Perdita as illegitimate, stands out even more when it is measured against Greene's narrative source.

In *Pandosto*, the king has plausible reason for suspecting his wife of infidelity, though the queen, Bellaria, is not visibly pregnant when Pandosto's doubts begin to mount. The narrator, for example, tells of Bellaria's recurrent but honest visits to Egistus's (Polixenes') bedchamber. Over time, she befriends Egistus in the name of hospitality (237). This familiarity progresses to an intimate attachment: "there grew such a secret uniting of their affections, that the one could not well be without the company of the other" (237). Their united affection engrosses them almost daily in private communications, and the intensity of their rapport triggers Pandosto's jealousy (237-38). Although Pandosto acts despotically, his suspicion of Bellaria's disloyalty originates in a logical and concrete series of events.

By contrast, Leontes' suspicions of Hermione's falseness escalate quickly to a "diseas'd opinion," as stated by Camillo. (1.2.297). Yet the king insists on the truth of his ill suspicions: "My wife is nothing, nor nothing have these nothings, If this be nothing" (1.2.295-96). Leontes impatiently thinks that his so-called ocular proofs, such as "paddling palms, and pinching fingers" (1.2.114), "leaning cheek to cheek," "meeting noses," and "Kissing with inside lip" (1.2.285-86), amount to something: "circumstances" that "Made up to th' deed." (2.1.178-79). He believes in these proofs, although it is unclear whether these behaviors are even happening. Leontes' swift denunciation of the queen extends to his misgivings over Perdita's legitimacy. Immediately given the stigma of bastardy, Perdita is instantly labeled a product of adultery. Leontes calls her "bastard" eight times, "brat" three times in Acts 2 and 3. (As it happens, Pandosto refers to Fawnia as a "bastard" four times, "brat" twice). "Brat" in the early modern period did not necessarily signify a child born out of wedlock, but, as specified by the *OED*, a child "called in contempt." The apparent justification for Perdita's rejection and subsequent abandonment is her reputed illegitimacy.

The crux of Leontes' cruelty against Perdita is the king's assault on the infant's illegitimate identity. This assault once again links mother and daughter in adulterous sin. For Leontes, Perdita's existence owes itself to lewd fornication, rather than lawful procreative sex: "My wife's a hobby-horse, deserves a name / As rank as any flax-wench that puts to / Before her troth-plight" (1.2.277-78). To his court, Leontes proclaims the queen an "adulteress," "thing," "traitor," and "bed-swerver" (2.1.82-95). Even the Shepherd, who first discovers the "pretty barne" Perdita, comically attributes her abandonment to scurrilous hank-panky, to "some stair-work, some trunk-work, some behind-the-door-work" (3.3.73-75). In the opinion of Leontes, the consequence of Hermione's transgression is her child's fatherless state: "Thy brat hath been cast out, like to itself, / No father owning it (which is, indeed, / More criminal in thee than it)" (3.2.87-89). The king's verbal assault strips Perdita of her paternal identity and royal heritage. Moreover, the idea that Perdita has "No father" contrasts sharply with Hermione's identification with her own father, the Emperor of Russia, or possibly Ivan the Terrible. Ironically, the queen invokes her dead father's memory at trial when she is in need of pity and perhaps fatherly compassion. (3.2.119-123). Daryl W. Palmer stresses Leontes' lack of compassion by comparing him to Hermione's notoriously cruel father: "The queen knows the emperor of Russia and still imagines a sympathetic gaze."[20] If the play suggests the primacy of the paternal bloodline, then Perdita's fatherless condition marks her as inferior at birth, adding to the psychologically adverse conditions of her infancy.

The anti-parallel pattern in the first half of *The Winter's Tale* sets up a theme of Perdita's mistreatment as an infant. Here, Shakespeare is far from the pastoral epitome of kindly birth and exposure. This alteration is made the more interesting in light of research by the social historian John Boswell. In *The Kindness of Strangers*, Boswell argues that the Greek romances of the Roman Imperial period, particularly *Daphnis and Chloe*, reflected a very real cultural problem that related to child abandonment. By way of example, he cites Roman legislation that prohibited wealthy citizens from casting off children to rural shepherds.[21] As in fiction, the rationale of child abandonment in this period appears to be relatively benign: a desire "to limit the family" and a fear of "adverse circumstances."[22] Although some exposed children were undoubtedly sold into slavery and prostitution, many were welcomed into households as family members or integrated into the system of domestic servitude.[23]

We have seen that in Daye's Elizabethan version of *Daphnis and Chloe*, the natal fathers cast off their newborns with the benevolent hope for the children's survival and recovery. At least in literature, tokens helped to identify the social status of the foundling or the child's natal parents; Daphnis's father, for instance, adorns his infant with royal ornaments: a purple cloak, gold clasp, and ivory dagger. While Dionysophanes alleges that these tokens were intended for the infant's funereal decoration, he "registers only delight" when reclaiming Daphnis as an adult (Daye's version omits the reference to funeral ornaments).[24] Likewise, Chloe's tokens, "curiously wrought and imbroidred with golde, jewels and other precious things, not to be despized" (Daye, sig. Cv), assist in her recognition and felicitous recuperation. In these literary instances, the circumstances of abandonment, along with valuable and poignant tokens of identity, give rise to the favorable expectation of a dramatic *anagnorisis*, the reconciliation of parents with child. Likewise, tokens of recognition are placed with Perdita: her fardel contains Hermione's mantle, her jewel, letters, and gold (3.3.120, 5.2.33-35). These mementos ensure the family's reunion; however, tokens also function as emblems of loss: they represent a past from which the exposed child has been cast out.

Perdita's adversity also includes deprivation on a more material scale. The power Leontes has to hurt his wife and daughter also involves increasing their physical discomfort during childbirth. This discomfort has less to do with the curse of Eve-- woman's pain in child labor--than with Leontes' denial of any material comfort during and after Hermione's delivery. Thus far, Perdita's misuse by her natal father has taken the form of verbal affronts. Leontes' vituperation against his daughter, threats like "The bastard brains with these my proper hands / Shall I dash out" (2.3.139-40), exemplifies the nature of the king's revilement. Likewise, Leontes' vitriol against Hermione, the "most cruel usage of [his] queen" (2.3.116), jeopardizes Hermione's reputation, including her children's honor. As Hermione says at her trial defense, "for honour, / 'Tis a derivative from me to mine, / And only that I stand for" (3.2.43-45). In addition to verbal attacks, Leontes causes mother and daughter to suffer the injury of physical abuse. This offense is interconnected with Leontes' psychological maltreatment of the two, and it touches upon the female experience of birthing.[25]

The shock of Leontes' accusation of adultery forces Hermione into premature labor. Emilia relates that "on her frights and griefs / (Which never tender lady hath borne greater) / She is, something before her time, deliver'd" (2.2.23-25).[26] Having given birth in jail, Hermione later asserts that she had lacked the dignity of "child-bed privilege," or lying-in, a right that belongs "To women of all fashion" (3.2.103-04). Compelled to stand public trial after delivery, Hermione further complains of bodily weakness: "hurried / Here, to this place, i' th' open air, before / I have got strength of limit" (3.2.104-06). In an analogous scene, the narrator in Greene's *Pandosto* makes no specific mention of the queen's childbed suffering in prison, nor of the daughter's premature birth. The text simply states, "Bellaria was brought to bed of a faire & beautifull daughter" ( 251). Needless to say, in Shakespeare Hermione's affliction translates into her daughter's affliction, a child "Starr'd most unluckily" (3.2.99). Besides imprisonment and enforced isolation from her son, the queen protests that her infant daughter had been ripped from her breast, from the substance of maternal nourishment and care: "(The innocent milk in it most innocent mouth) / Hal'd out to murder" (3.2.99-100). We recall that the queen Persinna in the *Aethiopica* deliberately exposes her daughter in order to protect the infant from the king's jealousy. She places trinkets beside the baby girl: precious gems and an embroidered waistband, a band that chronicles the child's heritage and the story of the mother's sorrow. As Carol Gesner writes, "Fear of being accused of adultery caused Persina to abandon the infant Chariclea, and so began the chain of events which made up the plot of the romance."[27] But the ruthless act of separating mother and child after parturition is more than a plot device in *The Winter's Tale*; the separation encompasses Hermione's pain, and it stands for a wider violation of human decency.

The abandonment of Perdita exceeds in cruelty even beyond material deprivation. The mistreatment of mother and daughter reflects a larger imbalance in the physical world, and the exposure introduces a moment of cosmic disorder. Effectively, this imbalance contributes to the anti-parallelism of the play's first half. The sense of disorder becomes clearer when the scene of Perdita's ostracism is compared with a correlative scene in pastoral romance. In *Daphnis and Chloe*, the disposing of children reveals the harmonious operation of nature. Chloe is securely stowed away in a cave sacred to the Nymphs. The shepherd Dryas stumbles upon the female newborn, who is contentedly suckling an ewe. Similarly, the goatherd Lamon gathers up the baby Daphnis, who has been gingerly deposited in a nest of foliage by a milking goat. The exposure of children in Longus demonstrates nature in harmony with human actions. Not surprisingly, the story's tutelary deities, Pan and Eros, preside over the infants well into young adulthood.

By way of contrast, Perdita's exposure demonstrates nature in disharmony with human affairs. When Leontes charges Antigonus to carry the child to a "remote and desert place," far from "our dominions," without "more mercy" (2.3.175-77), he conjures up an image of desolation in opposition to the amity and fecundity of "great creating nature" (4.4.88). Instead of kindly sheep and goats that give suck to abandoned infants, Antigonus prays that "kites and ravens" or "wolves and bears" nurse Perdita (2.3.185-86).[28] The subversion of the pastoral order continues in the inversion of nature. The storm that is occasioned by Perdita's abandonment mixes together earth and sky in a violent blending. The Clown reports that the tempest has uncannily melded together the elements: "betwixt the firmament and it you cannot thrust a bodkin's point" (3.3.84-86). The chaos of the sea storm is a visual metaphor for the imbalance of Leontes' jealous rage, an anger that underlies the motive for Perdita's rejection. Moreover, in Act 5 the violent storm undergoes an interpretative reevaluation. As the Third Gentleman reports, "all the instruments which aided to expose the child were even then lost when it was found" (5.2.70-72). The storm now represents providential justice, in that it has destroyed all the participants and tools involved in the abandonment.

Shakespeare associates Perdita's abandonment with sinister forces. The macabre depiction of the event points to the unusual cruelty of her spurning. Paulina describes the exposure of Perdita as a crime that ranks below the villainy of a fiend. In her words, "a devil / Would have shed water out of fire, ere done't" (3.2.192-93). Paulina's hyperbolic rhetoric reinforces the depravity of the abandonment, but it also links the infant's exposure to the preternatural, to Hermione's ghostly appearance on the eve of Perdita's casting away. In a dream vision, Hermione visits the "affrighted" Antigonus since he is the reluctant agent of catastrophe, the "thrower-out" of the queen's "poor babe" (3.3.36, 3.3.29-30). Like a tormented spirit, Hermione gasps, shrieks, and melts into air, and her utterances forebode Antigonus's death by a marauding bear. (He will never see his wife Paulina again [3.3.35-36]). Because Perdita's rejection by her father is both unnatural and unnecessary--the Oracle declares the princess "an innocent babe truly begotten" (3.2.133-34)--the abandonment exemplifies the destructive side of human behavior. As Ruth Nevo writes, Antigonus actualizes the king's "destructive, ambivalent will in the abandonment of the babe."[29] Although Perdita's name connotes sorrow, " for the babe / Is counted lost for ever, Perdita, / I prithee, call't" (3.3.32-34), it is Hermione who internalizes her daughter's loss. The apparition of the queen embodies this idea: Antigonus compares her otherworldly figure to "sanctity" and to a "vessel of like sorrow," whose her eyes have turned into somatic "spouts" pouring forth "fury" (3.3.21-26). Injured by Leontes, Hermione's body is a metaphor of affliction, the suffering brought on by the wrongdoing of another. Leontes' destructive tendency is entombed in Hermione's person, whether or not she is actually dead, as Antigonus guesses. The king's violence opposes the life-affirming character of mother and daughter. As Carol Thomas Neely writes, "[T]he play's central miracle--birth--is human, personal, physical, and female."[30] And according to Paulina, Perdita is the progeny of "great nature," by whose authority the princess lives "Free'd and enfranchis'd" from the maternal womb that gave her life (2.2.60-61).

Shakespeare invests the exposure of Perdita with a greater tragic element. Whereas in Greene's *Pandosto* the narrator consigns the female infant to fortune, Shakespeare reinterprets his source, so that the child's destiny is largely dependent on willful human intervention. Commentators have pointed out that, in Greene, the abandonment of Fawnia calls attention to the agency of chance: secured in a small boat without sail or rudder, Fawnia is carried by "the wind & wave as the destinies please to appoint" (254). Yet in Shakespeare Antigonus purposely takes the baby Perdita to the shores of Bohemia because the apparition of Hermione has implored him to do so: "Places remote enough are in Bohemia, / There weep, and leave it crying" (3.3.31-32). Stanley Wells aptly observes that Shakespeare humanizes Greene's narrative by emphasizing the characteristic of "personal responsibility" over fortune.[31] One might augment this point. In *The Winter's Tale*, the highest form of cruelty issues from the individual's willingness to enact harm.[32] The sequence of events that lead up to the disowning of Perdita shows characters exercising their judgments, but their judgments are willfully misguided or incorrect. We have seen how Leontes chooses to follow his delusions about his wife's reputed extramarital affair. "I have drunk, and seen the spider," he admits (2.1.45). More naively, Antigonus willfully misinterprets--he uses the phrase "superstitiously, / I will be squar'd by this" (3.3.40-41)--Hermione's deathlike apparition as evidence of her guilt and punishment: "I do believe / Hermione has suffer'd death [ . . . ] this being indeed the issue / Of King Polixenes" (3.3.41-44). Leontes stubbornly blames the exposure of Perdita on the workings of fortune, not on his own violation.

The king shows a perversion of natural causality when he orders Perdita to be cast off. To Antigonus, he states:

> As by strange fortune
>
> It came to us, I do in justice charge thee,
>
> On thy soul's peril and thy body's torture,
>
> That thou commend it strangely to some place
>
> Where chance may nurse or end it.  (2.3.178-82)

Leontes' role in the abandonment has been removed from the equation. In this passage, he substitutes the mother's body for the mechanism of chance: fortune has engendered the "It" that has "came to us." Again, it is "chance," acting in a maternal capacity, that may nourish the child. Since Leontes confuses the maternal body with fortune, he transfers the guilt of forsaking the infant from himself to the realm of the feminine. Antigonus later echoes this logic when he blames Hermione for Perdita's misfortune: "poor wretch, / That for thy mother's fault art thus expos'd" (3.349-50). As a father figure (Antigonus has three daughters, whom he will ridiculously "geld" if they prove false [2.1.147]), he betrays Perdita to "loss" and to the uncertainty of "what may follow" (3.3.51).

These instances of paternal abuse demonstrate in part a basic dissimilarity in Perdita's beginnings and those of her male counterpart, Florizel. The pattern of character asymmetry between Florizel and Perdita can be seen in the contrasting relationships they have with their birth fathers in the first half of the play. Unlike Perdita, who suffers from parental condemnation, Florizel enjoys the privilege of king Polixenes' wholehearted affection. Briefly mentioning his son at the Sicilian court, Polixenes gives an endearing description of the young prince that illustrates the loving rapport between father and son. About his young boy, Polixenes says:

> He's all my exercise, my mirth, my matter:
>
> Now my sworn friend, and then mine enemy;
>
> My parasite, my soldier, statesman, all.
>
> He makes a July's day short as December;
>
> And with his varying childness cures in me
>
> Thoughts that would thick my blood.  (1.2.166-171)

At a young age Florizel has already taken on the mantle of adulthood, poised for political life as a soldier or statesman: whether friend or enemy, the boy stands, figuratively speaking, on an equal footing with the king. Florizel, however, is still a playfully audacious child: a mock "parasite" and source of pride. It seems that the prince alleviates his father's graver fears by reminding Polixenes of generation, that the king's bloodline will continue through his son. In short, Florizel is a facsimile of the king. Heir to the throne of Bohemia, the young prince benefits from the entitlements of his royal birth status.

The example of royal privilege can be viewed in the characterization of Perdita's birth brother, Mamillius. This portrayal is worth emphasizing, because it sharpens the sense of incongruity between the play's female and male child. Like Florizel, Mamillius mirrors his kingly father. "[T]hey say we are / Almost as like as eggs" (1.2.129-30), states Leontes after noting a similarity in noses. On the one hand, Leontes' preoccupation with the idea of family resemblance emphasizes his fear of Hermione's sexual infidelity. On the other hand, it strengthens the assumption that Mamillius is descended from princely lineage. Since Mamillius appears physically to favor the king, his paternal identification brings him closer to the world of male privilege and royal prerogative. Comparatively, Paulina's conviction that Perdita is a "copy of the father" holds little sway with Leontes (2.3.99). The Bohemian courtier Archidamus makes it clear that the young boy Mamillius will one day fit the role of king well: "It is a gentleman of the greatest promise that ever came into my note" (1.135-36). Camillo responds in agreement and with equal praise: "it is a gallant child; one that, indeed, physics the subject, makes old hearts fresh" (1.1.38-39).

The picture of Mamillius as heir apparent to the throne of Sicily is complicated, however, by his association with women. Because Mamillius remains fundamentally connected to the play's female sphere, he pays the price of his father's abuse with death. Shown as essentially feeble, Mamillius's characterization lacks the resiliency of heroic prowess. At court, Mamillius is affiliated closely with the feminine. For example, the boy is precociously adept in the art of cosmetics, evidently having spent time in the company of Hermione's attendants (2.1.8-10). Even on a linguistic level, the name "Mamillius" conveys an image of maternal breasts. More significantly, Mamillius strongly empathizes with his mother's tribulation in prison, transferring Hermione's pain onto himself. He feels the queen's anguish so intensely that his body literally cannot withstand the torment: "The prince your son, with mere conceit and fear / Of the queen's speed, is gone" (3.2.144-45). In this instance, Susan Synder points to "a direct connection between physical death and the psychological identification with the mother."[33] Mamillius is deeply affected by Leontes' distrust of Hermione's sexuality. Although the young prince suffers death, his affliction does not involve direct assaults to his person, as in the case of Hermione and Perdita. In fact, Leontes deems himself his son's protector, guarding the boy from his "infected" mother by prohibiting their visitation (3.2.96-98). In terms of genre, the death of children in pastoral romance is usually the plot mechanism of providence: the miraculous recognition of the lost child provides the birth family with an heir. In Longus, for example, the recovery of Chloe reestablishes her as the family's surviving descendent (Daphnis has one living brother). Similarly, the recovery of Perdita sixteen years after the death of Mamillius restores her as sole heir to the Sicilian throne, as decreed by the Oracle (3.2.131-35).

One of the dominant readings of *The Winter's Tale* concerns the romantic pairing of Perdita and Florizel. The young lovers are instrumental in effecting the dramatic transition from the play's tragic first half to its restorative second half. Perdita, especially, is the focal point of this transition: she represents the theme of renewal and the triumph of true love over adversity.[34] The dramatic movement from tragedy to romance coincides with a shift in relations between characters, one from anti-parallelism to a state of character equality. In Act 4, Shakespeare reverses the pattern of female suffering and patriarchal abuse: Perdita's abandonment transforms into Florizel's self-imposed banishment, Leontes' cruel jealousy into Polixenes' imperious rage. These changes serve to equalize the experience of adversity between the young hero and heroine. In the process, the motif of mutual love operates as a backdrop against which the reversals take place.

The transition to parallelism involves the motif of role reversal. In keeping with the festive spirit of the sheepshearing feast, the lovers put on holiday costumes. Florizel wears the apparel of a rustic "swain" (4.4.8), becoming the shepherd Doricles. And Perdita arrays herself with flowers; she fashions herself in the likeness of the goddess Flora "in April's front" (4.4.3). Beyond their festive utility, these costumes adumbrate the couple's class equality, as each character moves either up or down on the social scale to meet in the middle. Evidently, Florizel has played the country shepherd's part for more than a day, but long enough for the Shepherd to be deceived. He believes that "Doricles" has a large estate, or "a worthy feeding" (4.4.171). At court, Camillo's observation that Florizel "is of late much retired" bears witness to the prince's continuous role-playing as Doricles (4.2.32-33). Although Camillo reckons that the prince has been absent from court for three days (4.2.30), he also notes that Florizel has frequented the countryside for longer. Polixenes agrees: "he is seldom from the house of a most homely shepherd" (4.2.38-39). According to Perdita, Florizel's homespun costume makes him appear "Viley bound up" (4.4.22). Her observation underlies the risk and degradation of his disguise, and it shows Florizel's willful relinquishment of his position as prince.

Just as Florizel humbles himself as Doricles, Perdita is transfigured into a queen. She is more than a mere holiday maid, who is "Most goddess-like prank'd up" in "borrowed flaunts" (4.4.10, 4.4.23). As Florizel reminds her, "This your sheep-shearing / Is as a meeting of the petty gods, / And you the queen on't (4.4.3-5). Although Florizel

uses playful imagery, his words give an indication of Perdita's grace and true royal birth.
Certainly, Florizel admires her majestic manners:

> Each your doing,
>
> So singular in each particular,
>
> Crowns what you are doing, in the present deeds
>
> That all your acts are queens. (4.4.143-46)

Echoing this adulation, Camillo enthusiastically calls Perdita, "The queen of curds and cream," intuiting, even in mirth, her princely status (4.4.161). By contrast, Perdita masquerades as "Mistress o' th' Feast," but only for a day (4.4.68). "I'll queen it no inch farther," she resolves when Polixenes uncovers Florizel's disguise (4.4.450). Despite her uneasiness with kingship, Perdita will be Florizel's "fair princess" in marriage (4.4.545). As the examples show, there is a thematic movement toward class equality in these scenes, even though Florizel remains a prince, and even though Perdita's birthright, as "the king's daughter," is not yet unveiled (5.2.40).

The development toward parallelism also entails reversing the pattern of authoritarian cruelty. In Shakespeare's Bohemia, the abandonment of Perdita corresponds to the pastoral convention of benevolent exposure. First, the Shepherd rescues the infant Perdita from possible destruction. "I'll take it up for pity," he muses (3.3.76). The Shepherd's compassion for the newborn recalls the goodwill of Chloe's foster father in Longus's romance. In that story, the shepherd Dryas affectionately cares for the infant Chloe until her marriage to Daphnis. In *The Winter's Tale*, the Shepherd's pity resembles the mercy of foster fathers in the pastoral model, though it differs from Hermione's plea for fatherly pity, where Leontes' lack of mercy was a sign of "The flatness of [the queen's] misery" (3.2.122). Moreover, the Shepherd takes up the infant--"Mercy on's, a barne!"--before he discovers the "fairy gold" in Perdita's bundle (3.3.69, 3.3.121). The Shepherd's initial ignorance, that gold is tucked away with the newborn, points to the genuine selflessness of the deed. By comparison, in Greene's version the shepherd father, Porrus, raises Fawnia on account of the riches he uncovers in her fardel: "for what will not the greedy desire of Gold cause a man to doe? So that he was resolved in himself to foster the child, and with the summe to relieve his want" (266-67).[35] Shakespeare omits any specific reference to the shepherd's greed in relation to Perdita's rescue; instead, the playwright stresses the notion of benevolence over self-interest. In return for the Shepherd's charity, rearing Perdita, he prospers beyond human expectation: "A man, they say, that from very nothing and beyond the imagination of his neighbours, is grown into an unspeakable estate" (4.2.38-40).

It is not clear from the text whether the gold found with Perdita has caused the Shepherd's wealth, or whether the Shepherd's act of benevolence has contributed to his prosperity, or both. In any case, it is tempting to speculate that kindly fairies have placed gold next to the baby Perdita. The Shepherd has been told that he "should be rich by the fairies" (3.3.114), and the courtiers who report the recovery of Perdita in Act 5 do not list "gold" among the tokens of identity found with her (5.2.33-40). Truly, the items placed by Perdita at her exposure possess an element of mystery. Fearing Polixenes' wrath, the Clown urges his father to "Show those things you found about her (those secret things, all but what she has with her)." Or, "We must to the king and show our strange sights" (4.4.695-97. 4.4.820-21). Again, the Shepherd refers to the tokens as secrets: "there lies such secrets in this fardel and box, which none must know but the king" (4.4.695-97,

4.4.757-58). The mention of an extra bundle or "box" is curious. Can one not postulate that this secret box contains gold left by fairies? Do these supernatural entities represent the kind of "better guiding spirit" on which Paulina calls before the child's exposure (2.3.126)? However farfetched this idea may be, the Shepherd's strange and "unspeakable" wealth, which befalls him after Perdita's rescue, implies the protective care of nature in concord with human affairs, not against it.

The pattern of reversal is also viewed in the Shepherd's verbal expression of kindness to his foster daughter. The invectives that Leontes had used against his child are now counterpoised by paternal flattery. To the Shepherd, the newborn he chances upon is a "very pretty barne [ . . . ] A pretty one; a very pretty one" (3.3.70-71). Later, the Shepherd boasts of his daughter's superior disposition and talent: "If young Doricles / Do light upon her, she shall bring him that / Which he not dreams of" (4.4.180-82). Although the Shepherd calls Perdita a "cursed wretch" when she presumes to "mingle faith" with a prince (4.4.459-61), he casts the greater blame and censure onto Florizel, who is "no honest man" to make the Shepherd "the king's brother-in-law" (4.4.700-02). Likewise, Greene's shepherd-father, Porrus, lays most of the blame on Dorastus.[36] In *The Winter's Tale*, the Shepherd's vexation with Perdita also serves as a plot device to advance the play's dramatic *anagnorisis*: the foster father must relinquish his paternal bond with the daughter, so that she can be recuperated by her birth parents. The Clown takes this one step further by rhetorically breaking the bond of nurture that had previously tied the family together. About his foster sister, he says to the Shepherd, "She being none of your flesh and blood, your flesh and blood has not offended the king" (4.4.693-94). Earlier, Leontes' belief in Perdita's bastardy, that the infant was not his "flesh and blood," was the catalyst that sparked her abandonment. Perdita, however, turns the appellation of bastardy on its head. At the sheepshearing feast, she refutes the notion of impure breeding: Perdita will not grow "nature's bastards," or "streak'd gillyvors" in her garden (4.4.82-83). She compares these hybrid flowers with tainted sexuality, with "painted" women who entice men "to breed" by them (4.4.101-03). Even though the various speeches about nature and art are almost always contradicted at some point in the sheephearing scene, Perdita inadvertently negates Leontes' accusation of her bastardy by disapproving of adulterated breeding, or the process by which seeds are fused and coupled to create a new entity.

In the first half of the play, Leontes correlates procreation with illicit sexuality. This correlation leads directly to the "death" of Hermione and the expulsion of Perdita. Conversely, in Act 4 the abandoned Perdita is brought up in household that does not denigrate the female. In a brief passage about holiday sociability, the Shepherd fondly remembers his deceased wife in a vignette that evokes her festive sexuality:[37]

> when my old wife liv'd, upon
>
> This day she was both pantler, butler, cook,
>
> Both dame and servant; welcom'd all, serv'd all;
>
> Would sing her song and dance her turn; now here
>
> At upper end o' th' table, no i' th' middle;
>
> On his shoulder, and his; her face o' fire
>
> With labour, and the thing she took to quench it
>
> She would to each one sip.  (4.4.54-62).

Apparently, the wife's hospitality went as far as lusty merrymaking. While Perdita refrains from emulating her foster mother's liberality as hostess, the princess has at least been positively influenced by her legacy. (It is not textually clear if Perdita grows up while the Shepherd's wife is still alive, though in *Pandosto* Fawnia has a foster mother). In the pastoral landscape of Bohemia, Perdita elevates the wife's comic sexuality to an ideal vision of erotic love: she wants Florizel "quick, and in [her] arms" and pictures the prince strewn with flowers much like "a bank, for love to lie and play on" (4.4.130-33). Janet Adelman interprets this passage as the play's central expression of sexual regeneration: as Florizel "quickens in her embrace, she herself imagistically becomes quick with him, restoring him through the pregnant fecundity of her own body."[38] This image of embracement not only constructs romantic love as a mutually life-giving pleasure; it evokes the orthodox, biblical symbol of two persons grafted into one matrimonial body.

The movement toward parallelism, Perdita and Florizel's symmetry in character, requires that each lover suffers paternal abandonment. Instead of Leontes' rejection of Perdita, we have Polixenes' castigation of Florizel. In effect, Florizel is cast off by Polixenes, who flagrantly disrupts the lovers' marriage contract: "Mark your divorce, young sir, / Whom son I dare not call; thou art too base / To be acknowledg'd" (4.4.418-20). Again, "we'll bar thee from succession; / Not hold thee of our blood, no, not our kin" (4.4.430-31). This kind of abandonment, in which the parent disowns or disinherits his adult child, repeats the basic pattern of abuse that occurs when Leontes mandates Perdita's exposure as an infant. While Polixenes may have good reason to disapprove of his son's lowly marriage, his anger betrays a larger distrust of female sexuality. Peter

Lindenbaum argues that Leontes and Polixenes share a fear of sexual love.[39] Indeed, Polixenes repeats Leontes' vituperation against woman. Instead of being designated as a product of adultery, Perdita is now transformed into the adulteress or whore. She is "the angle" that "plucks" Florizel (4.2.47); a "sheep-hook" (4.4.421); a "fresh piece / Of excellent witchcraft" (4.4.423-24); a "knack" (4.4.429); and an "enchantment" (4.4.435). More than as a rare strumpet, Perdita's body is construed as a monstrous thing, an entity that would rape Florizel. Polixenes believes that her "rural latches" will force the way to the prince's "entrance" (4.4.439), or that she will unnaturally "hoop" his body like an overpowering creature (4.4.440), an image that recalls "the foul witch Sycorax, who with age and envy / Was grown into a hoop" (1.2.259-60).[40]

Perdita is the recipient of a father's cruelty once more. Polixenes' abuse, however, also impinges on Florizel. The young prince opposes his father's denunciation of Perdita by upholding his commitment to her, a loyalty that he defends over family and civil duty: "From my succession wipe me, father; I / Am heir to my affection" (4.4.481-82). By the end of Act 4, Florizel has reversed the theme of child abandonment by becoming the author of his father's casting off. The prince's determination to remain constant to "affection" precipitates his self-imposed exile: "I mean not / To see [my father] any more . . . I am put to sea / With her whom here I cannot hold on shore" (4.4.496-500). In Act 5, the suggestion of paternal abandonment becomes fact: Florizel has "[h]is dignity and duty both cast off-- / Fled from his father" (5.1.182-83). The prince's disobedience to Polixenes, his renunciation of the father, permits him to share (almost joyfully) in Perdita's suffering. "O, the thorns *we* stand upon!" he exclaims before the two sail to Sicily (my emphasis, 4.4.586). Perdita's apprehension of elopement is partially due to the threat of Florizel's rejection. There is the possibility that the prince's words lack substance, or that he will forgo standing on his proverbial "thorns." To be sure, Perdita fears that the prince has wooed her the false way (4.4.150-51).[41] Yet rather than shrinking from adversity, Florizel presents a united front, and he persuades Perdita of his sincerity more than once: "I'll be thine, my fair, / Or not my father's. For I cannot be / Mine own, nor anything to any, if / I be not thine" (4.4.42-45). While it can be inferred that Perdita is the object of Polixenes' raw anger--he says, "I'll have thy beauty scratch'd with briers" (4.4.426) and "I will devise a death as cruel for thee / As thou art tender to 't" (4.4.441-42)--Florizel eases the burden of her ordeal by blurring the boundaries between self and other. He constructs selfhood by incorporating Perdita into the "I" of his person. Because she is an integral component of him, Florizel builds on the image of unity, a joining of two autonomous selves that reaches beyond private pleasure, or a bank where love lies and plays, to shared fortitude in calamity.

The couple's flight to Sicily should prefigure their adventure and peril at sea. Camillo sums up the usual outcome of children who flee from parental authority. Like generic romance lovers, the two should expect "a wild dedication of yourselves / To unpath'd waters, undream'd shores; most certain / To miseries enough; no hope to help you, / But as you shake off one, to take another" (4.4.567-70). Camillo's admonishment describes dangers that typically assail the Greek romance hero and heroine: the betrothed couple escapes obstacles to their union by sailing to a foreign shore where they are beset by additional pitfalls. (Renaissance readers would have known this formula best from the *Aethiopica* and *Leucippe and Clitophon*). As one critic observes, Camillo can see no "beneficent power" beyond the "sway of courtly art," but only the "rule of indifferent

Fortune."[42] That the romance pair overcomes trials virtually unscathed is a testament to their conventionalized virtues of chastity and fidelity, as well as to the benevolent design of providence.

In *Pandosto*, Dorastus and Fawnia run away from paternal opposition and are nearly shipwrecked at the harbor of Bohemia. At the king's court, they meet with a harsh set of trials: the imprisonment of Dorastus, the incestuous lust of Pandosto, and the near murder of Fawnia. Florizel acknowledges the possibility of such impending hazards: "we do profess / Ourselves to be the slaves of chance, and flies / Of every wind that blows" (4.4.540-42). But Shakespeare cuts further adversity from the play. The misfortune that fleeing lovers often confront is replaced by a theoretical emphasis on these young lovers' admirable strength of will. At the court of Leontes, Florizel maintains that his commitment to Perdita is a stronghold against the whims of fortune or the prerogative of Polixenes:

> Though Fortune, visible an enemy,
>
> Should chase us, with my father, power not jot
>
> Hath she to change our loves. (5.1.215-17)

In Act 4, Camillo misinterprets the pair's commitment when he predicts that Florizel and Perdita will buckle under duress. He sententiously warns that "Prosperity's the very bond of love, / Whose fresh complexion and whose heart together / Affliction alters" (4.4.574-76). Perdita immediately corrects him: "I think affliction may subdue the cheek, / But not take in the mind" (4.4.577-78). Perdita reiterates Florizel's resolve to prevail in love despite Polixenes' disapproval of the match. Earlier, the prince had set forth a similar conviction, one akin to Perdita's belief that affliction cannot "take in the mind." He declares to Camillo his fixity of purpose: "[not] for all the sun sees, or / The close earth wombs, or the profound seas hides / In unknown fathoms, will I break my oath / To this my fair belov'd" (4.4.490-93). Florizel uses imagery of physical containment to suggest the inviolability and enormity of his faith. He balances the will of the individual with the natural order; by his analogy, the subduing of the mind is tantamount to unveiling the inscrutable laws of nature and retrieving its riches.

*The Winter's Tale* begins by exposing the depth of Leontes' cruelty against his wife and daughter. The traditional model of benevolent abandonment, which can be traced back to ancient pastoral romance, is modified to assimilate the theme of patriarchal abuse. The persecution of mother and daughter is rooted in a suspicion of female sexuality that associates her body with the impurity of fallen woman. In the first half of the play, Shakespeare creates character asymmetry between Perdita and Florizel by emphasizing male privilege and female wretchedness. This pattern is neutralized in the pastoral episodes where the young hero and heroine suffer mutually for romantic love. The class disparity between the pair is rectified by the recognition of the heroine's royal identity.

The dramatic *anagnorisis* in *The Winter's Tale* establishes the formation of a new family that includes both birth and foster parents. While the shepherds are absent from the scene of Hermione's restoration, the Clown acquaints Autolycus with this novel, hybrid household:

> For the king's son took me by the hand, and called me brother; and then
> the two kings called my father brother; and then the prince, my brother,

and the princess, my sister, called my father father; and so we wept.

(5.2.140-44)

The reunion of family members seems to lack the presence of mothers. Hermione has not

yet been integrated into the reconstituted family, and Florizel's mother continues to stay

unrepresented. Yet Hermione's incorporation into the domestic circle is contingent upon

a final reversal. As Paulina observes, Hermione becomes the initiator of the reconciliation

between husband and wife: "When she was young you woo'd her; now, in age, / Is she

become the suitor?" (5.3.108-09). Hermione overturns the memory of courtship that had

haunted Leontes in Act 1; according to the king, the queen would not reciprocate his

amorous overtures until three "crabbed months had sour'd themselves" (1.2.102). Grown

with age, their marital reconciliation is still not wholly complete. At the recognition

scene, Hermione does not speak to Leontes, but only to their daughter:

> for thou shalt hear that I,
>
> Knowing by Paulina that the Oracle
>
> Gave hope thou wast in being, have preserv'd
>
> Myself to see the issue.  (5.3.125-28)

Ultimately, there is the sense in this passage that Leontes and Hermione will remain

asymmetrical in marriage because they have suffered irreconcilably in life. While

Leontes does goes through hardship, his tribulation is one of intellectual repentance.[43]

Conversely, Hermione suffers profound abuse as does her daughter; she experiences

"death" as does her son. Paulina even speaks of the queen's affliction in terms of great

anguish: "What wheels? racks? fires? what flaying? Boiling? / In leads or oils? What old

or newer torture / Must I receive, whose every word deserves / To taste of thy most worst? Thy tyranny" (3.2.176-80). Hermione has withstood oppression and tyranny to behold Perdita once again. Like that of the younger generation, her patience in adversity gives her the temerity to persevere. In *The Winter's Tale*, the human will is the most mysterious of all--despite everything, holding on to hope, to faith, and above all to love.

The next chapter addresses how Imogen in *Cymbeline* suffers both from parental abuse and cruelty from a jealous husband. Shakespeare in this play combines the figure of wife and daughter into one character: as a wife, Imogen is made to confront her husband's violent condemnation of her loyalty; as a daughter she is made to endure her family's threats to her clandestine marriage. Shakespeare shapes this heroine by joining two romantic traditions, one rooted in Greek romance, the other in medieval folk tale. I find that in *Cymbeline* the dramatic focus turns with even greater emphasis on the erotic suffering of the young heroine: her heroism consists in an inviolable fidelity to her partner in marriage, a husband who has cold-heartedly forsaken her in spirit.

---

[1]Lennox, Charlotte, *Shakespear Illustrated*, vol. 2 (London: A. Miller, 1753-54), 75. For more recent discussions of Greene's *Pandosto* as primary source of *The Winter's Tale*, see Geoffrey Bullough, *The Narrative and Dramatic Sources of Shakespeare*, vol. 8 (London: Routledge, 1966); and Kenneth Muir, *The Sources of Shakespeare's Plays* (New Haven: Yale University Press, 1978), 267-279. For a discussion of Greene's prose pamphlets as sources for the play's dramatic structure, see Steven R. Mentz, "Wearing Greene: Autolycus, Robert Greene, and the Structure of Romance in *The Winter's Tale*," *Renaissance Drama* 30 (1999-2001): 73-92. For discussions of the play's secondary sources other than Greene, see E. A. J. Honigmann, "Secondary Sources of *The Winter's*

Tale," *Philological Quarterly* 34 (1955): 27-38. Honigmann argues for *Amadis de Gaule*, along with Francis Sabie's "The Fisshermans Tale" (1595) and its second part, "The Fisher-mans Tale" (1595), as probably sources. See also Thomas E. Mussio's "Bandello's 'Timbreo and Fenicia' and *The Winter's Tale*," *Comparative Drama* 34 (2000): 211-244. Mussio finds that Shakespeare looks to Bandello's novella for his handling of such themes as repentance, regeneration, and forgiveness (212).

[2]I cite the title from *The Life and Complete Works in Prose and Verse of Robert Greene*, ed., Alexander B. Grosart, vol. 4 (London: Hazell, Watson, & Viney, 1881-86), 227. Further citations of *Pandosto* refer to this edition, and they will be cited parenthetically.

[3]The first printing of *Pandosto* may have occurred as early as 1585, and its popularity continued throughout the seventeenth century. See Lori Humphrey Newcomb, "'Social Things': The Production of Popular Culture in the Reception of Robert Greene's *Pandosto*," *ELH* 61 (1994): 753-81, 756. Newcomb examines Greene's romance and its relationship to the emerging commercial market of the sixteenth century. For further discussion of Greene's prose fiction and its relation to popular culture, see David Margolies, *Novel and Society in Elizabethan England* (London: Croom Helm, 1985), 105-142.

[4]Walter Davis, *Idea and Act in Elizabethan Fiction* (Princeton: Princeton University Press, 1969), 139. Davis identifies three other major periods in Greene's non-dramatic writings: "experiments in the Euphuistic mode (1580-84);" "collections of short tales or novelle (1585-88);" and "pamphlets of repentance and roguery, in the main nonfictional

(1590-92)" (139). Paul Salzman concurs with Davis's classification in *English Prose Fiction, 1558-1700* (Oxford: Clarendon Press, 1985), 59.

[5]About Greene's use of Euphuism, Nicholas Storojenko writes, "'Dorastus and Fawnia' belongs to the central period of Greene's literary labours, when he was still under the influence of Lylly [*sic*]. The pamphlet is written in language so euphistic as to be inferior in nothing to the 'euphues' of the great Lylly [*sic*] himself" (*Robert Greene: His Life and Works: A Critical Investigation*, in *The Life and Complete Works in Prose and Verse of Robert Greene*), 250-51. See also Inga-Stina Ewbank, "From Narrative to Dramatic Language: *The Winter's Tale* and Its Source," in *Shakespeare and the Sense of Performance: Essays in the Tradition of Performance Criticism in Honor of Bernard Beckerman*, eds. Marvin and Ruth Thompson (Newark: University of Delaware Press; London and Toronto: Associated University Presses, 1989), 29-47. Ewbank argues that Shakespeare translates Greene's Euphistic style into a thematic structure: "This style Shakespeare has absorbed and transmuted, not so much verbally as [ . . . ] structurally: into that two-part structure of parallels and contrasts which, as such, has so often been commented on" (32).

[6]Frank Kermode, ed., *The Winter's Tale*, The Signet Classic Shakespeare, ed. Sylvan Barnet (New York and Scarborough, Ontario: New American Library, 1963), xxiv-xxv. See also Geoffrey Bullough, *Narrative and Dramatic Sources*, 119, and J. H. P. Pafford, ed, *The Winter's Tale*, The Arden Shakespeare (London: Methuen & Co., 1963; London: Thomas Nelson and Sons, 1999), xxxvi, lxv. Robert M. Adams mentions *Daphnis and Chloe* as a possible minor source (*Shakespeare: The Four Romances* [New York and

London: W. W. Norton & Company, 1989], 90-91). For studies that see in *The Winter's Tale* the influence via Greene of Longus' *Daphnis and Chloe* and Heliodorus's Greek romance, the *Aethiopica*, see the following: Carol Gesner, *Shakespeare and the Greek Romance* (Lexington: University Press of Kentucky, 1970), 116-125; Samuel Lee Wolff, *The Greek Romances in Elizabethan Prose Fiction* (New York: Columbia University Press, 1912), 367-447. Wolff maintains that in *Pandosto* Greene takes his "structure" from "solid Heliodorus and "incident and ornament" from "decorative Longus" (456). For studies that observe a general thematic or structural influence of Greek romance in the play, see Barbara A. Mowat, *The Dramaturgy of Shakespeare's Romances* (Athens: University of Georgia Press, 1976), esp, 31-33; Northrop Frye, "Shakespeare's Romances: *The Winter's Tale*," in *Northrop Frye on Shakespeare*, ed. Robert Sandler (New Haven and London: Yale University Press, 1986), 154-70, 158-59. Frye notes that the Greek romances, "fashionable in Elizabeth's time," are an offshoot of Greek New Comedy (159); Ernest Schanzer, ed., *The Winter's Tale* (Harmondsworth: Penguin Books, 1969), 10; Stanley Wells, "Shakespeare and Romance, " in *Later Shakespeare*, eds. John Russell Brown and Bernard Harris (New York: St. Martin's Press, 1967), 49-79, esp. 50-51; Hallett Smith, "The Romance Tradition as it Influenced Shakespeare," in *Shakespeare's Romances* (San Marino, Calif.: The Huntington Library, 1972), 1-20. For the influence of Greek romance and the concept of adventure time in *The Winter's Tale*, see Michael D. Bristol, "In Search of the Bear: Spatiotemporal Form and the Heterogeneity of Economies in *The Winter's Tale*," *Shakespeare Quarterly* 42 (1991): 145-67. For studies that discuss Greek sources other than romance, especially Greek tragedy, see Sara Hanna, "Voices Against Tyranny: Greek Sources of *The Winter's Tale*," *Classical and Modern Literature* 14 (1993-94), 335-344; and Louis L. Martz, "Shakespeare's Humanist Enterprise: *The Winter's Tale*," in *English Renaissance Studies Presented to Dame Helen Gardner in Honour of Her Seventieth Birthday*, eds. John Carey and Helen Peters (Oxford: Clarendon Press, 1980), 114-31.

[7]John Lawler, "*Pandosto* and the Nature of Dramatic Romance," *Philological Quarterly* (1962): 96-113, 103-04. Fitzroy Pyle also observes that Shakespeare alters his source in order to create a greater sense of mutual trust and loyalty in his young lovers (*The Winter's Tale: A Commentary on the Structure* [London: Routledge & Kegan Paul, 1969], 161). About this alteration, see also Hallett Smith, "*The Winter's Tale* and *Pandosto*," in *Shakespeare's Romances*, 96-97; Stanley Wells, "Shakespeare and Romance," 67; and Ernest Schanzer, ed., *The Winter's Tale*, 26-27. Schanzer writes that the resurrection of Hermione is, however, the main element that brings the play closer to the world of Greek romance (11-12).

[8]J. II. P. Pafford, *The Winter's Tale*, xxx. Citations of the play refer to Pafford's Arden edition, and they will be cited parenthetically. I follow Pafford's dating of the play between 1610-1611.

[9]Massimo Fusillo, "The Conflict of Emotions: A *Topos* in the Greek Erotic Novel," in *Oxford Readings in The Greek Novel*, ed. Simon Swain (Oxford: Oxford University Press, 1999), 60-82, 62. Fusillo does not include *Daphnis and Chloe* in his analysis of the conflict of emotions in Greek romance; yet, the concept of parallelism certainly applies to Longus's romance, since the protagonists experience near identical situations and similar

mishaps. For a study that discusses *Daphnis and Chloe* as a generic hybrid of Greek romance narrative and pastoral set pieces, see Paul Alpers, *What is Pastoral?* (Chicago and London: University of Chicago Press, 1996), esp. 323-48; and Lia Raffaella Cresci, "The Novel of Longus the Sophist and the Pastoral Tradition," in *Oxford Readings in the Greek Novel*, 210-42.

[10]For a discussion that complicates the issue of Hermione's unequivocal innocence, see Howard Felperin, "'Tongue-tied, Our Queen?': The Deconstruction of Presence in *The Winter's Tale*," in *Shakespeare and the Question of Theory*, ed. Patricia Parker (New York: Methuen, 1985), 3-18.

[11]For publication dates of Amyot's translation of Longus, see Gesner, *Shakespeare and the Greek Romance*, 161.

[12]For the influence of Spenser's Book 6 on the pastoral material in *The Winter's Tale*, including the theme of the exposed child, see Bullough, *Narrative and Dramatic Sources*, 121; Pafford, *The Winter's Tale*, lxxvii; and Stephen Orgel, ed., *The Winter's Tale*, Oxford World Classics (Oxford and New York: Oxford University Press, 1996), 43. Bullough also postulates that *The Second Part of the Mirrour of Knighthood* (1583) served as a possible source for the lost child raised by shepherds (121).

[13]Joseph Jacobs, ed., *Daphnis and Chloe: The Elizabethan Version from Amyot's Translation. By Angel Day Reprinted from the Unique Original* (London: David Nutt, 1890), sig. X1. Further citations of *Daphnis and Chloe* will refer to this edition, unless indicated otherwise, and they will be cited parenthetically.

---

[14]Christopher Gill, trans. Daphnis and Chloe, in *Collected Ancient Greek Novels*, ed. B. P. Reardon (Berkeley and Los Angeles: University of California Press, 1989), 285-348, 347.

[15]It is helpful to review the similarity of the storylines. Two years prior to Chloe's exposure, the shepherd Lamon discovers a baby boy and brings the bundle to his wife, Myrtale. The pair raise the child as their own until Dionysophanes, the birth father, apprehends by tokens that Daphnis is his son. Dionysophanes had abandoned the infant eighteen years previously on account of an already existing large family and its resulting monetary strain: And "as yet he had not attempted the fortune of the worlde" (sig. U2v).

[16]Brian P. Levack, *The Witch-Hunt in Early Modern Europe*, 2nd edition (London and New York: Longman, 1995), 90-91, 55. Levack notes that most witches were not burned alive, but were "garrotted," or strangled, before their purification by flames (91). For further discussions on the relationship between woman and witchcraft in this period, see Keith Thomas, "Witchcraft in England: The Crime and its History," in *Religion and the Decline of Magic* (1971; London: Penguin Books, 1991), 517-558; and James Sharp, "Women and Witchcraft," in *Instruments of Darkness* (London: Penguin Books, 1997), 169-189.

[17]Marianne Hester, "Patriarchal Reconstruction and Witch Hunting," in *Witchcraft in Early Modern Europe*, eds. Jonathan Barry, Marianne Hester, and Gareth Roberts (Cambridge: Cambridge University Press, 1996), 296. For a discussion of witchcraft and its relation to female sexuality in the play, see Kirstie Gulick Rosenfield, "Nursing Nothing: Witchcraft and Female Sexuality in *The Winter's Tale*," *Mosaic* 35, no.1 (2002): 95-112. Rosenfield argues that Shakespeare's play subverts witchcraft belief by

exposing the artifice that sustains those beliefs and the male fear that produces them. See also David Schalkwyk, "'A Lady's 'Verily' Is as Potent as a Lord's': Women, Word and Witchcraft in *The Winter's Tale*," *ELR* 22 (1992): 242-72. Schalkwyk argues the bewitching influence of woman in the play subverts the transcendental unity of language, since women's words are shifting and unreliable.

[18]Nevill Coghill, "Six Points of Stage-Craft," in *Shakespeare The Winter's Tale: A Casebook*, ed. Kenneth Muir (London: Macmillan & Co., 1968), 198-213, 201.

[19]Charles Frey, "Tragic Structure in *The Winter's Tale*: The Affective Dimension," in *Shakespeare's Romances Reconsidered*, eds. Carol McGinnis Kay and Henry E. Jacobs (Lincoln and London: The University Of Nebraska Press, 1978 ), 113-124.

[20]Daryl W. Palmer, "Jacobean Muscovites: Winter, Tyranny, and Knowledge in *The Winter's Tale*," *Shakespeare Quarterly*, 46 (1995): 323-339, 331. Palmer argues here that Hermione's invocation of Ivan the Terrible only serves to highlight Leontes' lack of pity toward his wife.

[21]John Boswell, *The Kindness of Strangers* (London: The Penguin Press, 1988), 97. Boswell finds that the most common way to expose a child in late antiquity was to place it in a public place (110). This reference was brought to my attention by Mark Fortier in "Married with Children: *The Winter's Tale* and Social History; or, Infacticide in Earlier Seventeenth-Century England," *Modern Language Quarterly* 57 (1996): 579-603. Punning on the idea of critical "infacticide," Fortier explores the problem of reading *The Winter's Tale* as a historically representative text on marriage and children, though he says little on actual infanticide.

[22]Ibid., 109.

[23]For the full complexity of the argument, see Boswell's chapter, "Rome: Literary Flesh and Blood," 95-137.

[24]Ibid., 126, 130.

[25]For a historical account of childbirth as woman's dominion in the early modern period, see David Cressy, "Childbed Mysteries," in *Birth, Marriage & Death* (Oxford: Oxford University Press, 1997), 15-34.

[26]Helen Hackett points out that early modern commentators on childbirth believed that imprisonment could be detrimental to the unborn child ("'Gracious Be the Issue': Maternity and Narrative in Shakespeare's Late Plays," in *Shakespeare's Late Plays: New Readings*, eds. Jennifer Richards and James Knowles [Edinburgh: Edinburgh University Press, 1999], 25-39, 28).

[27]Gesner, *Shakespeare and The Greek Romance*, 119. In Sidney, Pastorella's birth mother, Claribell, willfully exposes her child in order to save the newborn from her father's anger (6.6.6-7). Like Hermione, Claribell gives birth to a daughter while imprisoned.

[28]The pairing of wolves and bears seems more comedic than "kites and ravens," especially since it was a she-wolf who had famously nursed the twins Romulus and Remus, brothers brought up by a shepherd family. The pairing may point to the comic underpinning of the abandonment in that Perdita's exposure is ultimately governed by providence.

[29]Ruth Nevo, *Shakespeare's Other Language* (New York and London: Methuen, 1987), 118.

[30]Carol Thomas Neely, "Incest and Issue in the Romances: *The Winter's Tale,"* in *Broken Nuptials in Shakespeare's Plays (*New Haven and London: Yale University Press, 1985), 166-209, 191.

[31]Stanley Wells, "Shakespeare and Romance," 66. For a similar view, see also Gesner, *Shakespeare and The Greek Romance*, 121.

[32]Anne Barton argues that in *The Winter's Tale* the human imagination, the spider in the cup, has the potential to engender harm: "Whether visible or not, the spider in the cup is itself innocuous: it is the human imagination that is destructive and deadly" ("Leontes and the Spider: Language and Speaker in Shakespeare's Last Plays," in *Shakespeare's Styles: Essays in Honour of Kenneth Muir,* eds., Philip Edwards, Inga-Stina Ewbank, C. K. Hunter [Cambridge: Cambridge University Press, 1980], 131-50, 133).

[33]See Susan Snyder, "Mamillius and Gender Polarization in *The Winter's Tale*, in *Shakespeare Quarterly* 50 (1990): 1-8, 5. Snyder locates Mamillius tragically in the middle of the play's male and female gender domain: "In a world that ruthlessly polarizes male and female, Mamillius can't survive. Unable to be an ally, he can only be a victim" (8).

[34]E. M. W. Tillyard epitomizes this critical viewpoint: "It is through Perdita's magnificence that we accept as valuable the new life into which the play is made to issue"("The Tragic Pattern," in *Shakespeare's The Winter's Tale: A Casebook*, ed. Kenneth Muir [London: Macmillan & Co., 1968], 80-97, 85). Tillyard further argues that

*The Winter's Tale* completes the tragic pattern of "prosperity to destruction, regeneration, and still fairer prosperity" (80). See also G. Wilson Knight, "'Great Creating Nature': An Essay on *The Winter's Tale*," in *The Crown of Life: Essays in Interpretation of Shakespeare's Final Plays*, vol. 3 (1947; London and New York: Routledge, 2002), 76-128. Wilson views the "creative spirit in man" as the force that binds the individual to "'great creating Nature'"; the return of Perdita to Sicily helps to institute the release back to nature (127). See also Sir Arthur Quiller-Couch, *Shakespeare's Workmanship* (Cambridge: Cambridge University Press, 1931), 230. For a discussion of the play's two movements from destruction to prosperity, see Ernest Schanzer, "The Structural Pattern," in *Shakespeare's The Winter's Tale: A Casebook*, 87-97. Schanzer writes: "Shakespeare has divided the play into a predominantly destructive half and a predominately creative and restorative half; into a winter half, concentrating on the desolation that Leontes spreads at this court, and a spring and summer half, concentrating on the values represented by the mutual love of Florizel and Perdita and the reunions at the finale" (88-89). See also Richard Proudfoot, "Verbal Reminiscence and the Two-Part Structure of *The Winter's Tale*," in *The Winter's Tale: Critical Essays*, ed. Maurice Hunt (New York: Garland, 1995), 280-97.

[35]In *Daphnis and Chloe*, the shepherd Lamon sees the baby Daphnis with his expensive tokens, and at first he desires only the riches, not the infant. But Lamon is overcome with great shame and compunction; his humiliation occurs when he realizes that a nursing goat has demonstrated greater humanity than him (Book One).

[36] Greene's narrator state that "the young prince had allured her [Fawnia] to folly: he went, therefore, now to complain to the king how greatly he was abused."

[37] C. L. Barber's description of the festive atmosphere in Elizabethan holiday revels bears a likeness to Shakespeare's depiction of the wife's bawdy jollity: "A saturnalian attitude, assumed by a clear-cut gesture toward liberty, brings mirth, an accession of wanton vitality [ . . . ] The holidays in actual observance were built around the enjoyment of the vital pleasure of moments when nature and society are hospitable to life" [*Shakespeare's Festive Comedy* (Princeton: Princeton University Press, 1959), 7.

[38] Janet Adelman, *Suffocating Mothers* (New York and London: Routledge, 1992), 230.

[39] Peter Lindenbaum, "Time, Sexual Love, and the Uses of Pastoral in *The Winter's Tale*," *Modern Language Quarterly* 33 (1972): 3-22, esp. 10.

[40] *The Tempest*, cited from *The Oxford Shakespeare*, eds. Stanley Wells and Gary Taylor (Oxford: Clarendon Press, 1988).

[41] In *Pandosto*, Dorastus has been contracted to marry the princess of Denmark, Euphania. While the prince objects in spirit to this arranged betrothal, this arrangement underscores the duty of the prince to marry royalty (271-73). For a study that discusses Perdita's fear of rejection, see B. J. Sokol, "Perdita's Tale: dubious piedness," in *Art and Illusion: The Winter's Tale* (Manchester and New York: Manchester University Press, 1994), 116-41, esp. 127-35.

[42] John Anthony Williams, *The Natural Work of Art: The Experience of Romance in Shakespeare's The Winter's Tale* (Cambridge Mass.: Harvard University Press, 1967), 31.

[43]See Joan M. Byles, "*The Winter's Tale*, *Othello*, and *Troiolus and Cressida*: Narcissism and Sexual Betrayal," *American Imago* 36 (1979): 80-93. Leontes does not suffer the anguish of seeing a marriage and family destroyed because he "has no ideal view of love" (89).

## CHAPTER 6

The Comedy of Romantic Suffering: Imogen in Shakespeare's *Cymbeline*


O how full of briers is this working-day world!

--Rosalind, *As You Like It*


Unlike *Pericles* and *The Winter's Tale*, Shakespeare's *Cymbeline* is not based on

prose romance. The play's well-documented sources, Holinshed's *Chronicles* and the

wager story in Boccaccio's *Decameron* and *Frederyke of Jennen*, derive from

Renaissance annals and medieval folk tale, respectively.[1] In addition to this material, the

Arden editor J. M. Nosworthy argues persuasively that an early Elizabethan play, *The*

*Rare Triumphs of Love and Fortune*, provided a dramatic influence for *Cymbeline*. More

radically, Nosworthy contends that *Love and Fortune* should even be "regarded as

Shakespeare's primary source or impulse."[2] What is sure is that *Cymbeline* and *Love and*

*Fortune* share striking similarities.[3] One of the main correlations between the two plays

can be located in the romance structure of their plots, which are both centered around

separation, adventure, and reunion. As Nosworthy states, "The dramatic conduct of

*Cymbeline* requires that Posthumus and Imogen should be parted and re-united [ . . . ] and

that all discordant circumstances should be resolved into a final invulnerable unity"

(xxvii). The romantic scheme of separation and reunion draws specifically on the plot

pattern of Greek romance. In fact, among the three surviving romance dramas produced at court between 1570-1585, two, it would seem, stem directly from ancient romance: *Common Conditions*, printed in 1576 (based on the lost prose romance *The most famous historie of Galiarbus Duke of Arabia*) and, important for this study, *Love and Fortune*, performed for Queen Elizabeth I in 1582.[4] The plot formula of Greek romance, with its basic tripartite pattern of love, separation, and marriage, was adapted to the episodic and progressive morality play structure of the sixteenth-century commercial theater. As David Bevington observes, "From the romantic saga of separation, wandering, and reunion, [popular dramatists] extracted a formula similar to the moral theme of fall from grace, temporary prosperity of evil, and divine reconciliation."[5] Within the romance framework of love-leading-to-marriage, *Love and Fortune* invokes the characteristic three-part structure of separation, adventure, and reunion. While this early romantic play does serve as a source for *Cymbeline*, it is not the exclusive source.

As scholars have noted, the sources for *Cymbeline* are diverse and complex.[6] This study will focus on two of the play's analogues: the wager story, rooted in medieval folk literature, and the love story, rooted in Greek romance. The fusion of these storylines brings into sharp focus an interpretative crux, the critical issue of inconsistencies in Imogen's characterization. As early as *Shakespeare's Heroines* (1832), Anna Jameson had perceived that the character of Imogen is "varied and complex." According to Jameson, Imogen shows "vivacity of temper" and at the same time "delicacy, sweetness, and submission."[7] More recently, Janet Adelman reads Imogen's inconsistent characterization as problematic. Adelman argues that Imogen, although initially "shrewd, impetuous, passionate," is later divested of her autonomy, becoming "directionless" and "passive": when she is disguised as the boy Fidele, Imogen's resourcefulness and volition

are subordinated to an ascendant male power that dominates the second half of the play.[8]
Paula S. Berggren finds that Imogen's role reflects a split between Shakespearean
comedy and romance: Imogen's male disguise effects the transition from the "resourceful
virgins" in romantic comedies to the wives or "beatified mothers" in romance: the
heroine's "supposed death and apparent resurrection" bind her to the tragicomic sphere of
"life-in-death," the rhythmic pattern of destruction and regeneration.[9]

These critical evaluations point to a fundamental disjointedness in Imogen's
character, both in her psychological flux from activity to passivity and in her social
transition from maiden to wife. This study argues, however, that Imogen's character is
irregular precisely because Shakespeare constructs the heroine from disparate sources:
*Love and Fortune* on the one hand, the wager story on the other. The conflation of these
stories gives Imogen her complexity; specifically, it creates a heroine who responds
differently to erotic suffering. Imogen's suffering is correlated with what I will refer to as
"external" and "internal" obstacles, deterrents that block young love. In *Cymbeline*,
external obstacles have a foundation in the adventure plot of Greek romance, while
internal obstacles, psychological in nature, evolve from the "deceived wife theme" of the
medieval wager story.[10]

As previously stated, *Love and Fortune* has roots in the generic formula of Greek
romance. In this model, external forces, such as bandits, evildoers, or family members,
obstruct the union of the primary couple. These perilous obstacles test the absolute worth
of the pair: their ability to overcome tribulation and still remain true to their mutual
commitment. Aptly, Mikhail Bakhtin's name for the genre, the "adventure novel of
ordeal," embodies the idea that obstacles or "ordeals" must be overcome before the lovers

reunite: "There are the usual obstacles and adventures of lovers [ . . . ] a storm at sea, a *shipwreck*, a miraculous rescue, an attack by *pirates*, *captivity* and *prison*, an attempt on the innocence of the hero and heroine . . . recognition and failures of recognition, presumed betrayals, and attempts on chastity and fidelity . . . "(Bakhtin's emphasis).[11] Although these impediments threaten the very fabric of the romantic relationship, the plot design of the "adventure novel of ordeal" stipulates, in conventional terms, that the lovers will triumph over adversity. In Bakhtin's words," The novel ends happily with the lovers united in marriage."[12] In Greek romance, the hero and heroine are inundated by outside or external obstacles. Their suffering for love possesses a comic undertone in accordance with the genre's formulaic, fairy-tale conclusion.

The wager story in *Cymbeline* introduces an element outside the Greek romance formula, a psychological or internal component of marital jealousy and cruelty. The best-known version of the wager story is found in Boccaccio's *Decameron* (Second day, Ninth tale). It is interesting that the stories that belong to this day tell of people who triumph over fortune.[13] According to one critic, "the topic itself of the Second Day seems to formulate the fundamental principle of the Greek romances: 'those who after suffering a series of misfortunes are brought to a state of unexpected happiness.'"[14] While the wager story has aspects of the adventure of ordeal, for instance in the villain's assault on the heroine's chastity, it departs from the Greek romance paradigm that emphasizes an outside threat to the stability of the love relationship. In Boccaccio, the major obstacle that the heroine (Zinevra) encounters originates from within the confederacy of marriage: the crucial assault on her chastity is anchored firmly in her husband's (Bernabò's) exploitation of her person. When Bernabò places a wager of five thousand florins against his wife's chastity, he virtually authorizes the villain, Ambrogiuolo, to seduce his wife.

The suffering that Zinevra goes through--shame, attempted murder, exile, hidden

identity--has a potentially tragic aspect. The heroine's ordeals, serving a didactic purpose,

situate the individual in an uncertain and hostile world: they remind the reader how

"disaster can be brought about by another's malice" and how it can be "reversed by one's

own efforts."[15]

    In *Cymbeline*, Iachimo's assault on Imogen's sexuality represents an external

obstacle, one over which she prevails. On the other hand, Posthumus's participation in

the game of testing Imogen's chastity is an internal obstacle that threatens to destroy the

marriage. The external obstacles, which correspond to adventure romance, relate to the

drama's comedic form. The generic function of these obstacles assures that Imogen will

overcome her enemies or opposition, so that her suffering is fundamentally non-

threatening. When Imogen confronts an exterior barrier, such as a parent or seducer, her

expression of suffering is demonstrably sensational and stylized. As Arthur C. Kirsch

states, "[Imogen] is repeatedly called upon for histrionic displays . . . ."[16] By contrast,

Posthumus's role in the wager story goes beyond the traditional formula of romance. It

unleashes the unpredictability of the individual and with it the potential for tragedy.

When Imogen faces marital betrayal, her suffering takes on an insidious reality as she

struggles to come to terms with the cruel events that besiege her. This different sort of

obstacle produces a heroine who moves in both a tragic and comic sphere, and the result

is a character who can appear more dislocated than uniform.[17]

# I

A close look at the play *Love and Fortune* sheds light on Shakespeare's use of the "adventure novel of ordeal" tradition in *Cymbeline*. *Love and Fortune* follows the basic schemata in Greek romance of mutual love, separation, and reunion. The following summary of the plot highlights the external obstacles that block the hero and heroine's marriage. The separation of the lovers begins immediately upon the disclosure of Hermione and Fidelia's clandestine love pact.[18] Because the relationship is deemed "Unequall," Fidelia's family opposes the union. Hermione has made a "conquest of a Princes childe," for the princess has been "beguilde" in love (l. 320). Armenio and Phizanties, Fidelia's brother and father, contend that Hermione has usurped his position as Fidelia's husband.[19] Since the orphaned hero has been raised by the heroine's father, and is thus considered inferior in blood, Phizanties reminds Hermione of his low station, among other issues:

> For my sake cease to love Fidelia still.
>
> Unequall love is enemie to rest,
>
> She is too young to love thee as she should:
>
> And thou Hermione canst conceive the rest
>
> My meaning is she loves not as we would.

> (ll. 450-54)

Despite the father's polite warning and kind meaning, Phizanties orders the hero banished from court. Notwithstanding accusations of "Unequall love" (l. 450), Hermione and Fidelia prove that their devotion to each other is predicated on reciprocal and symmetrical sentiment. The following passage not only illustrates the mutual love of the hero and heroine, but it also calls attention to the primary obstacle that Fidelia and Hermione face together, her brother Armenio:

> The lady of my life, Fidelia is.
>
> Of whome I am, I know belov'd no less,
>
> Then she of me my gratious mistresse.
>
> Severde by Fortune and our cruell foe,
>
> My Lord her brother Prince Armenio.  (ll. 517-21)

Hermione requests that the Vice, Penulo, "bring my Lady to the cave. / Where whilome lovers we were wont to meete, / in secret sorte eche other for to greete" (ll. 522-25). When the Vice double-crosses the hero by informing Armenio of this covert encounter, the brother's anger toward Hermione and obsession with Fidelia's illicit alliance point to his desire for vengeance: "Now serves the time to wreak my foe, / My dastard foe that to dishonour me: / in privie corners seekes to shame me so, / that my discredit might his credit be" (11. 760-64).[20] When Fidelia arrives at the appointed cave before her brother, she reiterates the theme of mutual suffering, unaware that further trouble awaits her. In an apostrophe to Hermione, she says, "Beholde the shiftes that faithful love can make, / See what I dare adventure for thy sake" (ll. 779-780). Hence, she determines to

> draw in equall portion still,
>
> Of both our Fortunes either good or ill.
>
> And sith the lots of our unconstant fate,
>
> Have turned our former blisse to wretched state,
>
> I am content to tread the wofull duance,
>
> That soundes the measure of our haplesse chaunce.  (ll. 796-800)

As her name implies, Fidelia even acquires an allegorical dimension in the play,
representing the precept of fidelity and constancy.

Instead of finding Hermione at the appointed cave, Fidelia comes upon an old
man, Bomelio, who is Hermione's father, exiled years before by the king. When an irate
Armenio discovers his sister in the appointed cave and forces her to return home,
Bomelio casts a spell on him, and he is struck dumb. At this point, the heroine's ordeals
culminate in a bizarre ritual that pits brother against sister. In order to restore Armenio's
speech, Fidelia must be pricked under her "paps," her blood drawn, and washed in her
brother's mouth. According to Bomelio, who speaks here in a comic Italian accent,

> Tis in her pappes, her dugges for der be de tenderest parte,
>
> And de blood de deerest, it comes from de hart.
>
> So she be prickt a little under de brest,
>
> And wash his tunga he speak wit de best.  (ll. 1217-1220)

The pricking of the heroine's blood from her "tenderest parte," I would argue,
metaphorically enacts the ritual deflowering of her virginity. When Fidelia refuses to aid
her brother by undergoing this procedure, she triumphs in a figurative test of her chastity.
Ultimately forced to obey her father's will, Fidelia submits, but she prays that death will
deliver her from such degradation:

> I am content my deerest blod to spill.
>
> Deferre not then, holde take thine ayme at mee,
>
> And strike me through, for I desire to dye.  (ll. 1300-03)

Bomelio saves Fidelia from this violence and symbolic deflowering. The bond, however,
between the two families is ultimately solidified when Fidelia makes a sacrifice of her

blood. Because Armenio remains unable to speak and because Bomelio lies in a stupor (induced by Mercury on account of the destruction of his magic books), Fortune provides a remedy: "the shedding of thy daughters deerest blood, / Shall both to him and to this man doo good" (ll. 1781-2). Hence, Fidelia agrees to being pricked under her "paps" in order to reverse her brother's dumbness. She acts as a sacrificial object in the cure of Bomelio's and Armenio's illnesses and as the redeemer of the two families in lawful marriage. Due to the hero's new-found aristocratic standing as son of the banished courtier Bomelio, Venus requests that the couple "together be conjoyned still" (l. 1756). Phizanties repents his bad conduct toward Hermione and endorses the matrimonial alliance by offering amends to Bomelio: "In token of our faithfull amitie, / We will be joyned in neere affinitie" (ll. 1819-20). After the lovers' separation and subsequent mishaps, the conclusion of the play turns on the parental consent of the couple in marriage.

**II**

Like Fidelia, Imogen confronts external obstacles and surmounts them. These obstacles are comedic in nature precisely because they are successfully defeated. In Act 3 of *Cymbeline*, Pisanio receives a letter that maligns Imogen's reputation. Tricked by the "false Italian" Iachimo (3.2.04), Posthumus is deceived into slandering his wife's chastity. As Pisanio says, "She's punish'd for her truth; and undergoes, / More goddess-like than wife-like, such assaults / As would take in some virtue" (3.2.07-09). Ordered by Posthumus to murder Imogen with his "own hands" (3.4.33-35), Pisanio believes that the sharp edge of slander has already cut his mistress's throat (3.4.33-35). This personification of murder, one in which slander wounds "sharper than the sword," is one of many graphic images in the play that creates the motif of death. In terms of genre, it is commonplace in the Greek model of romance for the hero and heroine to idealize death as a virtuous alternative to life without the other. Equally, the plot device of presumed death commonly acts as an obstacle that delays the reunion of separated lovers. Just as the protagonists of Greek romance endure deathlike "assaults" for "truth" or fidelity, Imogen suffers for her unyielding truth to Posthumus: "O, that husband, / My supreme crown of grief! and those repeated / Vexations of it!" (1.7.04-05). This passionate exclamation of grief is characteristic of the overwrought tone of Imogen's erotic suffering in the face of external blocking forces.

As the play opens, exterior obstacles have already attacked Posthumus and Imogen's private alliance. Imogen endures assaults from many directions. King Cymbeline has confined her and banished Posthumus on account of their clandestine marriage. Since the pair have wedded without parental approval, Imogen predicts that she will be the object of the court's hostility and disapprobation: "You must be gone, / And I shall here abide the hourly shot / Of angry eyes: not comforted to live, / But that there is this jewel in the world / That I may see again" (1.2.19-13). Interestingly, these lines are the first that Imogen speaks to Posthumus. It is noteworthy that Imogen emphasizes her distressed state, a despair that has gone past hope, and even further, "that way past grace" (1.2.68). In this abject despair, Imogen links Posthumus's absence with death; only in anticipation of his return will she continue to live. Moreover, she daily fears Cymbeline's retribution: "I something fear my father's wrath, but nothing (Always reserv'd my holy duty) what / His rage can do on me" (1.2.17-19). In this passage, Imogen makes a significant distinction between her father's "wrath" and his "rage." While Imogen's reference to "wrath" in this statement suggests the king's frustration or indignation, "rage" implies his violent action against Imogen. Even the Queen notes that the "fire of rage is in him" (1.1.08). Indeed, Cymbeline's outbursts of anger threaten Imogen with mortal harm: "Away with her, / And pen her up" (1.2.84-85), or "let her languish / A drop of blood a day, and being aged / Die of this folly" (1.2.88-89). Such prolonged torture would culminate in a languorous and drawn-out death. The strong emphasis on Imogen's erotic suffering in these initial scenes is part of the play's romance/comedy frame. It enables Imogen to emerge as a non-tragic victim of her family's prejudice against Posthumus.

Posthumus is the first among several characters in the play to describe Imogen as a victim of love. To his new wife he says, "I my poor self did exchange you / To your so infinite loss" (1.2.50-51). During this exchange of commitment tokens, Posthumus observes that the pair's secret marriage has exposed Imogen to loss.[21] The idea that Imogen is subject to injury is so pervasive in Cymbeline's court that her suffering becomes uncomfortably amusing. For example, the Queen excuses Imogen's absence at court due to her heartache, believing that the frail princess would be a likely victim of Cymbeline's "sharp speeches:" "She's a lady / So tender of rebukes that words are strokes, / And strokes death to her" (3.5.39-40). As the Queen's disingenuous words suggest, the nature of Imogen's victimization also has a comedic undertone. Because the Queen, the cardboard "crafty devil" (2.1.51), conspires to have her son Cloten marry the princess, Imogen's victimization carries the threat of the "clotpoll's" (4.2.184) violation. The Second Lord, who curses the many evils that Imogen "endur'st"--including a hateful wooer, a browbeating father, and a plotting stepmother--hopes that her marital chastity can withstand the onslaught:

> The heavens hold firm
>
> The walls of thy dear honour, keep unshak'd
>
> That temple, thy fair mind, that thou mayst stand,
>
> T' enjoy thy banish'd lord and this great land!  (2.1.56-64)

The "standing walls" of Imogen's honor are equated with the preservation of her sexual integrity, while the "solid temple" of her mind refers to courage and faithfulness to Posthumus. The hyperbole of the passage indicates that the defilement of Imogen would result in a national crisis to "this great land," as if the violation of her person relates to the corruption of the entire body politic. The threat to the princess by Cloten, a veritable "puttock" (1.2.71), not only has a farcical quality, but is connected to the comic idea of Imogen's mock death.

According to Imogen, Cloten's attempts at wooing are "[a]s fearful as a siege" (3.4.136). The heroine's pseudo-distress arises from Cloten's clumsy attempts at lovemaking; consequently, her rebuffs provoke Cloten to mount a make-believe sexual assault in the following speech (although he actually hunts for her later). Cloten fantasizes that he will first kill Posthumus and then rape Imogen: "[Posthumus] on the ground, my speech of insultment ended on his dead body, and when my lust hath dined (which, as I say, to vex her I will execute in the clothes that she so prais'd) to the court I'll knock her back, foot her home again" (3.5.141-45). In this violent but absurd vision of revenge, Cloten blurs the boundaries between murder and molestation. By wearing the clothes of the dead Posthumus and wishing to ravish Imogen in these garments, Cloten visualizes the princess in a symbolic clasp of brutality and death. This sexualized charade recurs when Imogen transfers Posthumus's anger at her alleged immodesty onto her person: "I must be ripp'd:--to pieces with me!" (3.4.54). Her death wish recalls Posthumus's earlier urge "to tear her limb-meal!" upon learning of her supposed infidelity (2.4.147). Death, in this case the fantasy of dismemberment, is an expression of the heroine's overwrought despair, rather than a sadistic fantasy that constructs the heroine as a tragic victim of male resentment.[22]

Here Imogen's grief occurs in response to external obstacles. Her melodramatic suffering is a condition of passionate love, much as Rosalind, in *As You Like It,* identifies "careless desolation" as a symptom of lovesickness (3.2.368-69).[23] Whereas Rosalind understands that the conventional signs of heartache, such as a lean cheek and pale complexion, are merely well-worn conceits, Imogen candidly adopts the rhetoric of suffering-in-love as the bedrock of romantic affliction. In a manneristic gesture, she connects suffering to the poetic sphere of wronged love. For example, Imogen hopes that Posthumus, having been exiled, is distressed and shaken by their separation: "That we two are asunder; let that grieve him; / Some griefs are med'cinable, that is one of them / For it doth physic love" (3.2.32-34). If health and contentment do not "physic love," then desolation and grief will. Imogen pushes the idea of romantic anguish into the realm of worldly loss or death: "There cannot be a pinch in death / More sharp than this" (1.2.61-62). And her determination to stay "senseless" to Cymbeline's "wrath" even means a figurative death when "all pangs, all fears" are subdued (1.2.66-67). This ominous statement foreshadows Imogen's presumed death (as Fidele) when Guiderius and Arviragus say the dirge, "Fear no more the heat o' th' sun, / Nor the furious winter's rages" (4.2.258-59). Being senseless to pangs and fears, whether from love, nature or the tyrant's stroke, is tantamount to annihilation. Finally, Imogen's gift of a ring to Posthumus elicits a perverse request: "But keep it till you woo another wife, / When Imogen is dead" (1.2.44-45). Posthumus mirrors Imogen's language by calling upon the "bonds of death" to prevent him from ever loving another (1.2.47-48). As Harley Granville-Barker observes, the verse in *Cymbeline* is "rich in texture." He continues: "if sometimes it seems overrich, this suits it to the frank artifice of the play."[24] In effect, Imogen's luxuriant use of poetic images, ones that describe near-death suffering, brings an exaggerated artifice to the finality and tragedy of death. Fittingly, she feels a sense of "heaven" when Posthumus "encounters [her] with orisons" (1.4.32-33).

At Cymbeline's court, Imogen is cast as a victim of her "hand-fast" marriage to Posthumus (1.6.78). In itself, this theme is not remarkable. What interests us, though, is that Imogen reveals in her sense of victimization a preoccupation with romantic anguish, as she appropriates the mode of lovesickness. For Imogen, suffering keeps alive the ideal of mutual love, and thus pain--even death-- becomes a measure of the intensity of passion. Because the heroine wants to preserve the ideal of mutual affection between the pair, especially since Posthumus has been exiled, she embellishes the familiar topoi of love's misery. When Imogen considers Posthumus's banishment, she exaggerates an already sentimentalized image of departing lovers:

> I would have broke mine eye-strings, crack'd them, but
>
> To look upon him, till the diminution
>
> Of space had pointed him sharp as my needle:
>
> Nay, followed him, till he had melted from

The smallness of a gnat, to air: and then

Have turn'd mine eye, and wept (1.4.17-22).

Although Imogen imagines a depature that she has not actually witnessed, the emotionally-charged scene of leave taking is further telescoped in the next lines; here Imogen focuses her attention on the sentimentalized moment of the couple's good-bye: what she would say to Posthumus, what she would have him swear, and what she would charge him to do (1.4.25-35). In the same passage, Imogen places herself in the conventional, romantic scheme of young lovers who are thwarted by the elder generation, since Cymbeline and the Queen have disrupted the princess's contract to Posthumus. Imogen specifically compares her father to old man winter, the "tyrannous breathing of the north," who, as a figure of death, destroys springtime love by shaking "all buds from growing" (1.4.36-37). She later adds Cloten and the Queen to the list of malefactors who block young love: "A father cruel, and a step-dame false, / A foolish suitor to a wedded lady, / That hath her husband banish'd" (1.6.1-05). In that same speech, Imogen invokes Posthumus as her "supreme crown of grief," lamenting "those repeated / Vexations of it!" as previously noted (1.7.04-05). Imogen suffers expressly on account of her devotion to Posthumus. Her comic vexations, her crown of thorns, idealize pain in terms of the conventional plight of star-crossed love.

### III

The wager story accounts for two aspects of Imogen's erotic victimization. The first component derives from the stock material of adventure romance, particularly from the Greek paradigm. As mentioned, this paradigm revolves around a series of obstacles that obstruct the union of the primary couple. The second component deals with

Posthumus's violent reversal of love for Imogen, as well as his satiric hatred of the female sex in general ("I'll write against them, / Detest them, curse them"[2.4.183-84]). We will see that Posthumus's cruelty, his transformation from lover to enemy, causes Imogen to face the dire reality of betrayal and disaffection. This abuse, arising from within the boundaries of their marital alliance, marks a turning point in Imogen's response to suffering. The wager story begins when Posthumus defends Imogen's honor against the slurs of the villain Iachimo. Provoked by Iachimo's attack on Imogen's chastity, Posthumus submits to the bet, risking his marital ring for ten thousand ducats of gold: "I will wage against your gold, gold to it: my ring I hold dear as my finger, 'tis part of it" (1.5.129-30). Posthumus agrees to gamble on the inviolability of Imogen's chastity, while Iachimo stakes his gold on the ravishment of "the dearest bodily part of [his] mistress" (1.5.146-47). Iachimo admits that the wager has less to do with disproving Imogen's virtue than with crushing Posthumus's self-assuredness: "I make my wager rather against your confidence than her reputation" (1.5.107-08). Posthumus's acceptance of the wager indicates his desire for personal vindication over and beyond protecting his wife's good name; it also points to the selfish thrill of competition at his partner's expense. With such underlying reference to her objectification, Imogen becomes a pawn in a game controlled by men.

Iachimo's role in the wager plot will be examined first. That Iachimo has no apparent motive for sabotaging the relationship between Posthumus and Imogen places him squarely in the network of romance figures who exist as deterrents to the story's love match. Like a standard blocking figure, Iachimo aims to destroy the trust between the main protagonists, and his action follows in the pattern of romantic wrongdoers, villains who venture to seduce, rape, or destroy the hero or heroine. These villains cause the protagonists to suffer, and they suffer precisely because they oppose the forces that act against them. In *Cymbeline*, the obstacles that threaten the marriage of Posthumus and Imogen involve not only the malice of Iachimo, but also the wickedness of the Queen and Cloten. (Cymbeline, who is by Imogen's "step-dame govern'd," is a passive blocking figure [2.1.57]).[25] Because Posthumus is banished from court, Imogen takes the brunt of the abuse: the Queen, if unable to force her to marry Cloten, will poison her outright (1.6.80-81), and Cloten, if unable to wed Imogen freely, will possess her in revenge by force (3.5.79-80, 3.5.146-47). Iachimo's failed attempt at Imogen's seduction, the "assault" he makes "to her chastity" (1.5.159-60), aligns him closely with Cloten's comic blocking role as obstructer and violator.

Iachimo's failed seduction of Imogen compels him to steal into the princess's bedchamber while hidden in a chest. In the dead of night, Iachimo stalks over her as she sleeps: "O sleep, thou ape of death, lie dull upon her, / And be her sense but as a monument, / Thus in a chapel lying" (2.2.31-33). Like a necrophiliac, Iachimo finds sexual arousal in an image of death, and he wields his power by visually assailing the most defenseless of entities, a lifeless or slumbering body. Shakespeare intensifies this scene of voyeurism by associating Iachimo with the historical rapist, Tarquin. In the bedroom scene, Iachimo refers to himself as that very same Tarquin, the despotic Roman ruler, who had infamously "wounded" the matrimonial chastity of Lucretia: "The chastity he wounded" (2.2.14). Likewise, in Shakespeare's narrative poem, *The Rape of Lucrece*, Tarquin surprises Lucrece at night, and he defiles her as she lies "at the mercy of his mortal sting" (364). In that poem, Shakespeare makes the connection between death, sexuality, and victimization patently clear, specifically in phrases such as "Where like a virtuous monument she lies / To be admired of lewd and unhallowed eyes" (391-92) and "Showing life's triumph in the map of death, / And death's dim look in life's mortality" (402-03). In *Cymbeline*, however, Iachimo's "rape" of Imogen is reduced to a metaphorical anatomization of her body parts, notwithstanding that Iachimoe covertly kisses the heroine: her skin is whiter than "fresh lily"; her lips like "Rubies unparagon'd"; her breath like perfume; her lids "canopy" the "windows" that open to her soul "white and azure lac'd" (2.2.15-23). The telltale mole on her left breast, "cinque-spotted: like the crimson drops / I' th' bottom of a cowslip" (2.2.38-39), combines the delicacy of a flower (the female) with the stain of blood (deflowering), a symbolic ravishment of Imogen's virginity.

Iachimo's symbolic rape of Imogen lends itself to a less than tragic interpretation, in that her violation does not result in physical despoiling or death. This symbolic rape differs from Lucretia's brutal violation and tragic suicide, where self-slaughter is a heroic act that mitigates sexual degradation and humiliation.[26] Furthermore, the comedic underpinning of Iachimo's connivance can also be attributed to Imogen's role-playing as victim: she unconsciously participates in Iachimo's scheme. In the bedchamber, Imogen fashions herself in the tradition of wronged, enshrining herself in a type of death tomb. As Imogen extinguishes the candles and rests in darkness, she prays that the gods protect her from "fairies and the tempters of the night" (2.2.10). This prayer adumbrates Imogen's presumed death (as Fidele) when her brothers, Guiderius and Arviragus, summon female fairies to safeguard the lifeless body: "If he be gone, he'll make his grave a bed: / With female fairies will his tome be haunted" (4.2.215-16). Imogen also surrounds herself in a romantic heritage that underscores the danger of erotic love. Her

andirons are "winking Cupids" (2.4.89), an emblem of blind love and its recklessness.

Imogen's seductive and rich wall tapestries link passion with death: there is "Proud

Cleopatra, when she met her Roman" (2.4.70), and "Chaste Dian, bathing" (2.4.82).[27]

While Cleopatra commits suicide in sexual rapture over Antony, the picture of Diana

invokes the story of Actaeon, a youth who is punished with dismemberment for gazing

on the bathing goddess. Diana also represents the virtue of chastity for which women,

like Lucretia, sometimes do die. Moreover, Iachimo notices that Imogen's night reading

is Ovid's "tale of Tereus," the leaf turned down at the place where "Philomel gave up"

(2.2.46). Like Lucretia, Philomel is made wretched prey to male lust and ferocity.[28]

The correlation between comedic victimization and death had occurred earlier

when Iachimo tries to convince Imogen of her husband's infidelity. Iachimo feigns that

Posthumus's disloyalty has aroused his sincere compassion: "your cause doth strike my

heart / With pity that doth make me sick!" (1.7.118-19). In Iachimo's lewd jargon,

Posthumus's supposed falseness consists of base sexual exploits with prostitutes: to

"Slaver with lips"; to "join grips"; to "be partner'd / With tomboys" and "diseas'd

ventures" (1.7.105, 106, 121-22, 123). These acts of lust prove vile to the point of

destruction: "Such boil'd stuff / As well might poison poison!" (1.7.125-26). The poison

that underlies sexual depravity ties thematically back to the supposed poison that the

Queen concocts to kill Pisanio and, if necessary, Imogen. Cornelius deceptively refers to

the "poisonous compounds" he has prepared for the Queen as being "movers of a

languishing death" (1.6.09). In both instances, death by poison is punishment for either

romantic loyalty or disloyalty. In the former, poison or disease represents retribution for sexual faithlessness, and in the latter "languishing death" is a penalty for Imogen's constancy to her exiled husband and for Pisanio's trustworthiness. Nonetheless, this poison is a comic plot device because, relatively harmless, it manages to kill no one.

A further distancing from tragedy can be seen in the different circumstances between Imogen and her mythical counterpart, Philomel. Imogen has recourse to fatherly protection, whereas Philomel is taken far from her father, mutilated, and shut away in isolation. Philomel's family gives her no modicum of safety from the beastly lust of Tereus. Yet Imogen, when fearing the affront of Iachimo, takes refuge in the security of her servant and father: "What ho, Pisanio! / The king my father shall be made acquainted / Of thy assault" (1.7.148-50). Once her chastity is put under threat, Imogen immediately looks to the protection of her father (whom she was righteously condemning for his wrath only a few lines before). This sense of protection, along with Iachimo's relatively innocuous assault, gives rise to a comic scene, relegated to the realm of game as the nature of the wager suggests. Moreover, in 1.7, Imogen confronts Iachimo when she is assaulted by him, and she vigorously shields Posthumus from his accusations of infidelity. When the conniving Iachimo offers to "dedicate" himself to the princess's "sweet pleasure" (1.7.136), she sharply rebukes him: "Away, I do condemn mine ears, that have / So long attended thee" (1.7.141-42). Imogen effortlessly passes the all-important trial of sexual fidelity.

**IV**

The second and larger component of the wager story is Posthumus's treachery. To gamble on Imogen's chastity means that Posthumus cavalierly authorizes an attack on her honor, even condoning Iachimo's attempted "voyage upon her" (1.6.155). Posthumus not only hazards Imogen's safety and virginity (2.4.161-62), but he also becomes a detriment to his own wedded state when he destabilizes the trust and equilibrium of the relationship (in spite of the fact that the secret marriage had already given their union a measure of instability). The wager places Imogen at the center of a sexually-degrading game indiscriminately played out between her beloved partner and a stranger. This game reduces Imogen as princess to an object of exchange between men. Whether Posthumus views her as his prisoner--tied by a "manacle of love" (1.2.53)--or his pawn, Imogen's objectification conveys the same unsettling conclusion: it weakens the integrity of mutual love by involving woman's debasement. Posthumus summons "vengeance, vengeance!" (2.4.160) just before his misogynous "woman's part" speech. The belief in Imogen's infidelity causes Posthumus to transfer his jealous hatred of Imogen to womankind, who are all adulterous "half-workers" (2.4.154). Because woman is debased by birth, and because man is born from the female, it is woman who corrupts mankind: "for there's no motion / That tends to vice in man but I affirm / it is the woman's part" (2.4.172-74). Posthumus goes as far as to imagine Iachimo mounting his wife like a beast, so that she, by association, is equated with an animal. The treacherous threat of vengeance on Imogen, who stands for all adulterous "half-workers" (2.4.154), foregrounds Posthumus's psychological immaturity.

More than a mere game, the wager carries with it a gritty and destructive essence. Posthumus's wedding ring, his stake in the bet, is connected explicitly to the idea of Imogen's negotiable sexuality. Iachimo is the first of the two to equate the loss of the ring with Imogen's base defilement. He goads Posthumus thus: "you know strange fowl light upon neighbouring ponds. Your ring may be stolen too" (1.5.85-87). Although

Posthumus immediately denies that the ring can be exchanged for the immeasurable worth of Imogen's virtue, "the gift of the gods" (1.5.82), he all too easily capitulates to the wager: " I dare you to this match: here's my ring" (1.5.141-42). The ring transforms into a sign that stands for Imogen's sexuality and the sexual organ of the female body.[29] Imogen had earlier invested the ring with the symbolic virtues of traditional marriage: "This diamond was my mother's; take it, heart" (1.2.43). The circularity of the ring represents, it can be inferred, a solidarity between two people; it also suggests an ethic of sexual fidelity. For Imogen, the ring's symbolism of unity will dissolve only with her death: "But keep it till you woo another wife, / When Imogen is dead" (1.2.44-45). By contrast, Posthumus translates his gift to Imogen into the language of marital possession. In exchange for the diamond ring, he gives her the (less costly) token of a bracelet:

> For my sake wear this,
>
> It is a manacle of love, I'll place it
>
> Upon this fairest prisoner.  (1.2.52-54)

Although his speech is endearing, Posthumus describes the exchange of the bracelet in the hierarchal terminology of subordination: master and servant, jailor and prisoner. The idea of bondage that resonates in the phrase "manacle of love" calls forth the image of the chastity belt, a device that encapsulates male control and distrust of female sexuality. But it also reifies Imogen as a commodity: As Valerie Wayne states, "The very object that Posthumus intended as a means to reciprocate his wife's gift and simultaneously control her sexuality then becomes a means for her being put into circulation."[30] Even before Posthumus agrees to the wager, he has reduced Imogen to his possession, while simultaneously framing her as a "prisoner," already guilty of transgression.

Imogen's harrowing escape to Milford Haven serves as a catalyst for an essential change in her attitude about romantic suffering. Her staunch belief in suffering for love first comes under challenge in 3.4, when Pisanio discloses the devastating contents of Posthumus's letter: "Thy mistress, Pisanio, hath played the strumpet in my bed" (3.4.21-22). Posthumus endeavors to revenge his wife's so-called infidelity by entrusting his servant to kill her, or as Imogen bluntly puts it, he "Bring[s] me here to kill me" (3.4.119). This breach of faith takes Imogen to the nadir of her plight, from comic suffering to the possibility of death. Her response to the shock of the letter includes holding onto a sentimentalized conception of romantic suffering. Choosing death over life without her husband's adoration--"I am / Dead to my husband" (3.4.131-32)--she orders Pisanio to stab her in the breast: "I draw the sword myself, take it, and hit / The innocent mansion of my love, my heart: / Fear not, 'tis empty of all things, but grief: / Thy master is not there, who was indeed / The riches of it" (3.4.68-72). The poetic trope of the heart as the seat of love, along with the lover as its riches, is a conventional conceit, and Imogen's rhetorical posturing coincides with her idealization of suffering and death (here suicide by the hands of another) as constructions of passionate love. We have only to compare this scene with the attempted murder of Marina in *Pericles* to see Imogen's affected notion of loss, especially when Marina pleads with Leonine to spare her life: "I never did hurt in all my life. / I never spake bad word, nor did ill turn / To any living creature." Unlike those of Imogen, Marina's phrases lack stylistic flourish, and her simple pleas for mercy reflect a maiden's sense of humility. Imogen, though, employs a stylized metaphor of forsaken love in her plea for death, attempting to convey her grief and to evoke Pisanio's pity.

Imogen shifts her tone in this scene, however, as the realization of Posthumus's betrayal fractures her romantic illusion. The many caustic references to her impending murder display her ire as she becomes disillusioned with ideal love. Her rhetorical questions and wry observations reveal an astonishment at being the object of Posthumus's faithlessness. Imogen's anger perhaps originates in knowing that Posthumus has arranged this assassination without confronting her directly. To Pisanio, she effusively releases her indignation within a short space of 40 lines: "Why, I must die: /And If I do not by thy hand, thou art / No servant of thy master's (3.4.75-77); "Come, here's my heart [ . . . ] Obedient as the scabbard. What is here?" (3.4.79-81); "Prithee, dispatch: / The lamb entreats the butcher / Where's thy knife?" (3.4.97-98). "Why hast thou gone so far, / To be unbent when thou hast ta'en thy stand, / Th' elected deer before thee?" (3.4.109-111). Imogen's acrimony is motivated by her offense at Posthumus's treachery; her astonishment at her husband's disloyalty is exacerbated by Pisanio's benevolent duplicity: playing the ever-faithful servant, Pisanio has in reality not come to slay her at all.

In addition to Posthumus's callousness, Imogen's source of indignation also arises from her acute awareness that she has put herself at risk, tempted fate and her father's wrath, to marry Posthumus. In the meantime, he has neither respected nor trusted in the merit of such a bold sacrifice: "And thou, Posthumus, thou that didst set up / My disobedience 'gainst the king my father, / And make me put into contempt the suits / Of princely fellows" (3.4.89-92). Imogen's disobedient decision to marry Posthumus now seems maddingly ironic. For it was Imogen who, disdaining the suits of princes, had lowered herself to wed Posthumus: a "poor but worthy gentleman," according to the First

Gentleman (1.1.07), and perhaps worse, a "beggar," in the words of Cymbeline (1.2.72).

Still, Imogen's feelings of indignant frustration are rooted in her moral indignation rather

than fearing a chink in her elevated social rank. She makes it plain that her elopement,

her unshakable faith in Posthumus's worthiness, was "no act of common passage, but / A

strain of rareness" (3.4.93-94). Imogen's unfaltering belief and trust in Posthumus's

virtuous character changes what appears to be a rebellious choice of husband into a

unique and special decision. As Iachimo intuits, the marriage "must be weighed rather by

her value rather than his own" (1.5.13-14). But was Imogen's judgment sound? The play

does not give an easy answer; on the contrary, it complicates the issue of Posthumus's

worthiness.[31]

We recall that the Frenchman in Italy ascribes to Posthumus no particular

excellence above the courtly norm (1.5.10-11). On the other side, he is commendable and

a good part of his worthiness seems to derive from his family's military renown. The

First Gentleman explains that Posthumus is named after his dead father, Sicilius

Leonatus, a solider who had won much "glory and admired success" (1.1.32). Although

the mother dies in childbirth, the name given to the orphaned baby, "Posthumus," is a

tribute to the child's noble father; the child's full name, Posthumus Leonatus, testifies to

the legacy of his father's prowess and the bravery of his two brothers, who "[d]ied with

their swords in hand" (1.1.36). The deeds of the patriarch resonate in the play as a model

of masculine valor, so that the memory of the dead father acts as proof of Posthumus's

good character. The family's fame has grown from their martial reputation, not from

royalty or wealth. In fact, the princess later identifies Posthumus by his "Martial thigh"

(4.2.310), his "brawns of Hercules" (4.2.311), and his "Jovial face" (4.2.311) when she thinks he has died. Imogen has entrusted her welfare and future to reputation, but after the betrayal she grows exasperated that Posthumus has not fulfilled the expectation of his expected honor.

Instead of seeing herself as a victim of Posthumus's slander, Imogen infers that her "wound" has given her a forceful impetus to act: "I have heard I am a strumpet, and mine ear, / Therein false struck, can take no greater wound" (3.4.115-16). Injury no longer indicates the aesthetic of romantic suffering; it now spurs on the heroine to discover the rationale behind Posthumus's accusation of promiscuity. The Queen reinforces the idea that Imogen is the agent of her own destiny when she conjectures that the princess, "wing'd with fervour of her love," has flown from court to find Posthumus (3.5.62). While the Queen thinks that Imogen has gone "to dishonour" (or even to death if "despair hath sei'zd her"), Imogen actually flies from court to reunite with Posthumus and inadvertently to rectify her honor (3.5.64, 3.5.61). Since Pisanio suspects that some "villain" has plotted "cursed injury" against the pair (3.4.122-24), he urges Imogen to disguise herself as a boy to uncover the deceitful plot. Ironically, by following this plan, one that demands courage and pluck, attributes usually associated with the comic heroine, Imogen enters a scenario of palpable endangerment and peril. As Joan Carr writes, "The mean tricks that Shakespeare deliberately seems to be perpetrating on his heroine draw the absolutes of myth into a more problematical realm."[32] At this point, the regular, festive ending of romance (or the redemption of myth) totters in the balance.

One of the dangers that Imogen faces is the peril of cross-dressing. Her disguise suggests that she will need manly valor to survive, even though such valor is portrayed as light-heartedly waggish. To become a young man demands that Imogen submerge her true identity, wearing a mind as "[d]ark" as her "fortune." As Pisanio continues to warn, "to appear [your]self, must not yet be / But by self-danger" (3.4.146-48). Imogen prepares herself for the hazard and affront of the ordeal, not knowing yet that she must assume the guise of the opposite sex: "Though peril to my modesty, not death on't, / I would adventure!" (3.4.153-55). After Imogen leaves home to search for Posthumus, the journey takes the princess down a precarious path. As Pisanio comments plaintively, "O Imogen, / Safe mayst thou wander, safe return again!" (3.5.105-06). The primary danger that Imogen faces during her adventure, one that consists in "tread[ing] a course" near the "residence of Posthumus" (3.4.148-50), calls for the cultural traits of masculine bravado and venturesomeness. Thus, in order to find Posthumus, Imogen must "forget to be a woman" (3.4.156) and adopt the "waggish courage" of a young man: "Ready in gibes, quick-answer'd, saucy, and / As quarrelous as the weasel" (3.4.159-61). Imogen, as the boy Fidele, reacts to the accusation of her infidelity by taking action, which she describes as nothing less than warlike: "This attempt / I am soldier to, and will abide it with / A prince's courage" (3.4.185-86). At Cymbeline's court, the "pangs of barr'd affection" (1.2.13) are relegated to the domestic and female sphere of Imogen's imprisonment and bedchamber;[33] yet, in nature Imogen's suffering tests her masculine resiliency in hardship.

This initial resourcefulness, associated with the cross-dressed heroine of romantic comedy, quickly diminishes. Critics have often associated Imogen's weakness at this point with her passivity.[34] Despite her debility, Imogen is less passive than heartsick, and this emotional sickness is deeply intensified by the toilsome journey she embarks upon to find Posthumus.[35] The portrait that emerges of Imogen as Fidele depicts in broad outline the signs of the princess's physical distress, an ache that wracks her body. Far from the comfort of her bedchamber, Imogen has slept on the cold floor of the wild: "I have tir'd myself: and for two nights together / Have made the ground my bed" (1.6.02-03). Her journey down the mountain top to Milford Haven has exhausted her strength: "O Jove! I think / Foundations fly the wretched" (3.6.06-07). And her wretchedness would be devoid of heroic fortitude if it were not yoked to steadiness of purpose: "I should be sick, / But that my resolution helps me" (3.6.03-04). Imogen's sheer weariness is connected to her persistent, stabbing hunger. The pain of hunger brings the princess near death, and these references to hunger occur so often in this scene that they consolidate as a leitmotif. The references to starvation or food privation run as follows: " I was / At point to sink, for food" (3.6.16-17); "yet famine, / Ere clean it o'erthrow Nature, makes it valiant" (3.6.19-20); "Here's money for my meat, / I would have left in on the board, so soon / As I had made my meal" (3.7.22-24); "almost spent with hunger, / I am fall'n in this offence"(3.7.35-36); "thanks to stay and eat it" (3.7.40); "Discourse is heavy, fasting" (3.7.63). The sting of hunger drives Imogen into the cave of the outlaw Belarius--who dwells with Cymbeline's long-lost sons, Guiderius and Arviragus--where Fidele appears to collapse from fatigue and anguish. "He wrings at some distress" and "What pain it cost, what danger!" state Belarius and Arvigarus with bewildered concern (3.8.52-53). The pain of hunger and the danger of her ordeal become a distressing and life-threatening reality. Whether Imogen as Fidele suffers death from bodily weakness or from murderous intent signifies the same lamentable end. As she says to the mountaineers, "if you kill me for my fault, I should / Have died had I not made it" (3.8.29-30). Vulnerable, the heroine acknowledges that destruction surrounds her, and it hovers near her as a tangible threat.

Imogen's broken heart and sadness over Posthumus's treachery debilitate her body: "I am very sick" (4.2.05). Again, "I am not well" (4.2.07). Yet again, "I am ill" (4.2.11). Earlier, Pisanio had alluded to the concrete danger characteristic of romantic adventure: "If you are sick at sea, / Or stomach-qualm'd at land, a dram of this / Will drive away distemper" (3.4.191-93). Imogen believes that this potion, which cures ailments on land or sea, will work as an antidote to remedy love's injury. Drinking the potion, Imogen hopes to alleviate sickness together with the agony of ailing passion: "I am sick still, heart-sick; Pisanio, / I'll now taste of thy drug" (4.2.37-38). In Act 1, the Queen had falsely reported that the same drug had revived Cymbeline five times from death (1.6.63). When Imogen ingests the cordial, it produces the opposite effect: "have I not found it / Murd'rous to th' senses?" (4.2.327-28). The potion imitates the signs of death by "locking up the spirits a time" (1.6.41). This sham death represents the apex of the heroine's suffering and brings her to the brink of destruction. Her understanding that she has been betrayed by her husband, a man whom she has secretly married against her father's will, lies at the center of her disconsolation.

Belarius, eulogizing at the grave site of Imogen and Cloten, says that "their pleasures here are past, so is their pain" (4.2.290). The burial reminds the living of the reality of human frailty, bringing to the fore the inevitability of earthly decay and the inescapable fact of disintegration. For "[t]he ground that gave them first has them again" (4.2.289). Imogen's seeming death acts as a testament to the possible deadly outcome of a love-gone-wrong. The baleful lyrics of the dirge reinforce the relation between death and the tragic outcome of young love: "All lovers young, all lovers must / Consign to thee and come to dust" (4.2.274-75). Thinking that the decapitated body of Cloten is the headless corpse of Posthumus, Imogen wakens to the horrific reality of a dead husband: "Murder in heaven! How? 'Tis gone" (4.2.312). The final outrage of the situation occurs when Imogen mingles blood from the cadaver with the skin on her face in a grisly consummation of marriage in death. She asks Posthumus to "[[g]ive colour to my pale cheek with thy blood" (4.2.330). The stage image of sacrificial blood is also an echo of the wounded "pap" motif in *Love and Fortune*. This pathetic scene of death and anguish is made all too real by the discovery of a murdered body in the clothes of Posthumus.

It is true that the Greek romantic convention shows a heroine who wants to die when she learns of the death of her love partner. Imogen follows in this tradition when she literally embraces death, heaving herself atop what she thinks is the corpse of Posthumus. The Roman soldier Lucius believes that Imogen has in fact died: "How? A page? / Or dead, or sleeping on him? But dead rather" (4.2.355-57). At this moment, there is the implication that Imogen is dead, stretched across a headless and bloody body. Despite the grotesqueness of the situation, Imogen heroically gathers her strength. Through this volition and courage, she keeps her pledge to Posthumus as her adopted name, Fidele, suggests: "Thy name well fits thy faith; thy faith thy name" (4.2.381). Imogen's determination to bury her beloved teaches the soldiers virtue in suffering: "The boy hath taught us manly duties" (4.2.396). Her perseverance through betrayal and her survival of death imparts manly valor, even though she is a woman.

Even at the lowest point of Imogen's suffering, we are reminded that the play is moving toward a satisfactory resolution. Intermixed with Imogen's grievous sorrow, there is the sense that her erotic pain is set against an ever-present comic backdrop. From the start, the two brothers had depicted Fidele as a picture of enchanting sorrow: "How angel-like he sings!" (4.2.48). Arviragus notes that Fidele's sighs issue from a "divine temple," where ariel-like they "commix /With the winds that sailors rail at"; Guiderius observes that these murmurs spring from a deep well of "grief and patience" (4.2.55-57). In addition, Belarius presumes that Fidele has died from boyish melancholy: "Thou diedst a more rare boy, of melancholy" (4.2.208). Melancholy is a lover's disease and is therefore artfully feminized. When Fidele is presumably found dead, Arviragus describes him by using an image of picturesque otherworldliness. He looks "[n]ot as death's dart, being laugh'd at," but rather like an effigy with "his right cheek / Reposing on a cushion" (4.2.211-212). The brother's aesthetic portrait seems to echo Imogen's earlier affected statements of suffering, an idea that goes well with the almost telepathic bond Imogen appears to share with her brothers. Shakespeare overlays the potentially tragic scene of death with the suggestion of the family's enduring interrelationship.

A crucial aspect of *Cymbeline*'s comic resolution is built around Posthumus's atonement. First, he forgives Imogen for allegedly "wrying but a little" (5.1.05). Second, he takes responsibility for his past cruelty. These acts sanction the hero's reincorporation into the matrimonial covenant. When Pisanio falsely informs Posthumus that "Imogen was slain" (4.3.37) and sends "[s]ome bloody sign of it" (3.4.127), he succumbs to complete despair. Like Imogen, Posthumus now idealizes death, but his version of romantic suffering is embedded in a notion of stoical punishment. Posthumus connects pain, especially death, to the male world of battle and arms. As son to the soldier Sicilius, he longs to die in battle for his wrongdoing, while calling upon the "ugly monster" death to destroy him. Posthumus, however, remains steadfastly undefeated, unable to "find death where I did hear him groan, / Nor see him where he struck" (5.3.69-70). Although death is a projection of his guilt, Posthumus melds his love for Imogen with military gallantry: he sees the conflict between Britain and Rome as a way to combine his adoration for his wife with the virtue of soldiery. Disguising himself as a British peasant, Posthumus conflates victory in war with triumph in death, disdaining to "wound" Britain further as he has already killed its mistress: "So I'll fight / Against the part I come with: so I'll die / For thee, O Imogen, even for whom my life / Is, every breath, a death" (5.1.24-27). While Posthumus is apparently conscripted, his apparent disloyalty in combat, his changing sides from Rome to Britain back to Rome again, reflects a thematic feature that deals with the hero's changeability: his hasty misjudgment of Imogen's incontinency turns into his quick renunciation of her guilt. Because Posthumus has been unable to die by the sword, he seeks his own ruin by surrendering himself to the perilous tactics of a turncoat:

> For me, my ransom's death:
>
> On either side I come to spend my breath,
>
> Which neither here I'll keep nor bear again,
>
> But end it by some means for Imogen  (5.3.80-83)

Posthumus believes he has reached a higher level of loyalty beyond national fealty, and he counts on death to ransom him in exchange for the sanctified memory of Imogen, for "The temple / Of Virtue was she" (5.5.220-221).

Posthumus draws on the chivalric code of death in arms as a model of romantic allegiance, despite the fact that the enemy is his own consciousness: "My conscience, thou are fetter'd / More than any shanks and wrists" (5.4.8-09). Because Posthumous believes that death has a redemptive quality--it sometimes hides in "fresh cups" and "soft beds" (5.3.71)--it can release Posthumus from the bonds of his own guilt: "By th' sure physician, Death; who is the key / T' unbar these locks" (5.4.7-8). Death, the physician, becomes the healer of earthly sins, and its liberating power resides in spiritual penitence rather than mere stoic punishment. Accordingly, Posthumus looks to the gods to grant him release,

> The penitent instrument to pick that bolt,
>
> Then free for ever.
>
> ........................................................................
>
> Must I repent,
>
> I cannot do it better than in gyves,
>
> Desire'd more than constrain'd. (5.4.10-15)

Death in battle is converted into religious redemption, for Posthumus's crime will be expiated by self-sacrifice: "For Imogen's dear life take mine, and though / 'Tis not so dear, yet 'tis a life" (5.4.22-23). Not surprisingly, when the hangman is given orders to execute him as an enemy of the state, Posthumus welcomes the sentence: "I am merrier to die than thou art to live" (5.4.173). The fact that Posthumus personifies death as his ransomer and redeemer suggest that he views faith and erotic suffering as a type of quid pro quo, an exchange of guilt for salvation.

This salvation is emblematically represented in 5.5. when Posthumus and Imogen embrace. Posthumus envisions the caress as a redemptive act of conjugal unity: "Hang there like fruit, my soul, / Till the tree die" (5.5.263-64). Peggy Muñoz Simonds offers a symbolic interpretation of Shakespeare's stage image: "The emblem he gives us onstage is no longer that of woman as a clinging vine, no matter how fruitful, but of woman as an equal who has the strength and fortitude to sustain the elm after it dies, even as the tree now supports the vine."[36] Love and forgiveness join in a metaphysical entwinement of life-in-death, a figurative space where tragedy and comedy combine in an interconnected dependence.

———————————

[1] See Geoffrey Bullough, *Narrative and Dramatic Sources of Shakespeare*, vol. 8 (London: Routledge & Kegan Paul, 1975), 3-37. Bullough also discusses Geoffrey of Monmouth's account of the rule of King Cymbeline (7-12); he cites *The Faerie Queene* and *The Mirror for Magistrates* as possible sources for Cymbeline's rule (7-9). While Bullough places the wager story in the context of folk literature, he finds that Shakespeare drew primarily from two accounts of the tale: Boccaccio's *Decameron* (day 2, novella 9) and a German version, *Frederyke of Jennen*, translated into English in 1518 (16). See also Kenneth Muir, *The Sources of Shakespeare's Plays* (London: Methuen & Co., 1977), 258-266. Muir cites sources for King Cymbeline's reign in *The Faerie Queene*, *Albion's England*, and *The Mirror for Magistrates,* as well as Holinshed (259). Muir also points to the *Decameron* and *Frederyke of Jennen* as sources for the wager story ( 263-64). For studies that discuss the influence of historical narratives in *Cymbeline*, see David M. Bergeron, "*Cymbeline*: Shakespeare's Last Roman Play," *Shakespeare Quarterly* 31 (1980): 31-41; Jodi Mikalachki, "The Masculine Romance of Roman Britain: *Cymbeline* and Early Modern English Nationalism," in *Shakespeare's Romances*, ed. Alison Thorne (Basingstoke: Palgrave Macmillan, 2003), 117-44. Mikalachki explores gender and sexuality in relation to nationalism in the play and how powerful women are suppressed in the construction of national identity. For the influence

of Virgil in the play, and the relation of Aeneas to Posthumus, see Patricia Parker, "Romance and Empire: Anachronistic *Cymbeline*," in *Unfolded Tales*, eds. George M. Logan and Gordon Teskey (Ithaca and London: Cornell University Press, 1989), 189-207.

[2] J. M. Nosworthy, ed., *Cymbeline*, The Arden Shakespeare (1955; London: Methuen & Co., 2000), xxvii. Bullough also observes that *Cymbeline* and *The Rare Triumphs of Love and Fortune* possess "many minor points of resemblance," but he believes that these similarities occur by "contra-suggestion rather than by direct imitation" (*Narrative and Dramatic Sources*, 21). Muir points out the crucial correspondences between the two plays as follows: "initial situation," "pastoral scenes," and the "last act" (*Sources of Shakespeare*, 259). Roger Warren writes that *Love and Fortune* "provided a specific stimulus for *Cymbeline*." For Warren's discussion, see *Cymbeline*, The Oxford Shakespeare (Oxford: Oxford University Press, 1998), esp., 16-18. For Nosworthy's full discussion of the play's probable sources, see the editor's introductory remarks, especially pages xvii-xxviii. Citations of *Cymbeline* are from this Arden edition, and they will be cited parenthetically.

[3] In *Love and Fortune*, the goddesses Venus and Fortune, in their fight for supremacy, wreak havoc upon a pair of young lovers, Hermione and Fidelia. The allegorical interaction of the goddesses appropriately symbolizes true love tested by calamity. The dramatic action begins with the news of the couple's secret betrothal (The audience does not know what kind of contract has been made between the two). Upon discovery of the amorous alliance, the heroine's father and brother voice their disapproval of the match.

Hermione, an orphan, is banished from court, and his father, exiled by Fidelia's father, lives in a cave. When Jupiter urges the goddesses Fortune and Venus to reconcile their difference and unite the lovers with their families, providence wields its power in the form of a classical god. The families are reunited, and the lovers receive the benediction of all.

[4]See the introduction to *Common Conditions*, ed. Tucker Brooke, Elizabethan Club Reprints (New Haven: Yale University Press; London: Humphrey Milford; Oxford: Oxford University Press, 1915), ix-xv. See also the introduction to *The Rare Triumphes [sic] of Love and Fortune*, ed. W. W. Greg, Malone Society Reprints (Oxford: Oxford University Press, 1930), v-vi. When citing from the play, I follow the editor's line numbering, and the citations will be indicated parenthetically. See also Lee Monroe Ellison, *The Early Romantic Drama at the English Court* (Menasha, Wisconsin: George Banta, 1917), 96. The third romantic play, *Clyomon and Clamydes* (c. 1570-1583), originates in the medieval chivalric tradition; its source was the untranslated French prose romance *Perceforest*. See Betty J. Littleton's discussion of the play in *Clyomon and Clamydes: A Critical Edition* (Paris: Hague, 1968), 13-64.

[5]David Bevington, *From Mankind to Marlowe: Growth of Structure in the Popular Drama of Tudor England* (Cambridge, Mass.: Harvard University Press, 1962), 190.

[6]The Arden editor, Nosworthy, even calls the problem of tracing the sources "baffling" (xvii).

[7]Anna Jameson, *Shakespeare's Heroines* (London: George Bell and Sons, 1905), 158, 198.

[8] Janet Adelman, *Suffocating Mothers* (New York and London: Routledge, 1992), 209, 210. Adelman writes: "Because she has commanded as a woman, Imogen must simultaneously give up her command and her femaleness, as through her male disguise were the sign of her penitential obedience to male power" (210).

[9] Paula S. Berggren writes: "She [Imogen] participates in the miracle experienced by Thaisa and Hermione, but their agony and rebirth more directly exemplify the woman's role as savior of the race through childbirth" ("The Woman's Part: Female Sexuality as Power in Shakespeare's Plays," in *The Woman's Part: Feminist Criticism of Shakespeare*, eds. Carolyn Ruth Swift Lenz, Gayle Greene, and Carol Thomas Neely [Urbana and Chicago: University of Illinois Press, 1983], 17-34, 27-28).

[10] For a discussion of the dissemination of the wager story in early modern England, see William Flint Thrall, "*Cymbeline*, Boccaccio, and the Wager Story in England," *Studies in Philology* 28 (1931): 639-51. Thrall closely examines *Frederick of Jennen* as a possible Shakespearean source, but argues that Boccaccio's wager story provides the most convincing analogue (119). For analogues of the wager story, see also W. W. Lawrence, *Shakespeare's Problem Comedies*, 2nd edition (1931; New York: Frederick Ungar Publishing, 1960), esp. 180-88.

[11] M. M. Bakhtin, *The Dialogic Imagination*, ed. Michael Holquist, trans. Caryl Emerson and Michael Holquist (Austin: University of Texas Press, 1981), 87-88.

[12] Ibid., 88.

[13] David Wallace, *Decameron* (Cambridge: Cambridge University Press, 1991), 34. Critics see Fortune as the binding theme behind the tales of the second day. Thus, Wallace states

that "this movement from misery to joy, the movement of comedy, sees Boccaccio

working with Fortune, one of the most familiar and yet most elusive of all medieval

figures" (34). G. H. McWilliams, translator of the *Decameron*, also points out that an

"impersonal" and "capricious" goddess Fortune is the central motif of the second day

(*The Decameron*, 2nd edition [1972; London: Penguin Books, 1995], cxxxiv-cxxxv). He

also sees the idea of fortune in commercialism as a motif in these stories.

[14]Victor Šhklovskij, "Some Reflections on the *Decameron*," in *Critical Perspectives on

the Decameron*," ed. Robert S. Dombroski (London: Hodder and Stoughton, 1976), 66.

[15]Thomas G. Bergin, *Boccaccio* (New York: The Viking Press, 1981), 301. Wallace also

sees a somewhat tragic vein in the stories of the Second Day: "These longer, more

luxuriant narratives achieve effects of pathos by isolating a single, vulnerable individual

beneath a mighty framework of historical events" (*Decameron*, 35). See also Max

Alexander Staples's remarks on the importance of the individual in these stories: "In the

*Decameron, Fortuna* does not play a major role. Action is controlled by the person who

plans a series of events and then guides them through to achieve the desired end" (*The

Ideology of The Decameron* [Lewiston, New York; Queenston, Ontario; Lampeter,

Wales: The Edwin Mellon Press, 1994], 38). For the didactic nature of the novella, see

Corradina Caporello-Szykman, *The Boccaccian Novella* (New York: Peter Lang, 1990).

She explains the genre's characteristics as follows: "The main characteristics pertaining

to the novella which are discussed in this overview include *brevitas, didactica, imitatio*,

originated in Antiquity and the *exemplum*, the *fabliau* and the *lai* specifically proper to

the Middle Ages (29).

[16]Arthur C. Kirsch, "*Cymbeline* and Coterie Dramaturgy," *ELH* 34 (1967): 285-306, 296. Kirsh contends that Imogen's rhetoric of passion is part of the play's self-conscious art: "A self-conscious dramaturgy--including discontinuous action emphasizing scenes rather than plot, and exaggerated characters manipulated for debates and passionate declamations--seems to have been a common denominator of many if not most plays written for the private theater" (293). For an account of the play that sees *Cymbeline's* self-conscious dramaturgy as a spoof of romance, especially a mock of the revived play *Mucedorus*, see David L. Frost, "'Mouldy Tales': The Context of Shakespeare's *Cymbeline*," *Essays & Studies* 39 (1986): 19-38. I find that Imogen's response to suffering undergoes a change in tone, from overly passionate to heroic, when she realizes Posthumus's betrayal.

[17]For a discussion of the distinction between comic and tragic tone, see Frances Teague, ed., *Acting Funny* (Rutherford; London; Cranbury, N.J.: Farleigh Dickinson University Press; Associated University Presses, 1994), 9-26. In a related manner, Imogen's romantic characterization does not necessarily follow a tragicomic pattern, the kind that can be found in the drama of Beaumont and Fletcher. As Fletcher writes in the preface to *The Faithful Shepherdess*, "A tragicomedie is not so called in respect of mirth and killing, but in respect it wants deaths, which is enough to make it no tragedy, yet brings some near it, which is enough to make it no comedy." I cite from Kirsh, "*Cymbeline* and Coterie Dramaturgy," 287. Imogen's marriage to Posthumus follows the Greek plot of *Love and Fortune* until the hero's banishment. For the influence of Beaumont and Fletcher and tragicomedy on *Cymbeline*, see A. H. Thorndike, *The Influence of Beaumont*

*and Fletcher on Shakespeare* (Worcester, Mass.: n.p., 1901). See also Robert Y. Turner, "Slander in *Cymbeline* and Other Jacobean Tragicomedies," *ELH* 13 (1983): 182-202. Turner looks specifically at Guarini's tragicomedy, *Il Pastor Fido,* in relation to the slandered heroine in *Cymbeline*.

[18]The hero and heroine in Greek romance pledge vows of fidelity either before or during their adventures. For instance, in Heliodorus's *Aethiopica* Theagenes and Chariclea perform what appears to be a hand fast marriage (*verba de futuro*) before they elope (Book 4), and Leucippe and Clitophon in Achilles Tatius' romance pledge chaste love (*verba de futuro*) after they elope (Book Four). A vow that is made *verba de futuro* is a promise to marry in the future, while a vow that is made *verba de praesenti* with witnesses is a legal marriage contract. In Xenophon's and Chariton's romances, which were not fully translated in the vernacular in the early modern period, the hero and heroine are married with parental consent before they are beset by obstacles.

[19]For a historical look at a women's prerogative in choosing a husband in the early modern period, see Diane Elizabeth Dreher, *Domination and Defiance* (Lexington: University Press of Kentucky, 1986). Dreher's comments on young love in Shakespeare could very well apply to *Love and Fortune*: "The moral vision in Shakespeare's plays is not ironclad obedience to the *ancien régime* but a new moral order based upon free will, choice, and commitment, a personal bond of love and trust between two individuals that becomes an inspiration to their world" (38).

[20] The brother's unnatural aggression against his sister and extreme hatred of Hermione lead us to consider his motives for disliking the hero so fiercely. Is there not the

suggestion of an incestuous attachment? Consider the brother's hysterical outpour of emotion; "What Dame," asks Armenio, "are you not shameless in your shame? / No Mistresse, no, it will not past: / But wilfull Wench this new attempted game, / Eare it be wun wil aske another cast" (ll.339-42). To Hermione, he rages: "Goe wend thy wayes, obscurer than night: / And Fortune for revenge plague thee with spite" (11.488-90). This suggestion of incest coincides with the incestuous pairing of Cloten and Imogen; it also may echo the hint of an incestuous attachment between Imogen and her brothers, Arviragus and Guiderius. About the theme of incest in comedy in the early modern theater, Richard A. McCabe states: "The comic perspective works not merely to avert actual incest, but also to diminish the significance of the event itself through the casual ease of its potential occurrence" (*Incest, Drama, and Nature's Law, 1550-1700* [Cambridge: Cambridge University Press, 1993], 128). Although we never believe that Fidelia stands in imminent danger of fraternal incest, the scene serves as a test of the heroine's physical and emotional constancy by reinforcing our perception of her bond to Hermione.

[21] For a discussion of Posthumus and his language as conscious of his deficiencies, see Coburn Freer, *The Poetics of Jacobean Drama* (Baltimore and London: The Johns Hopkins University Press, 1991), esp. 112-17.

[22] For a discussion of the theme of dismemberment in *Cymbeline*, see Maurice Hunt, "Dismemberment, Corporal Reconstitution, and the Body Politic in *Cymbeline*," *Studies in Philology* 99 (2002): 404-31. Hunt explores the division in the play between a Pauline conception of the body politic and an authoritative or Jamesian view of the body politic.

[23]I cite from *The Oxford Shakespeare*, eds. Stanley Wells and Gary Taylor (Oxford: Clarendon Press, 1998).

[24]Harley Granville-Barker, *Prefaces to Shakespeare* (London: B. T. Batsford, 1972), 498. Granville-Barker finds that the verse in *Cymbeline* is a kind of "new Euphuism" of the imagination (498).

[25]Carol Thomas Neely rightly points out that Cymbeline acts as a weak blocking figure: "No one much heeds him, since his blustering does not seem to give him the power to enforce an estrangement; the marriage in fact will be finally ruptured only by Posthumus's jealousy." This point is part of Neely's larger argument that in the romances anxieties about courtship and marriage are treated in an "abbreviated or comic way" in comparison to the earlier plays ("Incest and Issue: *The Winter's Tale*," in *Broken Nuptials in Shakespeare's Plays* [New Haven and London: Yale University Press, 1985], 177.

[26]For a discussion of suicide in Shakespeare's *The Rape of Lucrece*, see Margo Hendricks, "'A word, sweet Lucrece': Confession, Feminism, and *The Rape of Lucrece*," in *A Feminist Companion to Shakespeare*, ed. Dympna Callaghan (Oxford: Blackwell, 2003), 103-118. Hendricks looks at the suicide in the context of confessional narratives and race.

[27]See C. W. R. D. Moseley, "Innogen's Bedroom," *Notes and Queries* 235 (1990): 196-98. Moseley argues that Iachimo describes the suggestive items in Imogen's bedchamber to "manipulate Posthumus from overconfidence to overcredulity" (197). See also R. J. Schork, "Allusion, Theme, and Characterization in *Cymbeline*," *Studies in Philology* 69 (1972): 210-216. Schork argues that the items in Imogen's bedroom symbolize through

their mythical allusions Iachimo's failure at seduction: "each allusion contributes to the establishment of Iachimo's character and ironically signals the futility of his schemes" (213).

[28]For a discussion of Ovid's Philomel myth, see Ann Thompson, "Philomel in *Titus Andronicus* and *Cymbeline*," *Shakespeare Survery* 31 (1978): 23-32; Carmine Di Biase, "Ovid, Pettite, and the Mythic Foundation of *Cymbeline*," *Cahiers Elisabethains* 46 (1994), 59-70.

[29]For a discussion of rings in Shakespeare, in terms of debt structure and the heroine's body, see Lynda E. Boose, "The Comic Contract and Portia's Golden Ring," in *Shakespeare Studies* 20 (1998): 241-54.

[30]Valerie Wayne, "The Woman's Parts of *Cymbeline*," in *Staged Properties in Early Modern English Drama*, eds. Jonathan Gil Harris and Natasha Korda (Cambridge: Cambridge University Press, 2002), 288-315, 291.

[31]For discussions of the irregular characterization of Posthumus, see Christy Desmet, "Shakespearean Comic Character: Ethos and Epideictic in *Cymbeline*," in *Acting Funny*, 123-41. Desmet analyzes Posthumus in terms of the rhetoric of *ethos* rather than from a perspective of physiological motivation. For a psychological analysis of Posthumus's character, see Ruth Nevo, "Cymbeline: the Rescue of the King," in *Shakespeare's Other Language* (New York and London: Methuen, 1987). Nevo reads Cloten and Iachimo as representing aspects of Posthumus's character, especially with regard to sexual displacement of his desire for Imogen. For additional discussion of Posthumus's similarity to Cloten, see James Edward Siemon, "Noble Virtue in *Cymbeline*,"

*Shakespeare Survey* 29 (1976): 51-61. For a discussion of Posthumus as a questionable hero, see Homer Swander, "*Cymbeline* and the 'Blameless Hero,'" *ELH* 31 (1964): 259-70. By examining how Shakespeare changes his source material to increase Posthumus's cruelty to Imogen, Swander challenges W. W. Lawrence's assumption that Posthumus's cruelty is part of his romance makeup.

[32]Joan Carr, "*Cymbeline* and the Validity of Myth," *Studies in Philology* 75 (1978): 316-330, 326. Carr discusses the Orpheus myth in *Cymbeline* in relation to the theme of resurrection. I find the theme of regeneration more directly connected to romance than to myth.

[33]For an analysis of domestic space in *Cymbeline* as feminine, see Georgianna Ziegler, "My lady's Chamber: Female Space, Female Chastity in Shakespeare," in *Textual Practice* 4 (1990): 73-90. Ziegler finds that female chastity in thet early modern period is associated with the enclosure of woman's domestic chamber, and this space is metaphorically linked to her body.

[34]See Nancy K. Hayles, "Sexual Disguise in *Cymbeline*," *Modern Language Quarterly* 41 (1980): 231-47, 238.

[35]About the harsh landscape that Imogen traverses, Rosalie L. Colie states: "This is unmitigated hard pastoral, a rocky, difficult terrain training its inhabitants to a spare and muscular strength sufficient to wrest their nutriment from its minimal, ungenerous, exiguous resources" (*Shakespeare's Living Art* [Princeton, New Jersey: Princeton University Press, 1974], 295).

<hr>

[36]Peggy Muñoz Simonds, "The Marriage Topos in *Cymbeline*: Shakespeare's Variations on a Classical Theme, " *ELR* 19 (1989): 94-117, 109. For the idea that the play goes beyond respresenting marital harmony by suggesting the universal harmony of Christ's birth, see Robin Moffet, "*Cymbeline* and the Nativity," in *Shakespeare Quarterly* 13 (1962): 207-18.

# CHAPTER 7

## Conclusion

The purpose of this dissertation is to consider the influence of Greek prose romance in Sidney and Shakespeare. I chose to discuss these writers together because they both explicitly use the Hellenistic romance paradigm of sexual love. In the *New Arcadia*, Sidney creates a heroic romance by incorporating the plot design of Helidorus's *Aethiopica*. Not only did Heliodorus impart to Sidney a chaste love story, but he also gave him a model of female heroism. Shakespeare, however, has a more intricate relationship to Greek romance. In *Pericles*, he draws specifically on the *Apollonius of Tyre* narrative (as retold by Gower and Twine), a story that has deep roots in ancient romance, especially in Xenophon's story, the *Ephesiaca*. In *The Winter's Tale*, Shakespeare refashions Greene's Elizabethan romance, *Pandosto*, a story itself influenced by the pastoral narrative of Longus. Finally, in *Cymbeline* Shakespeare looks back to an early Elizabethan romance play, *The Rare Triumphs of Love and Fortune*, for the Greek romance theme of erotic suffering. In the romances, Shakespeare invokes the romance paradigm of ideal love as a redemptive force, one that restores degenerate sexuality or patriarchal abuse. The erotic suffering of the young hero and heroine is a kind of atonement for the wrongdoing of the older generation. While the Shakespearean heroine is often made to suffer greater harm than her male counterpart, the heroic quality of the hero is also measured by his ability to surmount affliction.

I speculate that Renaissance writers such as Sidney and Shakespeare associated the virtue of erotic suffering with the feminine. To suffer is a feminized state because it is often associated with passivity. For example, Sidney creates heroes who fall madly in love, and they suffer great anguish due to their passionate obsession; however, Sidney is also insistent on reminding his audience that Musidorus and Pyrocles are courageous knights, young men who are world-renowned for their marital expertise and innate prowess. The lovesickness that Musidorus and Pryocles undergo as Cupid's novices is counterpoised by reminders of their martial skills. Even when Pyrocles sinks into love's madness, going so low as to dress as a woman, he wears the "manly" outfit of an Amazonian warrior. When Musidorus puts on the guise of a shepherd for the love of Pamela, we are quickly, and humorously, reminded that the young prince has an uncanny ability to kill a bear with just a knife. The idea, however, that erotic suffering is a passive state remains only partially true. The heroine who confronts danger for the sake of fidelity or sexual faithfulness rigorously defends her chastity from opposition. She is an active agent of her destiny. In fact, if the male lover grows weak from romantic suffering, the female becomes stronger by resisting the affronts of enemies. In the depth of hardship, Pamela and Philoclea prove their heroism by countering adversity with resolution and fortitude: their suffering is conceptualized as a triumphant battle. But in the *New Arcadia*, the world of actual combat remains the territory of male heroism; thus, when Parthenia desires to revenge the killing of her husband, she pays the price of death for masquerading as a chivalric knight. Although Sidney can imagine a female heroism, he still subordinates that virtue to the more active heroism in battle demonstrated by his male characters.

Sidney's New Arcadia is written contemporaneously with the early Elizabethan romance plays *Common Conditions* and *The Rare Triumphs of Love and Fortune*. Despite this kinship, it is Shakespeare's Jacobean romances that most closely resemble the early dramatic imitations of ideal romance. In *Pericles*, *The Winter's Tale*, and *Cymbeline*, Shakespeare returns to an earlier mode of romance, one that utilizes the marriage plot and erotic suffering of the Greek paradigm. While Sidney invests his heroic romance with the chaste love plot of Greek romance, he retains the medieval chivalric principle of male heroism. While Sidney remains more or less constant with this contraposition, Shakespeare finds a wider context in which to explore marriage and suffering.

In *Pericles*, Shakespeare does not polarize the paradigm of erotic suffering as much as Sidney does. Instead, he attempts to align the play more closely with the Greek romance ideal of symmetry in marriage and shared adversity. Pericles and Thaisa fall in love at first sight, and they exhibit the classic characteristics of beauty, virtue, and nobility. Their love-leading-to-marriage story fits the ideal romance model. Although Pericles is associated with knightly valor, he ultimately shows his heroism by growing spiritually through tribulation; his ordeals are a lesson in redemption. While Pericles suffers a psychological crisis in the play (partially due to his fear of incest), Thaisa's suffering is connected to bodily vexation. Because of a difficult childbirth, she "dies," is washed up in on the shores of Ephesus, and, after a miraculous resurrection, dedicates her life to sexual abstinence as a votaress of Diana. Even though Thaisa suffers, she does not undergo as many trials of fidelity and chastity as the Greek romance heroine. I find that Thaisa's trials are displaced onto her lost daughter, Marina--so that mother and daughter share in the unconscious wrongs of Pericles. Like an ideal heroine, Marina survives

adventure ordeals: parental abandonment, attempted murder, capture by pirates, assaults

on her chastity. The crucial difference between Marina and her prototype, though, is that

Marina does not fall in love. This displacement of erotic suffering onto the daughter

anticipates the shared suffering of another mother-daughter pair, Hermione and Perdita. I

speculate that the daughter's sacrificial suffering links the family unit together again, so

that the play's comic ending has a powerful and poignant impact.

In *The Winter's Tale*, Shakespeare continues to explore the displacement of erotic

suffering onto the daughter. What emerges in this play is a greater emphasis on the

redemptive role of the female child. Perdita and Florizel's symmetrical love provides a

contrast to the asymmetrical and power-based relationship between Leontes and

Hermione. Hermione not only suffers physical abuse from the jealousy of Leontes, but

her psychological distress is so great that she is overcome with anguish and "dies." On

the other hand, Leontes undergoes sixteen years of repentance, atoning for his crimes

against his family. Once again, a familiar pattern arises. The male suffers and repents for

his wrongdoing, while the female withstands injury against her. Within this framework,

Shakespeare inserts the idealized love story of Perdita and Florizel; the playwright

changes his source in Greene's *Pandosto* to make the irregular courtship between a

prince and shepherdess follow a Greek romance pattern of love-at-first-sight and shared

fortitude in adversity. Even Florizel's name suggests his feminization in love. The mutual

respect and passion between Perdita and Florizel rectifies the distrust and abuse that

Leontes levels against Hermione. Because Hermione's and Perdita's affliction is closely

related in this play, Perdita takes on her mother's pain in order to heal the wounds of the family. The mother's wretchedness is displaced on to the daughter, even though her son, Mamillius, is also sacrificed in the process. The heroic resolve of the younger generation, in particular Perdita's chaste virtue, harmonizes the broken bonds of the parents' marital alliance. In *The Winter's Tale*, Shakespeare develops the potential destructive element of sexual passion. The pattern of male hostility toward female sexuality is repeated in *Cymbeline*.

In *Cymbeline*, Shakespeare explores the problems that occur when an ideal love match is threatened from within. Whereas in *The Winter's Tale* tragic potential radiates from the older generation--Leontes' abuse--in *Cymbeline* the tragic element develops from within the bonds of young love. Here, Shakespeare departs from the Greek romance paradigm by introducing an element of psychological cruelty. Posthumus's willingness to wager on his wife's chastity initiates the series of mishaps that lead to Imogen's near demise. Posthumus, unlike Florizel, is characterized as a heroic soldier. His name connects him directly to his family's glorious fame as military leaders. When Posthumus realizes the folly of accusing Imogen of sexual disloyalty, he becomes feminized precisely because he uses battle as a means to die for Imogen's love. Again, Posthumus suffers by seeking repentance for his sins. By contrast, Imogen grows stronger in her resolve to find Posthumus. Her physical weakness only increases her fortitude to reunite with her husband. In order to represent this female sense of fortitude, Shakespeare places Imogen in the role of a young boy. In this play, comedy / romance and tragedy converge sharply. Perhaps this experiment in altering the model of ideal love gives the play its disjointed characterization. Even so, it is the erotic suffering of the young lovers that redeems the family by bringing them back in unity.

Although Shakespeare draws from Greek romance in his late plays, the conventions of the ancient love genre can also be discerned in some of his romantic comedies and tragedies. In *As You Like It*, for instance, Shakespeare uses Thomas Lodge's Elizabethan prose romance, *Rosalynde*, for his main plot line. While this romance includes the subplot of two estranged brothers who eventually reunite, the main story follows the Greek romance pattern of love, separation, and union. In Shakespeare's play, Rosalind and Orlando fall in love instantly, but they are unable to remain together due to a father (Duke Frederick) who blocks the union, though unintentionally. After a series of adventures in the Forest of Arden, the two young lovers untie in marriage with much celebration and solemnity. We can also see a similar Greek pattern in *The Two Gentlemen of Verona*: Julia is separated from Proteus, encounters adversity, and is eventually reconciled to her beloved in future matrimony. Interestingly, the conventions of Greek romance also arise in Shakespeare's romantic tragedies, specifically in *Romeo and Juliet* and *Othello*. In *Romeo and Juliet*, the intensity of the passion between the two lovers recalls the passion of the ideal hero and heroine of Greek romance, lovers who express mutuality in love and are faithful to their pledge of commitment. In *Othello*, the central protagonists are asymmetrical (Othello is older than Desdemona and culturally "other"), but the play invokes conventions of the Greek romance genre: near shipwreck, trials of fidelity, blocking figures, and an exotic locale. In both of these romantic tragedies, the ideal love between husband and wife restores a sense of social harmony even in the couple's mutual deaths. Shakespeare's use of material from ancient romance in his early and late plays invites us to consider how the playwright rewrites not only a wide variety of source material—based in the tradition of Greek romance—but also how he rewrites the romance material as it manifests itself in his own plays.

The Greek romances were a vital tool for conveying a "new erotics," a paradigm of sexual love that advocated the idealization of chaste marriage and mutual love. The humanists' interest in discovering examples of virtue in classical or ancient texts applies to the recovery of Greek romance. While Renaissance critics of romantic fiction denounced the wild improbability of Hellenistic adventure romance, the advocates of the genre championed these tales as a mirror of ethical conduct, or even a storehouse of plots and characterization. Although the tradition of Greek romance in Sidney and Shakespeare has been widely acknowledged, it is the variations with which these authors flesh out the hero and heroine that have been the topic of this study. Sidney utilizes the prototype of the chaste, suffering heroine as a model of female heroism, while his hero is perhaps more flatly rooted in the male heroic tradition. Shakespeare uses Greek romance source material to break into new paradigms of male and female behavior. In Shakespearean romance, the hero moves into arenas outside the formulaic plot as he grapples with a dark cruelty that brings him and his beloved to the point of tragedy. Finally, it is the heroine's erotic suffering that becomes both heroic and redemptive.